How the Stock Markets Work

Colin Chapman

RANDOM HOUSE

BUSINESS BOOKS

Copyright © Colin Chapman 1986, 1987, 1991, 1994, 1998, 1999, 2002
All rights reserved.

Colin Chapman has asserted his right under the Copyright, Designs and Patents
Act, 1988 to be identified as the author of this work

This book is sold subject to the condition that it shall not, by way of trade
or otherwise, be lent, resold, hired out, or otherwise circulated without the
publisher's prior consent in any form of binding or cover other than that
in which it is published and without a similar condition including this
condition being imposed on the subsequent purchaser

First published in 1994 by Century Limited.
This edition first published in 2002 by
Random House Business Books

Business Books
The Random House Group Limited
20 Vauxhall Bridge Road, London SW1V 2SA

Random House Australia (Pty) Limited
20 Alfred Street, Milsons Point, Sydney,
New South Wales 2061, Australia

Random House New Zealand Limited
18 Poland Road, Glenfield,
Auckland 10, New Zealand

Random House (Pty) Limited
Endulini, 5a Jubilee Road, Parktown 2193, South Africa

The Random House Group Limited Reg. No. 954009

www.randomhouse.co.uk

A CIP catalogue record for this book is available from the British Library

Papers used by Random House are natural, recyclable products made from wood
grown in sustainable forests. The manufacturing processes conform to the
environmental regulations of the country of origin

ISBN 0 7126 1450 8

Typeset by SX Composing DTP, Rayleigh, Essex
Printed and bound in Great Britain by
Mackays of Chatham plc, Chatham, Kent

To the firemen of New York

Contents

Introduction and Acknowledgements

The new millennium has been a mixed blessing for the world's stock markets. The chaotic damage that was predicted for computer systems at midnight on 31 December 1999 did not occur, and investors entered the twenty-first century without as much as a blip.

Yet many of those who took up share ownership in the nineties to ride the crest of the wave of one of the longest bull markets in history spent the first two years of the new century in fear and apprehension. Those who were seduced into believing that Internet stocks could only surge to new heights ended up with paper certificates that were almost worthless. A new phrase was introduced into the lexicon: ninety per centers. They were those unfortunate enough to lose nine tenths of their original investment, and there have been plenty of them. Even those who made what they supposed to be a relatively safe investment by buying into unit trusts that track the main stock market index have watched their savings wither. And those who used the most cautious of savings vehicles, bank deposits or gilt-edged securities, were able to hold on to their capital, but with poor returns because of the lowest interest rates in half a century.

Then came the worst act of terrorism in history, which struck at the heart of world capitalism in Wall Street. Two commercial airliners, piloted by suicide pilots, were flown into the twin towers of the World Trade Center, the headquarters of leading stockbrokers and finance houses. Around three thousand people died in the disaster, many of them courageous firefighters who ran into the crumbling tower blocks as those trapped inside tried to evacuate.

This calamity brought the American stock markets to a four-day standstill. Billions of dollars were written off the value of the world's major corporations. Those who have contributed to pension schemes have also found that so far these schemes have added little to their eventual pensions, because of falling stock market values.

Yet from the heroism of the New York firefighters, from the resilience of the stock markets in the face of economic uncertainty, it seems probable that long-term interest in shares will continue to grow. When the first edition of this book was published, electronic technology was a novelty, the Internet was known only to a few specialists in technological universities, and there were only five known investment clubs in Britain. Now Wall Street traders teach marine commandos how to make fast decisions, the Internet has brought online share trading to anyone with a personal computer and an ordinary telephone line, and Britain has 10,000 thriving investment clubs. At last schoolchildren are being taught about shares, although there is still nothing about the stock markets in the National Curriculum of England and Wales.

Many people have given me considerable help with this completely rewritten new edition of this book. Most of them are involved in the stock markets on a day-to-day basis. They are traders, analysts and salesmen. They are regulators at the new Financial Services Authority, market reporters for the *Financial Times* and editors on magazines like *Shares* and the *Investors Chronicle*. I would like to thank all of them for their readiness to spend time with me, and to talk freely about the way the markets work. I must add a special thank you to my publisher at Random House, Clare Smith. And the book would have been much more difficult to complete had I not had the total support of Susan and Max.

Colin Chapman
February 2002

1   What is a Share?

What is a share? It is a simple enough question, but one which many find difficult to answer. Even the *Concise Oxford Dictionary* fumbles over it. 'A portion that a person receives from or gives to a common amount' is its best shot. The *American Heritage Dictionary* prefers the slightly more didactic 'part or portion belonging to, distributed to, contributed by, or owned by a person or group'.

It's as if these dictionaries were compiled by lawyers! Yet everyone has shares. The principle of sharing is part of life itself. We share toys, library books, meals and homes. We share aircraft flights by buying a seat from an airline. We share the cost of petrol on trips by car. As magazines become more expensive we share subscription costs and the use of the magazine. Some people even share jobs.

These share arrangements all have a value. If I share the use of a sailing boat with three others on an equal basis, I will pay one quarter of the costs, and have the use of it for one week in four. If one of my co-owners moves to Australia, then I might increase my share to 50 per cent by purchasing his share. Or the three remaining owners may collectively buy his stake so as to reduce the number of owners, with the result that each ends up with a third. Or a new partner could be found who might be expected to pay more than the original amount paid for the one-quarter stake.

It could even get more complicated. It would not be unusual for the three remaining co-owners of the yacht to decide they want to reduce the time and money spent on sailing, so they may elect to bring in several more additional partners, creating ten shareholders rather than four. This would lead them to issue new shares at a price perhaps sufficiently high to ensure that although the original owners' holdings are reduced to one tenth each, they have still gained more than enough cash back to compensate for their shares being worth less. It would become more complicated still if there were restrictions on the newcomers' shares, preventing them from using the boat in the peak summer season, for example.

All of these situations are reflected in the world's stock markets, which first began through the same kind of sharing as in my sailing example. What happened, as I will describe in Chapter 2, is that adventurers planning a long sea voyage from Britain decided to find others to help them finance an expedition through the Arctic to see if they could find a northern trade route to China. This voyage was somewhat more risky than a shared yacht moored in the Helford River, but the principle was the same.

The only difference between these kinds of shares and those held in a modern corporation is that, for the most part, a company's shares are of equal value. No one ordinary share in BP is worth more than any other BP share. Sometimes, but seldom, there are special shares, and some of these have differing values, but this is an exception I will explain later (see Chapter 3).

The price of a company's shares is determined by the same pressures that govern the price of anything else – a boat, a house, a car or an airline seat. That price is the point at which the amount the buyer is willing to pay matches the sum the seller is prepared to accept. And this point will move up or down according to supply and demand. If fresh cauliflowers are in plentiful supply at the vegetable market, the price will be lower than would be the case if drought had affected the crop. On the demand side, a television cooking series might have recommended a dish using cauliflowers, producing greater consumer interest and forcing prices up.

In precisely the same way, if there is a belief that there is over-production of silicon chips so that there are many more than enough to meet the needs of computer manufacturers, shares in Intel, the world's leading chip manufacturer, will fall. Note the word 'belief'. It is the market's perception of what will happen to the balance sheet of a business in the near future rather than the current facts that determines price movements. In the example mentioned, there will be more sellers than buyers until the price of Intel shares reaches a level that investors feel reflects their true value.

There is one important difference between the way a company's share price is determined and the other values discussed earlier. An airline seat is only of value until the flight for which it is booked takes off. Once the flight has closed, the seat cannot be sold, so it has no value, or liquidity. Shares in a big corporation like BP are traded very frequently, so there is high liquidity, and their price changes every few seconds. A market is at its most liquid when there are large numbers of buyers and sellers, and where this is the case the value of shares is most accurately defined.

Shares are one of the two essential planks of global capitalism. The other is debt, largely defined in bonds. So what is a bond? Again, this is a simple question that deserves a straightforward answer. There is one. A bond is an IOU. You are out of cash to pay the man who came to fix your broken car at the roadside, so you put your name and address on a piece of paper, write 'IOU £25' and sign it. He trusts you to honour the debt and send him a cheque or postal order. A bond comes finely printed on good paper and promises to pay its owner its value plus interest at a defined future date. If the date is in the distant future, then the IOU is known as a long bond. Hence the US Treasury long bond is an IOU from the United States Government which promises to pay you back in fifteen years' time the amount you have lent it. Do not be put off by the jargon; everyone can understand the bond markets.

As with shares, the value of bonds can change very rapidly. Some find this harder to understand; after all, a debt is a debt and has to be repaid by the person who has borrowed the money. But loans can be traded almost as easily as shares. Effectively the loan you have made at the agreed interest rate is handed over to someone else. If you have a standard savings account with a bank or building society you have the right to withdraw your money by presenting yourself and your pass book at the counter during opening hours. However, these accounts offer very poor rates of interest. If you agree to keep your money on deposit for a fixed term of two years, the interest will be better, but still not at the level offered by a bond. A bond will pay significantly more, but unless you decide to keep it until its payback date, you will have to sell it on the stock market at its market price, which will be different from the price you paid for it. The main factor affecting its price will be the level of interest rates. If interest rates have gone down since you bought your bond, it will go up in value because of the better return it offers; if rates have gone up, its traded value will fall.

In today's world, anyone who has savings or the ability to save can own shares or bonds, and most of them do so, often without realising it. Only the very poor are excluded from the stock markets, for the same reason that they do not own telephones and television sets, cars and washing machines, books and magazines, and all too often exist below the poverty line in totally inadequate housing, without health care, nutrition or education. The operations of the stock markets have not constricted wealth; they have spread it, albeit unevenly, and will continue to do so. The problems of the world's poor cannot be solved by a financial system, but only by concerted action from politicians brave enough to impose sacrifices on the power groups that elected them.

In a global economy a Briton can own shares in an Australian gold mine, an Asian hotel chain, or a German motor manufacturer. He can buy a stake in the world's biggest company, General Electric, where his greatest risk may be that the dollar may fall against the pound, or he can chance his money on one of London's smallest football clubs, Charlton Athletic, where relegation to a lower division could mean the loss of television income and financial disaster. If he doubts his own judgement he can put his trust in professional fund managers, and buy a share in a collective investment, which will give him a stake in a wide sweep of companies or countries, or both.

This freedom of ownership, of course, extends to billionaires and to large corporations, who are relatively free to move their money across national boundaries at a second's notice. Not all countries allow total freedom of capital movements, and some, most notably the United States, have restrictions on foreign ownership of certain assets. There is a widespread popular belief that America is the 'land of the free' so far as money movements are concerned, but this is not the case. Foreigners cannot take over an American airline, for example, though an American airline could buy a British one. Similarly, when he was an Australian, Rupert Murdoch was allowed to acquire four major newspaper titles in Britain; no British publisher could acquire even one title in Australia. A Canadian, Conrad Black, could buy the *Daily Telegraph*; but Pearson, the British group owning the *Financial Times* was prohibited from controlling the Toronto daily newspaper *Financial Post*. The Swiss were able to buy the British confectionary group Rowntree Mackintosh; Cadbury Schweppes would not be allowed to buy Nestlé.

Even so, this kind of protectionism, which successive rounds of talks under the aegis of the World Trade Organisation have failed to address, adds up to a fairly minor restriction on world share ownership, and it is still possible for both individuals and companies to hold minority stakes in restricted sectors or companies. That means that the only enterprises in the major industrial nations in which international share ownership is proscribed are the diminishing number of corporations owned by the state, or private, family-held companies. Many of these exist in Europe and Asia, but the trend is towards open ownership, and by the end of the first decade of the twenty-first century, most large businesses are likely to be listed on stock exchanges.

The last ten years of the twentieth century will be remembered not just for the start of the Internet age, but also as the time when the world discovered shares. In the year 2000 the total amount held in shares on the global stock markets was $35 trillion.[1] This means that the total value of stock markets was more than the total world gross domestic product (GDP). How could that be? To understand, you will need to read the section on how shares are valued (see p. 34). GDP, the everyday measurement of wealth used internationally to rate the performance of countries, represents the total value of goods and services in the economy in any given year. Ten years earlier, the value of the stock markets was only 40 per cent of GDP.[2]

About half of the American population own shares, which is twice as many as in 1987, the year of the last big stock market crash. In Britain there are about 12 million private shareholders, three times as many as in 1987. Australia, a country that until recently was dominated by trade unions and the credit unions in which their members entrusted their savings, now holds the record for the greatest percentage of shareholders. In Germany, a country noted for cautious investors preferring bank deposit accounts and bonds, one in five adults are now share owners.

The enthusiasm for shares has been driven by what has seemed to be an inexorable rise in values, greater even than the rising price of property in the major democracies. A detailed study conducted by Barclays Capital, a subsidiary of the British high street bank, found that provided shares are owned for a period of three years, historically they have produced better returns than high interest deposits or bonds.[3] The study took a long view, looking at eighty years of performance since the end of World War I in 1918, and at both short and long periods within this epoch. Where investments were held for a decade or more, shares outperformed deposits in 97 per cent of ten-year spells, and did better than bonds for 94 per cent of the time. Even for short periods of only two years the incidence of shares performing better than either bonds or deposits was 70 per cent. One notable exception was after the 1987 global stock market crash, when it took six years for an investment in shares to outperform a high-interest deposit. One hundred pounds invested in

---

[1] The Economist, 10 March 2001.
[2] Ibid.
[3] Barclays Capital Ltd, London.

the British stock market at the end of World War I in 1918 would now be worth almost £100,000. The same amount placed in a bank deposit would have grown to about £750.

This analysis may not have been much comfort to those investing in the stock markets at the turn of this century. In 2001 the total return on equities in Britain was a loss of 8.6 per cent, after adjusting for inflation. Equities underperformed bonds by 30.4 per cent in the year 2000, the widest margin of underperformance since the 1930s. The Great Depression years of 1930, 1931 and 1937 are the only years that have been as bad.

Still optimists can have some faith in another study, available in much greater detail, which confirms that the longer the time interval, the greater the probability of a better performance from shares compared with bonds and bank deposits. The Table 'Equity Performance since World War I' looks at the probability of equities outperforming bonds and cash.

Equity Performance since World War I

Probability of:	2 yrs	3-yrs	4-yrs	5-yrs	10-yrs
Shares Outperforming Cash	73	71	81	82	97
Shares Outperforming Gilts	69	79	84	81	96

source: Barclays Capital

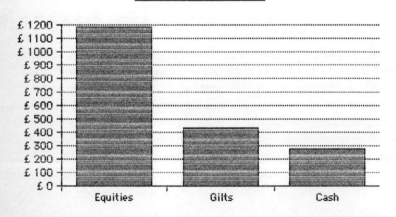

This table shows how £100 invested in 1979 in each type of investment has grown to £1180, £434 and £275 respectively

Over a 10 year period shares have outperformed gilts for 96 per cent of the time and cash for 97 per cent of the time. Even over short two-year periods the probability of equities outperforming cash has been 73 per cent and beating gilts 69 per cent. The chart 'How Shares Have Won' shows what has happened to £100 invested in October 1979 in each of these three types of investment. Shares substantially outperformed the other two.

The turn of the twenty-first century saw another sharp fall in stock market prices, provoking genuine fears of a world recession. Many of those who had staked their money on Internet and telecoms stocks in the belief that these would soar forever lost huge amounts of money. One reason for a crash that turned many investors into 'ninety per centers' – those who saw the value of their holdings fall to one tenth of what they paid for them – was that even though the companies in which they had invested had absurd valuations when they had never turned a profit. Another cause, most prevalent in the case of telecoms shares, was management blunders, for example bidding billions of dollars for third-generation mobile telephony licences when there was no certainty that this technology would ever deliver a satisfactory return. A third reason, applying to all stocks, was a downturn in the world business cycle. Even so, it is likely that in the long term stocks will outperform bonds. The short term might be different.

A study by the securities house Credit Suisse First Boston, found that during a twelve-month period in 1998–9, government bonds in Britain were a better investment than equities, generating total returns of 22 per cent, compared with 11 per cent. But over the long haul, equities did best.

These studies are undoubtedly correct, but I would insert two notes of caution. Most long-term studies are based on the performance of indices like the *Financial Times* 100 index, and not on companies that were part of an index years ago but may now either be out of business, taken over by another corporation, or whose market capitalisation has slipped so much that it is no longer qualified to be in it. If you go back and look at the *FT* 100 share index in 1984 you will find that 72 companies that were listed then have since vanished. A discussion of how indices work can be found in Chapter 4, from p. 60.

The second caution is that shares can be volatile. Two of Britain's big privatisation issues were trading in 2001 at substantially less than their value five years ago, and those who have these shares parked in government-sponsored savings schemes like personal equity plans have lost by holding on to them to 'save tax'. In many other instances investors can be caught out by bad timing. Ideally you sell out at the top of the market and buy in when shares are low, taking advantage of this volatility. According to Proshare, an independent not-for-profit organisation set up to encourage individual share ownership:

> There is a clear pattern to the way a market may behave in the future: stock market rises tend to be concentrated into relatively short time periods, and often occur just after the market has fallen sharply. Unfortunately this is often the time when many investors have sold; thus, having borne the decline they are uninvested when the market bounces back.[4]

This illustrates another very important point, which is often overlooked by investors: you do need to keep your eyes on the markets. This does not mean being glued to a computer monitor for ten hours a day, but it does require a daily look at the numbers in the financial pages. There are many techniques for spotting revived buyer interest. One of them is looking at the volume of trades as well as values. Suffice it to say the key point is to keep your eye on the ball.

So why did interest in shares not develop sooner? Shares used to be the preserve of the rich. Buying and selling them was expensive, and had to be carried out through a closed shop of stockbrokers, who preferred to deal with account holders of the same social class as themselves. Those who fared best on the stock markets were those in the know, or who had inside information. There was a clear pecking order for access to information. At the top of the list was the stockbroker himself and his preferred clients, either people who did him favours, such as supplying tickets for Royal Ascot or Wimbledon, or clients who traded often, thus providing him with high commissions. Next came people with connections, travelling companions in the first-class compartments of commuter trains to London from the 'stockbroker belt', and financial editors of major newspapers, who could be depended upon to write favourably about shares, thereby pushing the price up. Before the newspaper went to press, the financial editor would, of course, help himself to a few shares. The third layer for access to information were the readers of the broadsheet newspapers, particularly *The Times*, the *Daily*

---

[4] Performance of Different Types of Investments, Proshare, November 2000.

Telegraph, the *Financial Times* and the *Wall Street Journal*. At the bottom of the pile came everyone else. With this as the scenario, it is hardly surprising that Joe Public felt excluded from the stock markets. The average family was no more likely to buy shares than to venture on to the Yorkshire grouse moors on 12 August, the start of the British shooting season.

I agree with Justin Urquhart Stewart, formerly of Barclays Stockbrokers, who argues that the process of dealing in shares needs to be demystified.

> It's depressing that people still think deposit accounts make better investments. The US is much more clued-up about share dealing than the UK, but it is hardly surprising given the poor level of financial education available in Britain. We learn about home economics, but practical financial education is not even on the school syllabus.

It is an irony that in the forties and fifties, while the punters were excluded from the stock markets, they were indirectly contributing to the growing wealth of the privileged few. Each week the 'man from the Pru', a sallow foot soldier from what was then Britain's largest life assurance company, would call on homes in the mean streets of the country's towns and villages and collect a few pence towards a savings scheme. After the salesman's commission and other costs, the residue would be invested on the stock markets. The Prudential, and others who practised house-to-house selling, such as the Liverpool Victoria, Pearl Assurance and the United Friendly, were prime and favoured clients for the coterie of stockbrokers in the City of London – each treated the other well.

Thus collective investments were born on the argument that small people – later more politely referred to as small investors – could more safely channel their meagre savings into the stock markets through giant institutions. The collective might of these organisations could wield the kind of power in trading that no individual could aspire to. Rather than risk investing in any one share, those holding collective investments could have their savings managed by experts who would achieve better results.

The theory made sound economic sense, and for a while it worked. But by the 1980s as the financial services industry grew larger, and greedier, it began to sow the seeds for substantial public dissatisfaction. Many, if not most, financial products designed for the mass markets were sold by commission agents, who preferred to use

LIVERPOOL JOHN MOORES UNIVERSITY
LEARNING SERVICES

the euphemism of financial adviser. Most of them were rewarded not with fees geared to the quality of their advice or the amount of time spent with their clients, but with a sizeable cut of the first eighteen months' contribution. Many so-called financial advisers sold families packages that were totally inappropriate, a practice that later became known as mis-selling, and was to cost the companies dearly in fines.

In parallel with this, the British Government, in common with many others, burdened the financial services industry with a complex set of regulations, which added greatly to costs. Some of the new rules were sensible and long overdue, such as a total ban on insider trading, which was made a criminal offence. Others were poorly drafted, hard to enforce and an encouragement to unnecessary bureaucracy.

It became hard to run collective investment schemes profitably, but the burden of regulation was not the only cost pressure. The greater force pushing prices skywards was that created by inflated salaries paid in financial centres like the City of London. It became commonplace for City fund managers and other executives to earn in excess of £400,000 a year, supplemented by an annual bonus of an equivalent amount. In Wall Street pay is much higher, sometimes four times higher. The only way to avoid losses has been to increase charges to the investor.

This development coincided with a revolution in technology. It became possible for the private individual to buy and sell shares, if not on equal terms with the professional traders, at least swiftly and efficiently, and at reasonable cost. At the same time it also became easy for the individual investor to obtain a great deal of relevant information free of charge.

The technologies that were the catalyst for change were not particularly new: the first was the telephone, and the second was the Internet. What was new was the way in which one company, Charles Schwab, utilised these technologies for share trading by individuals, and then took the market by storm, transforming the industry as it did so.

Charles Schwab started his share trading business to serve cities and towns across America through bustling Main Street branch offices known as share shops. There, over a cup of coffee, a browse through the *Wall Street Journal*, and a look at the New York Stock Exchange prices running across a ticker, investors could buy and sell shares. Some sought advice from the Schwab staff on hand; others acted on their own.

By the early 1990s, the firm had become the largest out-of-town broker in the United States, but was hardly a threat to the titans of Wall Street, such as the giant Merrill Lynch Pierce Venner and Smith, known throughout the financial world as 'the thundering herd'.

Then Charles Schwab began to develop its telephone business, building call centres to accept buy or sell orders from customers, and executing trades immediately through its own team of traders based at the New York Stock Exchange. It also acquired the British company Sharelink, founded in Birmingham by the entrepreneur David Jones, to cash in on the interest in share trading created by the wave of privatisations in the years of Margaret Thatcher's Conservative government. Until Sharelink arrived, it had not been easy for ordinary Britons to trade shares, for the reasons mentioned earlier. Jones, helped by technologists from the University of Cambridge, created what was in effect a share trading factory on the first floor of an unpretentious building in a dreary quarter of the city mostly inhabited by insurance companies. Few people gave him much of a chance, and the London Stock Exchange, retreating only slowly from its old traditions of privilege and pretence, did its best to crush the business through a variety of legal manoeuvres. But Jones won through, built the business, and then sold it to Schwab.

Charles Schwab's real breakthrough came with web trading, when its technology group created new software that allowed a server to take an order from a web browser on a personal computer, route it through the company's sophisticated back-end systems and mainframes, execute it, and send a confirmation back to the buyer's PC. It now processes more trades online than through traditional means. The numbers of people using the Schwab web site are little short of astonishing. At the end of 1999 it was recording 76 million visitors each day, and had grabbed 42 per cent of the online business, adding 1.3 million new e-mail account customers in the year.

Schwab has not been without competition, but it has come from new companies rather than the financial services industry establishment. One of its major competitors is E-Trade, which had its beginnings at the Cambridge Science Park, and now operates in the United States, Britain, Australia and New Zealand.

Trading shares now could not be easier. Using one of the two major web browsers, Microsoft Explorer or Netscape Navigator, you open the Charles Schwab or E-Trade web site, select the market in which you wish to trade – for example, United Kingdom – and then log on using your account number and password. This will take you directly to the page containing the details of your account, including the latest prices of any shares you already own, and their value. If you wish to trade, you enter the name of the company whose shares you wish to buy or sell, and the number of shares to be traded. The next page to appear will provide you with the cost of the transaction, and ask you if you wish to proceed. If you accept the deal, the trade will be carried out and confirmed back to you.

It is as easy as purchasing an airline ticket, and a lot easier than booking a train journey. If you do not have computer access, buying and selling by phone is still available. All you need to know is what shares are, what makes them valuable one day and less valuable the next, how to pick and choose them and when to buy and sell. Now, a little history.

2　History

The howling of the wolf, the grunting of the hog, the braying of the ass, the nocturnal wooing of the cat, all these in unison could not be more hideous than the noise which these beings make in the Stock.

Anonymous commentator
on the scene in Change Alley, London, 1695

Stock-jobbing is knavish in its private practice, and treason in its public

Daniel Defoe.

Dictum meum pactum – My word is my bond.
Handbook of the London Stock Exchange

For most people the stock markets epitomise the concept of risk and reward. With a modicum of risk, and the chance of achieving a good reward, an investor can be on the road to riches. This has been true throughout the three centuries of stock market activity.

Those who took a billion pound risk in investing in satellite television in Britain at the end of the twentieth century were opting for the same choice as the few backers prepared to chance £3,200 apiece on the Concepcion adventure in 1686. Then, a whiskery sea captain from Boston called Phips sought investors for an expedition to the north coast of Hispaniola to salvage a sunken galleon. Nine months later the backers reaped their reward – £250,000 worth of fine silver.

Throughout history, one of the major threats to any investment has been that people cheat. There are big cheats and little cheats, and only a few of them have passed through the dock of the Old Bailey. The excitement that greeted the trial in London of the Guinness Five in 1990, or the humiliation of the president of the House of Nomura a year later – or the imprisonment of Ivan Boesky and Michael Milken in New York, Ronald Li in Hong Kong and Nick Leeson in Singapore – was only a latter-day repeat of events in Britain in the late seventeenth century.

The collapse in 1995 of Barings, a famous London investment bank, set regulators searching for new solutions and tougher rules. It was much the same in 1697, when, following a wave of market rigging and insider trading, the British Government brought in an Act designed to 'restrain the number and ill-practice of brokers and stockjobbers'.

This followed a report from a Parliamentary Commission set up a year earlier which had discovered that:

> the pernicious art of stockjobbing hath, of late, so perverted the end design of Companies and Corporations, erected for the introducing or carrying on of manufactures, to the private profit of the first projectors, that the privileges granted to them have commonly been made no other use of – but to sell again, with advantage, to innocent men.[1]

As a result of the 1697 Act, all stockbrokers and stockjobbers had to be licensed before they plied their trade in the coffee shops, walks and alleys near the Royal Exchange in London. These licences were limited in number to a hundred and were granted by the Lord Mayor of London and the Court of Aldermen. They cost only £2, and entitled the licensee to wear a specially struck silver medal embossed with the Royal Arms, once he had taken an oath that he would 'truly and faithfully execute and perform the office and employment of a broker between party and party, without fraud or collusion'.

The rules of operation were strict. Brokers were not allowed to deal on their own behalf, but only for clients. They could not hold any options for more than three days without facing the certainty of permanent expulsion. Commission was limited to 5 per cent, or less. Anyone who tried to operate as a broker without a licence was, if caught, incarcerated for three days in the City pillory.

The Muscovy and East India Companies

The trade in shares began with City traders and merchants spreading the risk of two major entrepreneurial journeys: an attempt to investigate the prospects offered by the uncharted White Sea and Arctic Circle; and a voyage to India and the East Indies via the Cape of Good Hope.

---

[1] Archives of the Stock Exchange.

These ventures were to lead to the world's first two public companies: the Muscovy Company and the East India Company. Until then companies had been privately owned businesses, or partnerships between individuals. These companies were new and different. Their owners contributed money to what was called 'joint stock', and these contributions were verified through certificates which became known as shares. If later unwanted, these shares were freely transferable to anyone who would pay a price acceptable to both buyer and seller.

The Muscovy Company was created to finance a brave, risky and costly attempt by Sebastian Cabot in 1553 to find a north-east trade route from Britain to China and what was then known as the Orient. Cabot and his crew would face the physical hazards, but others were needed to share the financial risk. As one of the first shareholders explained at the time:

> Every man willing to bee of the societie, should disburse the portion of twentie and five pounds a piece: so that in a short time, by this means, the sum of six thousand pounds being gathered, three ships were brought.[2]

Two of the three ships that formed the expedition sank off Norway, and things looked bleak for the 250 merchants putting up £25 each. Fortunately, one of the leaders of the venture did make it to Moscow, where he persuaded Ivan the Terrible to sign a trade agreement. This yielded some returns, though not as good as would have been achieved had they been able to get through the Arctic icecap to Asia.

The East India Company was more successful, and was the first company to find shareholders prepared to put up money on a substantial scale. It needed modern, armed ships for the difficult and dangerous voyage to the Orient, and a home base of substantial docks in London. Although some ships sank on voyages, and the company hovered close to bankruptcy in its early days, it managed to raise more than £1.6 million over seventeen years. As the silk and spice trade developed, those who had invested in the original stock enjoyed returns of 40 per cent a year.

This quickly led enterprising developers to realise that raising capital through shares was a good way to fund less risky ventures which were still too costly for one person, however rich, to finance.

---

[2] Alan Jenkins, *The Stock Exchange Story*, Heinemann, London, 1973.

Why not create more joint stock companies for domestic projects? One of the earliest was established by Francis, Earl of Bedford, to fulfil his bold plan to drain the East Anglian Fens. The aim of this ambitious scheme was to create thousands of hectares of additional fertile agricultural land, and to provide London with its first supply of fresh water. Others were persuaded to add to his own £100,000 contribution, and in 1609 the 'Government and Company of the New River brought from Chadwell and Amwell to London' was founded. It become Britain's first water stock. Although the water company operations were bought out by the Metropolitan Water Board in 1904, the company still exists as the oldest to be quoted on the London Stock Exchange.

Coffee Shops

By the end of the seventeenth century there were a number of large joint stock companies, and substantial dealing in their shares. The historian W. R. Scott estimated that by 1695 there were 140 joint stock companies, with a total market capitalisation of £4.5 million. When people wanted to buy and sell shares in these companies, the place to do it was usually one of two coffee houses in the heart of the City of London. One was called Garraway's and the other Jonathan's, and both were near Change Alley, a haunt favoured by City merchants and traders. Change Alley is still to be found today in the narrow spit of land between Cornhill and Threadneedle Street, close to the Bank of England.

The patrons of the coffee establishments of the seventeenth century had style and colour. There were no grey suits to be seen; even the tinkers dressed up. The atmosphere was convivial, the talk was of adventure and new ideas. The British Empire was expanding, and there was money to be made, and shares to be bought and sold. Over coffee you could also run your eye down a sheet of paper containing the latest prices of most commodities, and of those shares traded. The title of this daily sheet was also an accurate description of it: *The Course of the Exchange and Other Things*. It was to be the precursor of greater publications to come – the *Stock Exchange Daily Official List*, the *Financial Times* and the *Wall Street Journal*.

A writer of the day set the scene:

The centre of the jobbing is in the Kingdom of Exchange Alley and its adjacencies: the limits are easily surrounded in about a Minute and a half stepping out of Jonathan's into the Alley, you turn your face full South, moving on a few paces, and then turning Due East, you advance to Garraway's; from there going out at the other Door, you go on still East into Birchin Lane and then halting a little at the Sword-Blade Bank to do much mischief in fervent Words, you immediately face to the North, enter Cornhill, visit two or three petty Provinces there in your way West; and thus having Boxed your Compass, and sail'd round the whole Stock Jobbing Globe, you turn into Jonathan's again; and so, as most of the great Follies of Life oblige us to do, you end just where you began.[3]

The South Sea Bubble

This coffee society was to thrive for more than fifty years, and by 1720 Change Alley and its coffee houses were thronged with brokers. It was the place to be. Throughout the day the narrow streets were impassable because of the throng of lords and ladies in their carriages. The Act regulating and restricting their access to the narrow streets lapsed by default, because nobody took any notice of it, and no one tried to enforce it. The scene is described in an eighteenth-century ballad:

> Then stars and garters did appear
> Among the meaner rabble
> To buy and sell, to see and hear
> The Jews and Gentiles squabble,
> The greatest ladies thither came
> And plied in chariots daily,
> Or pawned their jewels for a sum
> To venture in the Alley.[4]

The principal attraction was the excitement caused by the booming share price of the South Sea Company, which started to be sold at the beginning of 1720 at £128 each, and swiftly rose as euphoria about the company's prospects was spread both by brokers and by the government. By March the price had risen to £330, by May it was

[3] E. V. Morgan and W. A. Thomas, *The London Stock Exchange*, St. Martin's Press, NY, 1969.
[4] Alan Jenkins, *The Stock Exchange Story*, Heinemann, London, 1973.

£550, and by 24 June it had reached an insane £1,050. The South Sea Company had been set up nine years earlier by the British Government, ostensibly with the aim of opening up trade and markets for new commodities in South America. It also had another purpose, which, these days, has a familiar ring about it. By converting it to a public company, rather than a government department, it reduced the Treasury's public debt by £9 million.

For eight years the company was moribund and unprofitable. Its shares were dormant. It had only one contract of any size: to supply black slaves to Latin America. The Government then adopted the concept of privatisation of a state-owned concern, something much more audacious than the sales of British Telecom or British Gas over 250 years later. It offered shares in the South Sea Company to the public, hoping that it would raise enough money to wipe out the entire National Debt of some £31 million.

The Government was persuaded to do this by a wily operator, Sir John Blunt, who was a director of the company, who effectively underwrote the issue. An underwriter in the financial markets guarantees that if there are not enough people willing to buy the shares on offer, he will do so at a discount. The issue was made on a 'partly paid' basis; which means an investor has only to find a small proportion at the time, but then pays for the full cost in instalments. The offer was heavily oversubscribed, and many people who had hoped to get South Sea shares missed out. There was considerable irritation when it was discovered that Blunt's acquaintances, and other people of influence, had been given an extra allocation, a circumstance that was to repeat itself in Britain during the Thatcher privatisations.

The Government realised it would be possible to raise even more money on the strength of the supposed bright future of the South Sea Company. To encourage wider share ownership, the company made loans to the public to buy its shares, with the loans secured on the shares themselves. Three centuries later the practice was to emerge again with the issue of junk bonds (see Chapter 11).

Sir John Blunt proved adept at adopting the techniques of public relations to push the share price up. There were hints of lavish dividends to come, prominent people offered thinly disguised bribes to buy shares and talk about it. Even the peace negotiations under way with Spain were frequently deployed for propaganda purposes, since the prospect of an end to conflict meant more trade with South America.

The astute reader will by now have guessed the inevitable outcome. The smart money, including that invested by the Prime Minister, Sir Robert Walpole, sold out at the peak of the boom. The Prince of Wales, the Duke of Argyll, the Chancellor of the Exchequer and many Members of Parliament made handsome profits. The bubble burst, and triggered off the first ever bear market. Within eight weeks of rising above the £1,000 mark, the share price plunged to £175. By December 1720 it had sunk to £124, bringing ruin to those who had seen the South Sea Company as the chance of a lifetime. There was an outcry, forcing the Government to introduce legislation in the shape of the Bubble Act, designed to prevent a rash of similar speculative ventures from springing up. There was the inevitable Parliamentary inquiry, which concluded that the accounts had been falsified and a government minister bribed. One of the few public figures to pay a penalty was the hapless Chancellor of the Exchequer John Aislabie. Before he had a chance to enjoy his £800,000 capital gain, he was committed to the Tower upon being found guilty of the 'most notorious, dangerous and infamous corruption'.

It was – and remains – the most fabled episode in British financial history. It took a while for investors to recover their nerve, and it was a long time before the fledgling stock market got back into its stride. Indeed, it wasn't until the next century that another large crop of joint stock companies was formed, and this only came about because of an acute shortage of capital for major projects both at home and abroad.

Mines, Railways, Canals

By 1824, the end of the cyclical trade depression, there were 156 companies quoted on the London Stock Exchange, with a market capitalisation of £47.9 million. In the following twelve months, interest in investment increased sharply. Prospectuses were issued for no fewer than 624 companies, with capital requirements of £372 million. The largest group were general investment companies, mostly with extensive interests overseas, which raised £52 million. Canals and railways came next, raising £44 million, followed by mining companies with £38 million and insurance, a new industry, with £35 million.

The insurance industry was founded on the same concept as the stock market: the pooling of risk. As the City became more built up and more congested, there were considerable fears that there could be a repeat of the Great Fire of London of 1666 when most of the City had been wiped out. Companies were formed to offer protection against fire, and this protection included the promotion of safety measures and the provision of fire brigades. With the chances of a repeat inferno much reduced, the fire offices began to accept premiums in exchange for taking on the risk of fire at individual premises. They insured not only buildings, but also the financial loss suffered by a business if it was forced to close or move as a result of a fire. Soon this concept spread to public and individual liability, theft, loss and accidental damage, and to individuals' lives. Thus the third major plank of the financial services industry was born, and expanded rapidly worldwide.

Meanwhile the railways proved to be a great benefit for the promotion of investment, even if most of the investors lost their money. The Duke of Wellington had opposed the development of railways, arguing imperiously that 'railroads will only encourage the lower classes to move about needlessly'. His words proved to be prescient. Not only did people start to travel, but the upper classes living outside London were spurred into owning shares. A new word entered the financial vocabulary: stag, a person who applies for an allotment of shares with the clear intention of selling them to someone else before having to meet the cost of buying them.

The stags were out in force in 1836 when George Hudson, a bluff Yorkshireman, raised £300,000 for the York and North Midland Railway under the slogan 'Mak' all t'railways coom t'York'. The £50 shares were oversubscribed and quickly traded at a premium of £4 each. Within three years the line was opened, and the bells of York Minster pealed out in joyful celebration. Much of the joy was short-lived. So many railway lines spread out across the country that many rail companies could not pay the wages of the train drivers, let alone dividends for shareholders. Many companies were overcapitalised, but instead of returning the cash to shareholders, managements found other ways to use the surplus funds, much to the chagrin of investors.

Despite these setbacks, by 1842 there were sixty-six railway companies quoted on the London Stock Exchange, with a capital of almost £50 million. During the boom in railway issues, the *Economist* was moved to publish an editorial which, with a change of name and date, might well have fitted into the British Telecom era of 1985: 'Everybody is in the stocks now,' it purred. 'Needy clerks, poor tradesmen's apprentices, discarding serving men and bankrupts – all have entered the ranks of the great moneyed interest.'

Provincial stock markets were also established. Local investment opportunities were featured in the advertisements for share auctions which regularly appeared in a Liverpool newspaper after about 1827. It was quite usual to use a property auction as the opportunity to dispose of a parcel of shares. By the middle of 1845, regional stock exchanges had been formed in twelve towns and cities, from Bristol in the south to Newcastle in the north, with Yorkshire claiming the greatest number. But only five of them were to survive the trading slump of 1845 to become permanent institutions.

Government Debt

All through this period government debt had been growing. Compensation to slave-owners whose slaves had been freed, the cost of the Crimean War and the purchase by the Government of the national telegraph system combined to blow out the deficit.

Raising the cash to fund it provided the most lucrative and reliable form of income for stockbrokers. By 1860, British funds amounted to more than all the other quoted securities combined, and created by far the widest market in the Exchange. Government stocks, or bonds, were bought daily from the Treasury by the City figure called the Government Broker, who then sold them on in the marketplace. The idea was that these stocks, to become known much later as gilt-edged securities, would be used to reduce or even eradicate the National Debt. Of course issuing these bonds had the opposite effect, because they added to the debt, but they quickly became a way of funding unpopular measures. Had the Government not been able to borrow money through these tradeable bonds, it would have had to resort to taxation.

It was not long before local authorities also jumped on the bandwagon. The City of Dublin was the first to raise money through bonds, followed by Edinburgh, Glasgow and the Metropolitan Board of Works.

The First Exchange

By this time the brokers and other money dealers had long since left their colourful but damp pitches in Change Alley. The friendly coffee houses had become too crowded for comfort, and everyone knew everyone else's business. The nature of the customers also changed, as Change Alley played host to people described by the established professionals as 'riff-raff'. When Jonathan's was finally burnt down after a series of major fires around 1748, the broking industry sought refuge in New Jonathan's, rebuilt in Threadneedle Street, where they were charged a sixpence-a-day entrance fee, a sum sufficient to discourage tinkers, money-lenders and the other parasites who had frequented the previous premises. Soon afterwards a sign was erected over the door: The Stock Exchange.

The stock market continued to operate in this way, more or less as a private club, for thirty years, until its members decided something more formal was needed. On 7 February 1801 the Stock Exchange was shut down, to reopen one month later as the Stock Subscription Room. The per diem entry fee was stopped: instead, members had to be elected, pay a fee of ten guineas, and risk a fine of two guineas if they were found guilty of 'disorderly conduct', the penalty going to charity. There does not seem to be an accurate record of how many charities benefited from this provision, or how many fines were levied.

The Stock Subscription Room had a short life, for members quickly decided it was too small, and in the same year laid the foundation stone for a new building in Capel Court. This stone records that this was also the 'first year of the union between Great Britain and Ireland', and notes that the building was being 'erected by private subscription for transaction of the business in the public funds'.

Not all members of the public were impressed by this new monument. The old lady who sold cups of tea and sweet buns outside Capel Court moved away because, she said, 'the Stock Exchange is such a wicked place'. But with monuments come tablets, and it was not long before members were forced to draw up new rules of operation. Adopted in 1812, these were to survive, more or less intact, for the next 150 years. Neither members nor their wives could be engaged in any other business, failures had to be chalked up above the clock immediately so that there could be a fair distribution of assets to creditors, and members were informed that they had to give up 'rude and trifling practices which have long disgraced the Stock Exchange'.

The Capel Court building was to last a century and a half, and in the end it was not size but ancient communications that made it unworkable. The decision was taken to rebuild, and a 'state-of-the-art' twenty-six-storey concrete tower was established as the new London Stock Exchange in Throgmorton Street almost on the spot where New Jonathan's had once flourished. Opened by Queen Elizabeth in 1972, it stood as a seemingly unassailable bastion of capitalism in a climate where the City of London was often under political scrutiny and attack, and where Britain was in deep economic and industrial decline.

The early years in 'Throg Street' were good ones for the practitioners in the market. While heavy industry had crumbled – and much of manufacturing industry had vanished under international competition from Europe and south-east Asia – the banks and other financial institutions that provided a large part of Britain's invisible exports thrived and prospered. Britain was still merchant banker to the free world, and overseas governments, corporations and individual potentates entrusted their dollars, gold and silver to financial houses in the square mile of the City. In the early 1980s more than £50 million worth of foreign currency changed hands each day in London, yielding banks and other dealers large sums in commission and making London the dominant market in foreign exchange with one third of world business.

The City was a club, as cosy and impenetrable as any of the establishments two miles away in St James's which served diplomats and the officer class. Those invited to share its mysteries at generous lunches or livery dinners sniffed an uneasy air of narrow bonhomie and patrimony. Above all it was a closed shop.

The members of the London Stock Exchange were particularly well protected. No one could buy or sell shares except through one of their member firms, most of which had been in the hands of the same family for decades. And as a consequence of a closed shop resembling a protection racket, investors had to pay twice for each transaction: a commission for the stockbroker and a mark-up for the stockjobber.

Commissions were fixed, in the manner of most professional fees at the time. For a broker to discount a commission, even to a friend, was as serious an offence as a doctor committing adultery with a patient or a farm worker poaching a landowner's pheasants. Stockbrokers brandished a pocket guide, published by Messrs Basil, Montgomery, Lloyd and Ward, which set out an elaborate sliding scale of charges. In 1975 the scale was generating average commissions of about 0.75

per cent, no matter how large the deal. Thus a £10,000 trade would cost £75 in commission; while the same trade today could be carried out for £12 or less. Ten years later in 1960 the commission rate went up to 1.25 per cent on small trades, penalising the small shareholder.

At these levels, and with the volume of business that was available to the limited number of stockbrokers, it was a profitable and relatively stress-free occupation. Advertising was banned, so clients were obtained through personal networking – usually over a substantial lunch, a game of cards in the first-class rail compartment on the way home, or a round of golf. The better broking firms used some of their profits to undertake detailed research into the activities of major companies, the results of which were made freely available to the investing institutions and more moneyed private customers.

The stockbroker did not have to involve himself in direct financial bargaining with other brokers; indeed, until 1986 he was prohibited from doing so. Share trading was in the hands of stockjobbers, shrewd and resilient characters who stood or perched on stools at the elevated benches on the floor of the London Stock Exchange. Many of them had a demeanour more akin to a barrow-boy or bookmaker than to a City gent, and their daily work had many similarities. The jobbers made the market, deciding at what price they would buy or sell the shares on offer. Their profit was the difference between the buying and selling price, known as the 'jobbers' turn'.

Jobbers never dealt with the investing public, at any level. They traded only with dealers, usually junior employees of stockbroking firms, who were based on the floor of the Exchange, and who took their instructions by telephone or by sign language from colleagues standing nearby. Trading started at nine and finished at four thirty, with an hour's break for lunch, and at peak times provided a colourful spectacle to visitors peering down from the gallery above. Occasionally trading would be punctuated by the ringing of a bell, signifying an announcement to the Exchange, which would usually be followed by a roar of approval or derision, a quick revision by jobbers of their prices and another burst of trading. In day-to-day trading, both dealer and jobber had to display a certain amount of guile.

Big Bang

October 1986 was the most momentous month in the long history of
the London Stock Exchange – a combination of forces for change
known as Big Bang. One force was the prime minister of the time,
Margaret Thatcher. As part of her assault on trade unions' restrictive
practices, she determined that fixed commissions charged by stockbrokers should be abolished, and that all major financial institutions
should have free and open access to the capital markets. The
principal barriers between banks, merchant banks, investment
institutions and stockbrokers should be broken down: all should be
able to set up as one-stop financial supermarkets if they wished to.
Why not allow one company to buy and sell shares for clients, raise
capital for business, invest in new ventures and trade in international
securities like eurobonds?

But by far the biggest force for change was technology: the combination of high-speed telecommunications and the microprocessor
meant that international deals could be carried out anywhere. There
was no need for any of the very large trades to pass through the Stock
Exchange at all.

Immediately prior to Big Bang, 62 per cent of the trading in one of
Britain's largest companies, ICI, was being transacted off the London
Exchange, mainly in New York. A large share of the buying and
selling of other major British companies had also been taking place
in the United States. This trading was by no means confined to
American investors, for some of the big British institutions found that
dealing across the Atlantic was a better proposition. An official of the
Prudential Assurance Company explained: 'When we have a
significant buying programme on we check all available markets. We
take the attitude that we deal wherever we can get the best price.'

Effectively the big traders had begun to bypass London, where the
complicated system of brokers and jobbers was costing them much
more in commission, government stamp duty and Value Added Tax.

For Sir Nicholas Goodison, chairman of the Stock Exchange,
sweeping reform was the only solution. If the Stock Exchange was to
compete with the giant American broking houses, it had to join them
at their own game. There was no choice when competition was
creaming off the top business, in both value and volume. Otherwise
there would be nothing left for the old-fashioned Stock Exchange,
and the jobbers would be left standing at their pitches.

Effecting the necessary changes took time and considerable

resolution. It meant ending a way of life that had been a tradition for more than a hundred years. Even though its members could see that the system was under threat, the Stock Exchange Council had to be given a firm nudge by the Government in the direction of change. This happened almost by accident. The Office of Fair Trading had argued that stockbrokers should be treated no differently from other sectors of the community – solicitors, estate agents, motor traders, soap powder manufacturers – who had been barred from fixing prices amongst themselves, and were now bound to offer some semblance of competition in the marketplace. When the Stock Exchange demurred, the Government decided on legal action, using the weight of the Monopolies Commission to take apart the entire rulebook of the Exchange as a litany of restrictive practices. It was estimated that the proceedings would take five years to complete, and cost at least £5 million in legal fees. It was, of course, like using a sledgehammer to crack a nut and an absurd way of challenging an entire trading system. As Sir Nicholas Goodison was later to say:

> It was a foolish way to study the future of a great international market. It was a matter which needed long and close study, and preferably a public examination not constrained by the requirements of litigation or the strait-jacket of court procedure. Unfortunately the government turned down the suggestion of such an examination, and we were forced into a position of defence of rules, not all of which we would necessarily wish to keep. Thus open debate became impossible because anything said could, as it were, be taken down in evidence and used in court. The case pre-empted resources, effort and thought.[5]

It did, however, concentrate the minds of the Council members of the Stock Exchange. The Government was clearly in no mood to set up a Royal Commission to inquire into the Stock Exchange; ministers saw that as a waste of time. If the legal case went on, with each side producing volumes of written evidence, as well as witnesses for examination, cross-examination and re-examination, the Stock Exchange would end up in an unwinnable situation. There would also be unfavourable publicity. And even if the Exchange won the legal battle, its joy would be short-lived, for such was the resolve of the Thatcher government to curb the restrictive power of trade unions that it could hardly spare a notorious City club, and would feel obliged to legislate to change the law.

---

[5] Interview with the author, 1985.

In July 1983, the Government offered Goodison a face-saver. It offered to drop the case against the Stock Exchange if the Council would follow the example of New York in 1985 and abandon fixed commissions. It did so, and the die was cast for the biggest transformation since the days of the Change Alley coffee shops.

With the abolition of fixed commissions, which provided a steady and solid income, more or less indexed to the rate of inflation, many stockbrokers could not survive. Competition over commissions might be acceptable in a bull market, but when the bears emerged in strength there would be trouble. 'Bull' is the name for the optimist who believes that prices are likely to go higher, and who charges into the market to buy; if there are enough bulls, their confidence is sufficient to push up prices, and commissions. A bear is the opposite market animal, who fears the worst, and expects a fall. When the bears run for cover, you have a bear market. For stockbrokers, a bear market generates fear, for although there are good commissions to be had when there is pronounced selling, the prices on which those commissions are based are lower, and interest dies.

From the perspective of the old-style broker, the future was grim. New technologies would force a change in the clubbish lifestyle. There would be fewer lunches at the club, and days out on the golf course. Those who wanted to survive would have to behave like Chicago futures dealers. Life would become unbearable – just like a job on the money or commodity markets, with young men and women arriving to a room full of telephones and computer terminals at 7.30 every morning, shouting at them and at each other for at least twelve hours, and leaving exhausted in the evening. This would be a world where the mid-life crisis could be expected at the age of twenty-six.

They also felt that competition would be so fierce there would probably be less profit. With no fixed commissions, firms would have neither the time nor the resources to undertake company or sector research, let alone visit a firm and enjoy a steak and kidney pie in a country hotel with the chairman and managing director. Instead they would spend their days peering at monitors, and yelling down the telephone.

As for open ownership, well, the senior partners would sell out, pocket their millions and go to live in Bermuda, whilst those left would not know who their bosses were, only that they worked for some large bank, almost certainly under foreign ownership. It was hard for brokers to imagine so great a change from the way things had been.

Despite their defeat over commissions, the old guard held out against other reforms. However, on 4 June 1985, the 4,495 members of the Stock Exchange were confronted with an historic choice: to face up to the future or face the consequences of living with the past.

Two resolutions were put to the members voting on the floor of the Exchange. For chairman Goodison, whose passion for old clocks belied his modern outlook, the issue was clear. It was about 'whether or not members want to keep the bulk of the securities business in this country and in the Stock Exchange', he wrote in a letter to all members of the exchange. 'It is about keeping and strengthening the Stock Exchange as the natural market in securities.'

The first resolution, which required only a simple majority, would enable outsiders – banks, international finance houses, money brokers – to own up to 100 per cent of a member firm, instead of only 29.9 per cent. The second resolution required a 75 per cent majority, and proposed changes in the constitution of the Stock Exchange to shift ownership from individual members to corporates. Plans were devised whereby members could sell their individual holdings in the Exchange to newcomers. The first resolution was passed by 3,246 votes to 681, but the second failed by a very small margin, achieving 73.64 per cent instead of the required 75 per cent. For Goodison this was a major setback, but for those who voted against it, it was an even greater blow.

Goodison had already warned members that to reject the proposal would be 'very serious and could cause substantial damage to the standing of the Stock Exchange', mainly because new entrants from America and elsewhere, if denied easy membership, would decide simply to bypass its activities. But he had one major card to play. Under his leadership the Stock Exchange's reputation and credibility had been high. In almost every other area of the City there had been scandal, but the Stock Exchange had retained its integrity, and had been shown to be a more effective policeman of those within its province than the Bank of England. Goodison was able to secure the Stock Exchange's right to self-regulation under the Conservative government's proposed financial services legislation, thus making it certain that those who wished to trade in British equities would want to be governed by its rules. The Exchange's Council then moved to create the new class of corporate membership effective from March 1986.

Under this, corporate members would each own one share, which gave them the right to take part in all of the Stock Exchange's trading activities, and to use its settlement and other facilities. There would be no need for any corporate member to have an individual member on either its board or staff, although all those in its employ who had contact with customers would have to be 'approved persons'. Thus, those members who had voted against the Council on the second resolution in the hope of getting better terms for selling their individual shares to new conglomerate members found that these shares were virtually worthless. The biggest group in the world could join the club for only one share, negotiating the price not with old members, but with the Stock Exchange Council.

The World's First International Exchange

No sooner had the new deal gone through and the day of Big Bang passed, relatively without incident, than Goodison achieved a major coup. As outlined earlier, one of the major threats to the London Stock Exchange was international equity trading bypassing London altogether. Even though the new rules made London more com-petitive than it had been – and electronic dealing systems forced traders to work faster – there was still a large group of securities houses trading international stocks who saw no good reason why they should be part of the new Exchange.

These houses had formed themselves into ISRO, the International Securities Regulatory Organisation, which, despite its grandiose title, showed very little affection for regulation. Its members traded in the stocks of about four hundred of the world's major corporations for the benefit of about eighty institutions. It was an exclusive club for the big boys, who argued that since they all knew each other, not many rules were needed.

Prior to Big Bang, ISRO and the London Exchange were not exactly the best of friends; indeed, they often traded insults. Since international equities were stocks which were traded beyond their own country boundaries, it was argued that they should not be subject to rigid domestic rules. And a new class of international equity was being spawned: issues by international corporations underwritten and distributed in overseas countries. The first really large issue of this kind was British Telecom; when it was floated off by the British Government, a large proportion of the stock was successfully offered to institutions in North America, Europe and Japan.

Such international equity issues were organised by investment banks and securities houses, who offered tranches of stock directly to favoured clients without touching the stock markets. Because of London's position at the centre of the world time zone, most of this business was conducted there. Goodison approached ISRO and suggested that sooner or later some form of ordered regulation for the conduct of global equity markets would be forced on it, if it did not form an international standard of its own; and since the London Stock Exchange offered the nearest thing to such a standard, why not merge with it?

From the Stock Exchange point of view, the proposed deal averted the possibility of the world's financial giants setting up a competing marketplace in London, and, according to Goodison, opened 'the way for a united securities market which will be a very powerful competitor for international business'.

On 12 November 1986, members of the Stock Exchange voted for the merger, and the combined body became known as the International Stock Exchange of the United Kingdom and Northern Ireland. The old guard knew there was no choice – the new Exchange was going to be dominated by foreigners, but so what? The previous changes they had approved had already allowed foreign financial houses to take over two thirds of large British broking firms, and so domination by the likes of Citicorp, American Express, Deutsche Bank, Merrill Lynch, Nomura and the Swiss Banking Corporation was anyway inevitable. There was also a sweetener of £10,000 for each member when they retired or reached the age of sixty.

The New Conglomerates

The establishment of giant new conglomerates which accompanied Big Bang led to an undignified scramble as City and international broking firms, banks and finance houses rushed to jump into bed with each other. So unseemly was the haste that some parted company with new-found, if expensive, friends within days rather than weeks, in a kind of financial promiscuity which must have left old faithfuls gasping for breath. One major bank bought a firm of jobbers only to find that, by the time the ink was dry on the contract, the best people had all left en masse to join a rival. Since these people had been almost the firm's only asset, the acquisition was more or less worthless. The Deputy Governor of the Bank of England, George Blunden, put his finger on the problem:

> If key staff – and on occasions whole teams – can be offered inducements to move suddenly from one institution to another it becomes very difficult for any bank to rely on the commitment individuals will give to implementing its plans, and adds a further dimension of risk to any bank which is building its strategy largely around a few individuals' skills.[6]

The banks and merchant banks were the predators, but they found even the very large broking firms only too willing to submit. Typical of the alliances formed was Barclays de Zoete Wedd, a merger between the investment banking side of Barclays Bank plc, the stockbrokers de Zoete and Bevan, and London's largest stockjobber in gilt-edged securities, Wedd, Durlacher & Mordaunt. Barclays became top dog, owning 75 per cent of the shares, but by the end of the decade had sold a big chunk of the business. Another group was Mercury Asset Management, formed by S.G. Warburg and Co. and three major broking and jobbing firms. Each of these two giants was able to issue securities, to place them with its large client base, and to buy and sell speculatively on its own account. MAM survived only one decade before being gobbled up by the world's largest securities business, Merrill Lynch.

All but one of Britain's top twenty broking and jobbing houses were absorbed into large new financial conglomerates. Among the leading firms, only Cazenove and Co. remained independent. By taking this step, it benefited from both institutions and private investors seeking out brokers with no commercial link, and therefore no potential conflict of interest with a bank, an insurance company or a unit trust management company.

What were created were new megagroups able to act as bankers to a corporation, raise long-term capital for it through debt or equity, make a market in its shares, retail them to investors, and buy them as managers of discretionary funds. The question at the time was how the public could be sure that those at the marketing end of the firm were not privy to insider information, and, if they were, how they could be prevented from acting upon it. Sensitive information does not, of course, have to be in written form in a report. A nudge and a wink over lunch is a more subtle and less detectable way of passing

---

[6] George Blunden, speech given at Mansion House.

secrets. The official Stock Exchange answer to this problem was that 'Chinese Walls' had to be erected between the various parts of a financial services company, so that the interest of the public or investors would always be put first. Whether this has happened is still open to debate.

The arrival of the new monoliths badly upset the staid City career structure. Salaries rocketed as a game of musical chairs for all but the most mundane jobs got under way. Staffs of merchant banks and broking firms, whose only regular bright spot had previously been the annual bonus payment, suddenly found, to their wonderment, that they had taken over from soccer professionals as the group in society most likely to be able to bid up earnings without lifting their game. 'The trick,' one twenty-six-year-old woman employed by a Swiss bank told me, 'is to always appear to be in demand. If they think you are about to leave, they will offer more without you having to ask for it.'

One might have expected the level of poaching to diminish over time. But more than ten years after Big Bang, generous offers were still being made to whole teams of analysts. One of those to suffer worst was Deutsche Morgan Grenfell, an institution formed out of an alliance between one of London's oldest firms and the powerful Deutsche Bank. In 1997 it lost its entire four-person emerging market bond team to the Japanese group Daiwa Europe. In the same month its deputy chairman, Peter Cadbury, responsible for some of Morgan Grenfell's most important relationships, left to become joint chairman of a large corporate finance institution.

Some of the individuals involved cut a very high profile, none more so than Nicola Horlick, mother-of-five from London, who made the headlines when she parted company with Deutsche Morgan Grenfell after being seen having lunch with senior officers from another company. It was alleged that she was planning to leave the company, for whom her team had quadrupled the value of the funds under management, a suggestion she strenuously denied. But within six months, after a series of tear-jerking stories in the tabloids about how as a woman in the City she had been 'picked on', she was leaving her £3 million home shortly after dawn each morning for a new job at DMG's deadly rivals, the French-owned Société Générale Asset Management. She was joined there by an old friend, John Richards, who had been on 'gardening leave', a euphemism for sitting at home doing nothing, after resigning as head of institutional investment management at another rival, Mercury Asset Management. Horlick's lifestyle, her £1 million a year income package and her huge responsibilities led to her being dubbed 'superwoman', a highly sexist remark because no one would ascribe the title 'superman' to a male with comparable responsibilities. On the other hand, few would agree with Nicola Horlick's own description of herself as 'an ordinary person doing an ordinary job'.

Another high-profile defection took place in 1999 when ABN Amro, the Dutch international banking group, lost its entire top-ranking banking research team to rival Morgan Stanley. For ABN Amro it was an unhappy year, for it had already seen the head of its oils team, and its entire pharmaceuticals team walk out. ABN Amro was philosophical. 'This is just part of the natural ebb and flow of analysts,' the company said.

Such is the new City: highly competitive, and with little loyalty.

Along with a move towards a superleague of financial conglomerates came another switch of attitudes – an obsession with short-term performance. It has become clear that fund managers – the men and women who manage the money in pension funds, life assurance companies and unit trusts – are no longer prepared to play safe by concentrating investments in large holdings in giant but dull corporations. The marketing men began to demand performance, as measured by league tables appearing regularly in the financial press. Fund managers' huge bonuses depended on achieving good returns. Not so long ago the average institutional investor shared his portfolio between government gilt-edged securities (interest-bearing bonds) and blue-chip equities (shares in well-known companies like Unilever, BP and ICI).

More recently, however, fund managers have been inclined to move the investments around, terrifying corporate treasurers who watch, helpless, as large blocks of their companies' shares are traded for what seems fashion or a whim. A fund manager may desert GEC, as many did soon after Big Bang, and buy into Siemens of Germany, Microsoft of America or NTT of Japan, thereby gambling on future currency movements as well as on the future profitability of a company or market sector. Or he may buy eurobonds. And because of the risk of volatile movements in exchange or interest rates, he may protect himself by an options or futures contract (see Chapter 9), or both. The result is that fund managers tend towards taking profits whenever they present themselves. The only goal is shareholder value. So how are shares valued?

3   Shares and Bonds

It's paper anyway. It was paper when we started and it's paper now.

Sam Moore Walton, founder of Wal-Mart

When stocks go down, shoeshine goes down. It's rough.

Wall Street shoe cleaner

Risks are explicit, and well priced. The skills of the bookmaker have proved more reliable than those of the banker.

Anthony Harris, *The Times*

From time to time television newscasters tell us in their breathless headline style that billions of pounds – or dollars, yen or euros – have been wiped off the value of shares. To most ordinary people, such stories are meaningless; since they are inclined to believe that shares are not for them and they do not take much interest. The minority of viewers who are economically literate may pause to ponder why BP or BT are worth hundreds of millions of dollars less today than yesterday, but will then shift their attention elsewhere. The broadcasters, adopting their self-styled mission to explain, never let such stories pass without interpretation, sometimes plausible but often wrong. They frequently take the opinion of a young market analyst, rarely slow to offer opinions and once described contemptuously by a former British Chancellor of the Exchequer, Nigel Lawson, as 'teenage scribblers'.

Each share represents a tiny but equal percentage of a company. The actual value of a public company whose stock is listed on an exchange will always be the price of each share at any given time multiplied by the number of shares in existence. A company's value can rise or fall by millions of pounds in a couple of minutes. When an individual applies for a mortgage, the lender assesses his net worth by aggregating his assets and deducting from that sum his liabilities. Perform the same operation with a company, and you get its net asset value – or NAV. Divide that by the number of shares, and you get

NAV per share. Neither figure is real value. Real value depends not on the assets-less-liabilities equation, but on the day-to-day perception of the market.

Often this real value seems illogical, especially when share prices appear to bear little relationship to the company's sales performance, or to the profit-and-loss account. Employees who see colleagues being made redundant at a time when share prices are at an all-time high are perplexed. This perplexity can turn to anger when they see their bosses reaping large bonuses when the share value is slumping.

But this lack of logic is what makes the stock markets fascinating. There are many reasons why shares move up and down, and here are some of them, starting with the obvious:

1. **The company is doing badly.** If a company has a poor year, as did British Airways in 2001, then the share price will fall. But remember that share price always reflects perception, or at least the investors' collective view as to where the company is going. So although British Airways' profits at the start of 1999 were not that bad, investors felt they would slip, and the share price fell. When BA announced a loss for the second quarter of the year, these investors were proved right, but the shares did not drop further because chief executive Robert Ayling was made the scapegoat and was replaced by Rod Eddington, whom institutions felt would do better. Much the same happened to Marks and Spencer in the same year. M&S was once a favourite share in many people's portfolios, but fell from grace when the perception of the company changed to the view that its fashions were stale, its goods too pricey and its buyers out of touch with the market.

2. **The company may be doing fine, but there is unease about the general direction of the economy and interest rates.** Frequently the market as a whole is unnerved by the prospects ahead. This could be because interest rates are believed to be on the rise, or because of a variety of global and regional economic factors which affect investor sentiment. Few shares move against a very significant downward trend in global markets, such as the world stock market crash of 1987, the Asian crash of 1998 or the bear market of 2001.

3. **The company has bold and strong leadership, which seems to know where it is going.** This has certainly been the case with many well-led large American companies, such as General Electric, headed until 2001 by the redoubtable Jack Welch; Microsoft, controlled by

Bill Gates; Michael Dell's Dell Computer, and Intel, inspired by Andy Grove. These high-profile personalities add an extra dimension to their corporations, and investors have faith in their leadership skills and management philosophies. Welch, for example, held the belief that GE should be either number one or number two in each sector in which it operated, or out of it altogether. Conversely, a company which appears to have weak leaders who lack strategic direction will lose investor support, and shares will fall. Such was the case with BT and Marconi in 2001.

4. The government may interfere with the company. Gone are the days when many large companies were in danger of being compulsorily acquired by the state. The march of privatisation has meant that governments have been busy divesting themselves of businesses. But governments love to interfere, and often pass legislation which will disadvantage some companies. Or government-appointed regulators tighten controls – and limit profits – of near-monopolies like British Telecom and British Gas. In Britain in 2000, strong government intervention in the affairs of Railtrack after two serious railway accidents depressed share prices and finally led to its collapse.

5. The shares are in a sector that is trendy. Once a sector has caught on as fashionable, sometimes the whole sector picks up investor enthusiasm, whatever the fundamentals may say. This happened with Internet stocks in the mid to late 1990s, when many companies that had never turned a profit suddenly built market capitalisations running into billions of dollars or pounds. Even though the companies' backers produced statements making it clear that profits could be some years away, investors, both large and small, piled in, creating vastly inflated values. Perhaps the best example was the on-line bookseller Amazon.com, formed to sell books and other goods at a modest discount to shop prices, with one attraction being that it could almost always deliver the book you wanted within a few days. At one point during the dotcom hysteria its market value rose to more than $1.5 billion, making it apparently worth more than some long-established successful corporations like Ford or Proctor & Gamble. On the eastern side of the Atlantic there was Freeserve, an Internet service provider set up by Dixons, the high street retailer. Freeserve's product was far from exceptional in terms of both technology and service, yet when it was floated off by Dixons at a well-chosen moment, its share price outstripped that of its parent.

All these Internet 'stars' were hyped in the media, none more so than lastminute.com, whose co-founder Martha Lane Fox developed a star quality of her own. The idea behind the company was a good one: it would provide anything anyone needed at the last minute – a holiday, an airline seat, a theatre ticket. Yet like many other Internet stocks, lastminute.com became a 'ninety per center'. When sanity returned to the markets and analysts started applying the normal rules of accountancy to valuations, there was a huge drop in prices, and many companies vanished from the scene as quickly as they had risen.

6. **Investment gurus like certain companies.** There are a number of well-known investment gurus whose investment and speculative skills have helped them to become multi-millionaires. These men include Warren Buffett, Henry Kaufmann, George Soros, Peter Lynch and Ron Brierley. All have a strong following, and when they act in the market, it sets a trend.

7. **Competition may be so tough that profits are hard to foresee.** There is such fierce price competition in some sectors that the companies' margins are always under threat. In Britain this is true of the food supermarket sector, where well-run companies like Tesco offer safe rather than spectacular profit growth, and therefore can be unappealing to the investor looking for above average returns. Worldwide airlines fall into the same trap. There is so much capacity – seats in search of a bottom on them – that air fares are too low to produce good yields.

8. **The company makes a major miscalculation.** Anyone can make mistakes, but sometimes the biggest blunders can be made by highly paid managements, often advised by well-rewarded management consultants. Usually the errors are as a result of strategic decisions – one of my former bosses, the current BBC Director-General, Greg Dyke, used to say to his team: 'Don't tell me you want to do something for strategic reasons, because I know then it will lose money.' It was for strategic reasons that BT, Vodacom and other companies overbid for third-generation telecoms licences, which loaded them with crippling debt and led, in one case, to the company being broken up. Marks and Spencer, mentioned earlier, adopted a new strategy designed to appeal to younger buyers, but ended up

upsetting their traditional customers while failing to attract new ones. British Airways' latest strategy of reducing capacity to serve business passengers at the expense of the wider public is far from proven, but if it fails it could seriously diminish the airline. As I have said, business is all about risk, but some managements take a risk too far.

9. **The company has been talked up in public relations campaigns**. Many companies employ investor relations managers or public relations consultants to put a favourable spin on their activities in order to keep share prices high. A high share price – with the resultant high market capitalisation – makes a company less vulnerable to takeover, and therefore leaves the executives in charge feeling more secure. It also boosts the value of their own stock options. Watch for profiles of chairmen and chief executives that are 'placed' in newspaper feature pages to enable them to talk up the company.

10. **The company may be under family control**. Families sometimes have motives which go beyond profit. A company may be a way of life. The Dow Jones Company, which publishes the excellent *Wall Street Journal*, has been criticised by shareholders for paying more attention to style than earnings. Family ownership tends to cause particularly severe problems in media corporations, where wilful and strange decisions are often taken. A power-hungry media mogul may overpay to acquire another prestigious title, for reasons of ego as much as anything else. When Rupert Murdoch bought the *New York Post* from Dorothy Schiff it lost money, and has been leaking dollars ever since. But it was the only New York daily available, and Murdoch enjoyed owning it, even if it benefited the shareholders little. Much the same could be said of his acquisition of *The Times* in London. News Corporation is also not renowned for paying generous dividends; the Murdoch family don't need the money, which would be taxable, and prefer to continue to risk it in the business. In Australia a scion of the Fairfax family seriously mismanaged the *Sydney Morning Herald*, until new shareholders provided new management. There are also problems of succession to consider in companies where a family is the principal shareholder. Many companies survive one or two generations, but not many go beyond three, for there are usually too many grandchildren to fight over the spoils or the jobs.

Gilts

Gilts is short for gilt-edged securities, which are, as the name suggests, units of a loan tranche issued by the government to fund its spending. Gilts are issued for a fixed term at a fixed rate of interest, though no one is obligated to hold them for the whole period. But like all fixed interest securities they offer the holder the security of regular interest payments, as well as repayment at maturity of the amount borrowed.

There are three types of gilts traded. Those with five years or less to run until redemption are known as shorts; those with a redemption period of between five and fifteen years are mediums, while longs are those stocks with a redemption date of more than fifteen years.

In the United States the equivalent to gilts are bonds known as Treasuries – because they are issued by the United States Treasury. Treasuries, particularly long bonds, have been popular over the years with Japanese investors, who have taken the risk that the rate of return in dollars will be greater than the decline of the dollar against the yen.

Large corporations also issue bonds, at rates of interest which are higher than government bonds, but which are also highly secure investments. Some of these offer the option to convert the bond to equities at a favourable price. It has also become fashionable for large corporations to raise money outside the country in which they are based and in another currency. These are known as eurobonds, and almost one third of these securities are listed on the London Stock Exchange.

Warrants

Another form of security is a warrant. This allows the holder the right to subscribe, at a fixed price, for shares in the company at some future date. Warrants are high risk, and offer the holder neither dividends nor voting rights. If the holder decides not to subscribe for the underlying shares, then the paper is worthless. These, and other more exotic securities, are known as derivatives, and the interested reader should look out one of the many specialist books devoted to them.

Warrants offer the opportunities and risks of options, but

generally over a longer period. It is usual for the specified exercise date to be a year or more in the future, and then on the same date in subsequent years. If share prices rise well above the exercise price of the warrant, a substantial capital gain can be made without further outlay, or the shares can be held, having effectively been bought at a discount. But the real benefit is the leverage you get by buying a large number of warrants for pennies.

Take the example of a share priced at £2, with a warrant to buy the share at the same price in two years' time for fifty pence. Buying 1,000 shares would cost £2,000. For that amount of money you could buy 4,000 warrants. If, by the exercise date, the share price has doubled to £4, you could exercise your right and buy 4,000 shares for £8,000. You could then sell them immediately for £16,000, making a profit of £8,000 for a capital outlay of £1,000. That is a profit of 700 per cent, compared with a gain of £2,000 (or only 100 per cent) had actual shares been traded. Things would not be so good if the basic share price were to fall to £1 by the specified date. If the investor had bought the shares he would be showing a loss of £1,000, but could live in hope that they might recover. The warrants would be worthless.

As with futures and options, which are discussed separately (see p. 121), it is as well to conduct some paper or pretend trades before taking the plunge with warrants. It is also as well to be careful at the end of a prolonged rise in share prices, as you could forfeit your investment.

Collective Investments

There are many people who hold no shares but nonetheless have a significant stake in stock market investment, although they may not realise it. Many older people hold with-profits endowment policies, having been persuaded to take them as part of a mortgage arrangement. Today more than £320 billion of our savings is tied up in these schemes. They are part life assurance and part savings, and were a favourite among financial advisers and insurance brokers because of the high rates of commission – usually 7 per cent – they were able to earn. Rather than taking a simple replacement mortgage, whereby the interest reduces as the capital is repaid, the endowment holder pays interest only, with the whole of the capital repayable from the sum assured upon maturity.

Money contributed to with-profits policies is invested in bonds, shares and property, but the policy holders do not get to know the details of these investments as life assurance companies tend to be secretive about their holdings. Unlike unit trust holders, who are free to sell their units at any time at the market price, an endowment policy holder has little choice but to stay the course, which could be twenty years or more. Policies can be surrendered, but the surrender value is likely to be less than the amount spent. Despite this, one in five savers give the policies up within the first five years. Brokers specialising in used policies will pay a little more than the official surrender value, but they expect to make high margins, not least because endowments are out of fashion and unpopular.

The attraction of endowments to investors took a heavy blow after the mis-selling scandals of the late nineties, when household name life assurance companies were fined heavily for foisting these products on those who could not afford them. Up to three million home-owners found that the policies would not produce enough money to pay off the mortgage – leaving them with a shortfall. What little favour they had was knocked again with the scandal surrounding Equitable Life, which was forced to close its doors to new business, downgrade bonuses and impose exit penalties after a series of decisions which left the competence of its management open to question. There is not space here to go into the whole Equitable Life saga in depth; suffice it to say that before anyone entertains a call from a life assurance salesman, they should spend a couple of hours on the Internet reading up about it. Better still, just tell the salesman to go away!

It is regrettable that life assurance companies, which, after all, are a core part of the City establishment, have behaved so badly, because the basic principle behind endowment policies is not a bad one. They offer a way of getting returns from the stock market without nail-biting direct exposure to the share markets. They do this through bonuses, which are paid annually based on the performance of the life fund, and of the life company itself. In good years the bonuses are not as high as they could be because money is held in reserve for poor years, when at least a modest bonus is paid. The bonuses are added to the value of the policy, and cannot be taken away. At the end of the policy's term a final or 'terminal' bonus is paid, at the company's discretion. In other words, policy holders are not told why the final bonus is the amount it is, or how the figure is made up.

Fortunately for the consumer, both the Financial Services

Authority and the Treasury have now dug their teeth into the life assurance industry. In 2001 the Treasury appointed Ron Sandler to investigate retail savings, with a special focus on with-profits policies. Howard Davies, the FSA's chairman, has spoken of life assurers' 'opaque superstructure, obscure marketing, and high charges'.[1] The industry is responding with some hesitation, but if the better companies become more open about their activities, there may be some future for these paper investments, though it will be a long while before they regain the trust of the public.

Unit Trusts

Unit trusts have become a cornerstone of personal investment in Britain. They allow savers to buy into the world's equity markets without staking their money in an individual company by spreading the risk across a wide range of shares, categorised by sector, region, or degree of risk. Putting it another way, they allow individuals to pool their money with others to share the risk. There is a unit trust for everybody, as a scan of the weekend newspapers will show. There are trusts that offer the prospect of capital gain; those that offer income; some that invest only in low-risk government bonds or those of blue-chip companies; those that specialise in technology stocks; and others that back high-risk stocks, often referred to by the euphemism 'recovery' or 'special situations'. There are trusts for those who will only invest in so called 'ethical' propositions. These eschew stakes in arms and tobacco companies, for example. Companies that conduct animal testing are often considered unethical, but this is a problem because only a small part of a very large corporation may conduct these tests.

There are about 1,500 unit trusts in Britain alone, managed by over 150 separate groups for more than seven million unit holders. Total unit trust investment is around £248 billion,[2] and some of the groups are very large. Almost all unit trust management companies, many of them owned by banks or other huge financial groups, operate worldwide, and have special country funds. The most popular are those with portfolios in the United States, Europe and Australia, or the more stable countries of Asia.

---

[1] *The Economist*, 24 January 2001.
[2] Association of Unit Trusts and Investment Funds, July 2001.

A good idea of the range available can be found by looking at the pricing tables in the Saturday editions of *The Times*, the *Daily Telegraph* or the *Financial Times*. The biggest group is Fidelity Investments, based in Tonbridge, Kent, which is a subsidiary of the eponymous group headquartered in Boston, United States. In Britain it lists forty-three unit trusts with £16 billion under management. Some of these funds have very specific investment goals, such as those that invest in growth in Europe, Japan, the ASEAN region, South East Asia, and the United States. There are higher-risk funds, such as American Special Situations, Japan Special Situations, European Opportunities, and one intriguingly named as the UK Aggressive Fund.

Many people still buy unit trusts through brokers, who take a substantial commission, but the industry has stepped up direct marketing through mail shots and the Internet. They are taking advantage of government savings schemes, known as ISAs, which allow individuals to save up to £7,000 a year in an approved scheme, and avoid both income tax on dividends and capital gains tax on profits. Some big unit trust groups run what amount to financial supermarkets, offering units in a range of competitors' products as well as their own. Henderson Global Investments, for instance, has a web site called www.ample.com which offers investments from Fidelity, Gartmore, Schroders, M and G and Invesco Perpetual as well as its own.

Another financial supermarket on the web comes from John Charcol, which invites investors to set out their requirements and will then recommend a portfolio of unit trusts and other investments. Their site offers a choice of 260 funds from eighteen groups. An attraction is that any money deposited with the company pending unit trust purchase or after dividend payout will earn interest on balances.

Investment Trusts

Often confused with unit trusts, but different in concept, are investment trusts. Like unit trusts, investment trusts allow the smaller private investor to benefit from having a stake in a large portfolio of widely spread shares. But there the similarity ends. Investment trusts are public companies like any other and their shares are traded on the stock markets.

Instead of making motor cars, running hotels, or operating department stores, an investment trust company exists purely and simply to buy and sell shares in other companies, for both short-term speculative gain and long-term capital growth. Those who manage investment trusts are full-time executives responsible to a board of directors, and they buy and sell shares on the world's stock exchanges, exercising their judgement as to what will be a profitable investment. Just like any other public company, they make profits and incur losses, and pay dividends to shareholders. Investment trust executives can borrow against the assets of their companies, and are able to take both a long- and a short-term view of the money entrusted to them. Capital gains on share trading are not distributed in cash but are used to build up portfolios and, through the generosity of the Treasury, escape taxation. This means that the fund manager can realise the profits on the trust's investment at the most opportune time. Trusts can also offset their management charges against tax. Investment trusts have about £50 billion under management with 250,000 investors.

Investment trusts are cheaper to invest in than unit trusts. Every £1,000 invested in unit trusts costs around £50 in an initial management charge. The same amount used to purchase shares in an investment trust would incur less than £30 in stockbroker's commission and government stamp duty. Unit trust managers also charge an annual fee of between 0.75 and 1 per cent for looking after their trusts; investment trust management charges are much lower.

Unlike individual investors, investment trust portfolio managers can take profits without paying tax, and move in and out of companies paying only dealing charges. There is also a very wide choice of funds across many markets and sectors.

So why do average investors not flock to investment trusts? The answer is hype. Unit trusts are prolific advertisers in the financial press, and therefore get much more than their fair share of space in the editorial columns. By contrast, investment trusts get comparatively little press attention. The serious newspapers provide free space to unit trusts to publicise their prices, acknowledging it a public service to do so, but provide only limited price information on investment trusts.

The investment trusts themselves have initiated advertising campaigns, but some of these have been less than impressive, and have not hit home. As one head of an investment trust company put it:

Investment trusts have been their own worst enemies: the people who run them and the investors who own them realise the large advantage they have over most other forms of savings, but they have been remarkably coy in spreading the good news to a wider audience.[3]

Moreover, unit trusts are, like most life assurance products, sold by middlemen – insurance brokers, financial advisers, even accountants and solicitors – who receive a handsome commission from this form of activity, most of it upfront. With the exception of investment trust savings schemes, there is no commission for intermediaries on investment trusts, so, for the most part, they do not recommend them. The 350 or so investment trusts in Britain deserve a place in everyone's savings portfolio, and, in many cases, offer a better return than the average with-profits policy.

Another important difference, seldom understood, between investment trusts and unit trusts is that while the latter tend to be priced according to their net asset value (NAV), investment trusts, like other equities, are valued according to what the market thinks they are worth, which is more often than not below the value of their underlying assets. The assets, of course, are the shares the trusts hold, which can be valued on a daily basis, thereby allowing their NAV to be calculated with the same frequency. Some investment trusts, particularly those with a strong following, trade at a premium. Buying at a discount does not always mean you are getting a bargain, although once the discount is more than 15 per cent, that probably is the case.

Within the investment trust sector are split capital trusts. These trusts, which have a limited life, contain two or more classes of share within them, each with different entitlements for shareholders on wind-up day. The types of shares common within split trusts are:

• Zero-dividend preference shares. There are no dividends from these securities but a fixed capital return at the end. Their price will be affected by changes in interest rates and bond yields, but they can generally be considered as safe as quality corporate bonds or gilt-edged securities. In effect a zero shareholder gives up the right to any income on his holding in return for a future capital sum.

---

[3] Jeremy Tigue, head of investment trusts at Home and Colonial, on *Bloomberg Money*, April 2001.

- Income shares. These are shares of companies that would be in a good high-income unit trust or investment trust.
- Growth shares. These are used to lift the value of the fund on wind-up.
- Warrants. These give holders the right to buy shares at a predetermined rate at a fixed future date. The risk with warrants is that the money spent on them could be completely lost, though they also offer the prospect of substantial gains.

In summary, splits allow investors to mix caution with risk. Zero-dividend shares will protect capital and generate a final income, while warrants will offer the chance of a big gain.

Tracker Funds

Tracker funds enjoyed a surge in popularity during the bull market in the nineties because they mirror the performance of the index they track, and most indices rose at that time by more than the average managed unit trust, especially when management costs were taken into account. During the early years of the twenty-first century, however, the story was rather different: indices tumbled by more than the better-managed defensive funds, and those who bought into trackers at the top of the market have lost value.

Managing a fund to follow precisely the path of an index is more a matter of mathematics than judgement, so costs should be less, but not all tracker funds are run in the same way. Some of the funds that track the FTSE 100, for example, hold all of the stocks that make up this index, in proportion to their strength in the index. This is called full replication, and should provide a line graph which is exactly the same as that on the FTSE. Others work more like an opinion poll, taking a representative sample in the hope that it will mimic the index.

There is another complication. Investors are happy when a tracker fund follows an index sharply up, but in a falling market would prefer that it falls less steeply. Some tracker funds use judgemental and technical skills to avoid the drop, for example selling stocks that look likely to be serious casualties of a recession. An example of the use of a technical tool would be identifying stocks which, because of their steadily falling market capitalisation, are likely to drop out of an index like the FTSE 100. Once gone, their prices tend to fall, if only because all the funds using the full replication technique will sell, so the astute manager will anticipate their departure and offload them. Conversely, stocks likely to replace them in the FTSE could be bought ahead of their entry.

Anyone considering a tracker should enquire about the tracking methods used, and, above all, consider the charges, which vary from a low of 0.3 per cent annually to a high of just under 1.5 per cent, which is extortionate for the amount of work involved.

Funds of Funds

Another concept is the fund of funds, designed to minimise risk for the small investor and to remove him one stage further from direct purchases of shares. Instead of having to pick and choose between many hundreds of unit trusts, the investor can buy units in a master fund, which in turn will buy units in one or more of its subsidiary funds. From the point of view of someone with a small amount of capital to invest – but no clear idea if and when to move out of a British equity trust and into a Japanese, German or American one – the fund of funds seems no bad idea. Let someone else do the worrying and save yourself the expense of having a stockbroker to manage a portfolio of unit trusts.

Like most bright ideas, the notion is not a new one, and has had to live down a bad reputation. Funds of funds first obtained notoriety as a result of the exposure back in 1962 of the international investment swindler Bernie Cornfeld, whose misdeeds are well spelt out in a brilliant book, *Do You Sincerely Want To Be Rich?*, by Charles Raw, Bruce Page and Godfrey Hodgson. This cautionary tale should be required reading for both investors and all those involved in the financial services industry. As the authors say:

> The salesman's rationale for the Fund of Funds was an unusually owlish piece of nonsense – one of those things that sounds impressive until you really think it through. Mutual funds, and all investment concerns, are sold on the proposition that the ordinary man needs investment advisers to make choices for him. The Fund of Funds went further and suggested that the ordinary man now needed professionals to choose the professionals who would make the choices. The Fund of Funds would take your money, and invest it in other mutual funds – but only in those whose values were rising most rapidly.

A lawyer from the US Securities and Exchange Commission exploded the fund of funds argument succinctly: 'If funds of funds are permitted to proliferate, how would an investor decide among the many companies seeking his investment dollar? Would he not need a fund of funds of funds to make this decision?'

Cornfeld's Fund of Funds, run by his Investors Overseas Services and given the hard sell by thousands of salesmen calling themselves 'financial counsellors', gathered in $100 million of people's savings within two years of its launch. The customer's money was transferred immediately into separate proprietary funds, for a brokerage fee which was pocketed by IOS. For the privilege of investing at all, the customer had to pay what has become known as a 'front-end load', much of which went in commission to the salesman who had persuaded him to part with his money in the first place. For every $3,000 invested in Cornfeld's Fund of Funds, $540 vanished immediately in fees. A further 10 per cent of any income generated also went in fees, as did 10 per cent of any capital gain. According to Raw, Page and Hodgson, an investor had to wait six years before he could even get his money out without loss. An investigation found that money which was supposed to be held on trust for customers was being used for the benefit of IOS itself, its directors, employees and friends; and that the IOS sales force was engaging in illegal currency transactions on a major scale, and constantly misrepresenting the investment performance of its largest fund.

The shock waves that surrounded the fall of IOS were such that the British Government introduced strict new rules. An approved fund of funds is restricted in its investments to its manager's own unit trusts, in total contrast with the United States, where master funds may invest in anything but their own in-house trusts. A new fund of funds must also be in a group holding at least four subsidiary trusts, and not more than 50 per cent of assets can be invested in any one of them.

These restrictions have narrowed the options, but one area where the fund of funds concept has continued to flourish is in investment trusts. There are several investment trusts whose *raison d'être* is to take shareholdings in other investment trusts. Instead of having to pick stocks for income or performance, a fund of funds unit or investment trust, such as Quilter's Growth IT, can pick off the best-performing and cheapest trusts, and buy and sell at discount prices.

In recent years the more reputable fund management groups have turned the argument against these vehicles on its head by giving investors a free hand to decide for themselves when they wish to switch from one type of inner fund to another. For instance, someone approaching retirement may decide to switch out of a growth fund and into one offering higher income. Here advantages come into play, because if the investor switching strategies was not in a fund of funds he or she would have to realise gains from one fund, pay capital gains tax of up to 40 per cent, and buy into another, paying stamp duty along the way. Though a sensible move in investment terms, it would decimate his savings. With a fund of funds the transfer could be carried out for only the charge made by the fund management company. These charges, which can be as much as 2.5 per cent of the value of the fund of funds, are not modest, but they do work out a lot cheaper than paying the taxes.

One problem that may arise is that not all funds within any one group have top-rate managers. A group may have an excellent European income fund manager, but a poor record in Americans. Once you are locked into one group, you cannot do much about that, other than assess the fund managers' overall performance.

Corporate Bonds

Corporate bonds are very similar to gilt-edged securities. They are generally issued by very large companies, and are, in effect, IOUs which promise to pay those who hold them an annual rate of interest during the life of the bond, and then to repay the money in full at the end of the fixed term specified in the bond. The interest stays the same throughout the term, but since general interest rates move up and down, the actual value of the bond will do the same. If general interest rates rise, making the rate on the corporate bond less attractive, then its value will fall, and vice versa.

Let me explain this further with a simple example. A company sells an issue of 8 per cent bonds at £100 each. That means holders will get £8 every year for each bond they own, so the yield is 8 per cent. Interest rates go up, and the price of the bond on the stock market falls to £93, reflecting the fact that its return is less attractive to the investor. If the original holder wants to switch investments and get out, he will only get £93 for each £100 bond he holds. On the other hand, someone buying the bonds at £93 each will still get the £8 per unit interest, and that means the yield is 8.6 per cent. If the purchaser holds on until the bond matures, he will also get the original value of

£100 per bond, which means he will make a £7 profit on each unit.

Corporate bonds are less safe than gilts because they do not have the guarantee of a government. But they are much safer than equities. The company issuing the bonds must pay the yearly interest on them in good times and bad, and before it pays a penny in dividends to shareholders. Even if a company goes into receivership, bond holders will get their money before anything is paid to shareholders.

Corporate bond prices are also more affected by general interest rate rises than they are by the performance of the company. If a company's share price plunges, it does not mean that the corporate bond value will change, even if its equity falls. Only if the company looks like becoming insolvent, and being forced to default on its debt, would this become a problem. That means there are degrees of risk, which became only too clear after the terrorist attack on the World Trade Center on 11 September 2001. A food company like Unilever or a retailer like Tesco saw shares slip, but were still financially sound. On the other hand many airlines, including British Airways, lost a large percentage of their business and, burdened with debt to pay for aircraft, were financially compromised.

Corporate risk is regularly assessed by ratings agencies like Moody's, and Standard and Poor's.

Although it is possible to buy some bonds on the stock markets, most traders are big institutions, because the minimum dealing level tends to be high. Many minimum lot sizes are as high as 10,000, which would mean that a purchase could not, for example, be put in an ISA. This is unfortunate, and another example of market discrimination against small investors. Therefore it is usually wisest to get into corporate bonds by subscribing to a corporate bond unit trust or investment trust. That is because the fund manager can afford to buy in volume, and also to spread bond exposure among those who are due to be repaid soon and those who still have many years ahead. This reduces the sensitivity of the fund to interest rate changes.

Details of corporate bond funds can be found on the web site of the Association of Unit Trusts and Investment Funds (www.investmentfunds.org.uk) and performance tables are published in some of the better investor magazines, such as *Bloomberg Money*. Details of individual bonds on offer are less easy to find and are readily available only to institutions.

4   How Shares are Bought

A weak sun rises over the strip of stone and cement that runs alongside the Thames from Blackfriars to Docklands in London. On the river itself there is little traffic, a far cry from two centuries earlier when the Pool of London was alive with clippers and merchantmen bringing goods and spices to what was then the capital of the English-speaking world. On this morning the only craft moving are the barges that transport waste from the City of London's depot in Lower Thames Street to be dumped on Essex marshlands close to the sea.

This grey scene is reflected in the glass-walled offices that are the throbbing heart of stock market trading in London. With the London Stock Exchange no longer providing a fixed centre for dealers to buy and sell, trading is all electronic, conducted from dealing rooms the size of football fields in clusters of buildings at Canary Wharf in Docklands, at the Broadgate Centre near Liverpool Street station, and in other office blocks in the City of London. The City, however, is no longer the focus of the stock markets, with an increasing number of financial houses following Fleet Street newspapers eastwards into the skyscrapers of the former docks area.

At Barclays Capital, sited at the Old Mint, where gold and silver coins for the merchants in the days of the Industrial Revolution were once minted, the morning meeting is underway. The head of European equities makes no attempt to put a brave face on the gloom everyone feels. The previous day saw the FTSE 100 index fall to its lowest level since the global financial turmoil of October 1998.

'It started as Black Monday again,' he says, 'the FTSE dipping below five thousand after the weekend press had been very negative. We saw some bargain hunting, and a bit of a recovery, but the market is all over the place.'

One by one his colleagues play their part. Present are the chief strategist, the acting head of UK equities, and specialist analysts. A Japan specialist seeks modest comfort in the news that Japan is at long last moving ahead with plans to privatise its railways. But the news from America is the familiar story of job losses. 'Four thousand have gone at Quest, two thousand at Michelin and one thousand and fifty at Gateway, we hear, and a couple of the governors of the Fed are saying things are slipping.'

The man chairing the meeting permits himself a hollow laugh. 'They are just putting in the rhetoric to make sure we get a cut in interest rates on October the second.'

Analysts report on profit figures that have just been published – ahead of the start of trading in accordance with the normal custom. Next have unveiled a 16 per cent increase in sales. 'The top end of expectations,' says the retail analyst, 'but there's concern as to whether this can be maintained. We've got it on hold and we will maintain it at that.' A similar judgement is made on results from Friends Provident, but concern is expressed about the management of Scottish Power's United States operations. 'But the price fall may be overdone so we have upgraded it from reduce to hold.'

Tuned into the conference are other centres like Barclays Private Bank in Mayfair, and parts of the organisation based in Peterborough and Glasgow. The meeting lasts twenty-five minutes, and then the participants disperse, ready to advise clients on their portfolios.

Across the markets in London and elsewhere, similar meetings are taking place. Most market professionals are at their desks by seven or even earlier, long before the commuter trains begin to deposit their cargo of office workers. Many of the young men and women striding through the Italian-marbled entrance halls of the securities houses have flushed faces and carry sports bags, evidence of a thirty-minute workout in a nearby gymnasium while most Britons are still in their beds. Before the morning meeting they will have flicked through the *Financial Times*, glanced at the other newspapers, and looked at Bloomberg or CNBC on the office television screens.

Some of the meetings, like that at Barclays, are designed to get business moving through the trading desks by persuading clients – many of them large investment institutions like life assurance companies, pension funds and unit trusts – to buy shares in the markets. This happens either by providing advice to those who call about their portfolios, or by equity and bond salesmen making buy and sell recommendations to clients.

Other meetings, more directly related to the day's trading, involve a degree of tension between the analysts and the market makers, the men and women who set the price at which their employers will trade shares. More often than not, the market makers ignore the logical arguments of the analysts. Analysts, some of them trained in accountancy, a few of them former financial journalists, are steeped in knowledge of the companies in which they specialise, and often have an almost scholarly approach to their work. Market makers are traders, and carry with them the air of the Cockney barrow-boy, many of them speaking in estuary English. Most are street smart, and have to make split-second judgements over share values.

While the analysts retreat behind their glass partitions to write their reports, the market makers dealing with all but FTSE100 stocks sit at their terminals keying in the prices at which they will buy and sell the shares in which they trade. The atmosphere is like a television portrayal of the newsroom of a big newspaper, though a trifle more tense, with more fever and bustle.

Most people appear to be on the telephone, their fitful dialogues always punctuated by taps at a keyboard, which reveal an array of coloured numbers on the bank of computer screens that dominates their desks.

Every few minutes someone gets up from his high-back swivel chair and shouts out a message – or, plastic coffee beaker in hand, wanders across the floor to talk with a colleague. For the most part these dialogues are friendly and unobtrusive, but the occasional sharp-edged rejoinder reminds the observer that this is a place where serious money is at stake. It is as well to get up and walk around, not only to stretch the muscles but also to avoid keyboard fatigue. Sometimes the latter can have dire consequences, as when in 1998 a Salomon Brothers trader slouched on his keyboard, firing off an order to sell $1.2 billion worth of French government bond futures. Realising his mistake, he bought them back immediately, but his temporary aberration had already cost his company several million pounds.

My description is of the equities floor of one of London's largest securities houses, where each working day tens of billions of pounds' worth of shares change hands. Most trading floors look the same. Large stakes in major companies are bought and sold; small allotments in privatisation issues are traded; money is won or lost.

Down on the floor, on the central desk, the lead salesman touches the flickering light on his telephone panel that indicates a call is waiting, picks up the phone and rests one foot on a drawer of his desk. The caller is a fund manager from one of Britain's largest life assurance companies. He is looking to pick up a million shares in one of the big breweries. The salesman keys into his computer the first three letters of the company's name, and the screen reveals to him that the price of the stock is higher than it has been for several weeks. But it also shows that the posted price is only available for the purchase of 50,000 shares or less. Buying a block twenty times that size could be difficult.

'Leave it with me, we'll see what we can do. The price is good, so someone might be prepared to sell,' he tells his client.

After ringing off, the salesman, a man in his early thirties, shirt-sleeved and displaying wide Wall Street braces, makes a few more keystrokes. In quick succession, two graphs appear on the screen – one of them portraying the movement of the share price of the brewery group over a five-year period; the other tracking it against the progress of the *Financial Times* Stock Exchange 100 share index, popularly known as the Footsie. The graph shows that although the shares have been rising, they have been outperformed by the index.

The salesman smiles, reflecting that one of the brewery's major shareholders may well be prepared to sell, given the higher price of the stock, and the prospect that by reinvesting elsewhere there will be a more profitable return. He keys in a few more strokes, and a printer at the end of the desk produces a sheet of paper with a breakdown of the company's major shareholders, in order of size of holding. Most of the names on the list are investment institutions, life assurance companies competing with the salesman's client, pension funds, and unit trust companies. But there are also some international com-panies and a handful of wealthy individuals. The salesman calls over a junior colleague and tells him: 'See if you can do anything with this. We need a million.'

The young man returns to his desk, picks up his telephone and starts making calls. Within forty minutes he is back. 'I've got them,' he says, glowing with pleasure at his swift if unexpected achievement. The salesman whoops with joy, hits his client's number on the phone pad and passes on the good news. He then walks over to market makers sitting at another, larger bank of computers, and asks them to execute the deal. The salesman is well pleased. His firm's com-mission on the transaction will be about £150,000. A small percentage of that goes towards his annual bonus.

Share prices vary according to who is buying, a little like the market for airline tickets. You can pay £1,200 for a fully flexible economy return ticket to New York, and find yourself sitting next to someone who has paid £225 for the same class of seat, the identical meals service and the same quarter-bottle of rough French red wine.

The differences are not that great in the stock markets, but they are there. Different investors buy the same share at prices which vary depending on the day or minute purchased, the volume bought, and the system used to buy them.

In share transactions in Britain, a class system exists. As you might expect, those with the most financial clout get the best deals. That this should be the case is of increasing concern to a number of consumer pressure groups and regulators. How the system works is a depressingly familiar story. Those dealing in large blocks of shares in the companies that make up the FTSE 100 will post on the London Stock Exchange's electronic trading system the price at which they are prepared to buy or sell their stock. By doing this they can directly influence the market. If they effect a trade at the posted price they save not only on brokers' commissions but also on the profit the market maker takes – that is, the spread between the price he buys at and that at which he sells.

The rest of us have to trade our shares through the market-making system, which means that we buy or sell at a price set by a man – it usually is a man – in a busy dealing room. Since we cannot deal with market makers direct, we also have to pay a broker's commission as well as a dealer's spread. Those without a stockbroker pay even more, directly or indirectly. This group includes the majority of those who have acquired popular shares through privatisation or the floating off of mutual assurance companies over the last few years. Abandoned largely to their own devices, they have sold out their shareholdings through high street banks and building societies, many of whose front counter staff not only are totally ignorant of the working of the stock markets, but compound their ignorance by attempting to persuade investors to buy unit trusts and other packaged investment products of doubtful quality. Such investors would be better off logging on to the vast variety of web sites available on the Internet, and then making their own decisions.

Internet Brokers

There are now large numbers of Internet brokers through whom private investors in Britain can buy and sell shares. There are as many opinions as to who offers the best service. The brokerages are fiercely competitive, and if it was just a matter of cost then the solution would be to pick those that offer to trade shares for a minimum charge of £10, no matter how large the trade. This is a huge reduction on the old percentage charges, where a sale of £100,000 worth of shares would once have cost £1,000 or more in commission.

But as in most services, cost is not the only factor. Accessibility is important. You need to be able to log on to the broker's web site quickly and trade immediately. You do not want to be getting messages like 'page unavailable: please try later' because the broker's server is locked up. Accuracy is also important. You do not want to find that you have sold all the shares in one company in your portfolio, rather than the 20 per cent you specified. This is a worryingly common type of error with some services.

The oldest of the online brokerages in Britain is Charles Schwab, which was built on the business of Sharelink, set up in Birmingham by David Jones (see p. 11). At one stage Schwab was conducting almost half of Britain's online trading. More recently it has encountered stiff competition, because its web site is not so information-rich as that of some rivals. Perhaps the best known of these are Barclayshare, part of the Barclays Bank group; E-Trade, another early entrant to the sector; TD Waterhouse, and DJL Direct, a subsidiary of Credit Suisse First Boston. New to the market is one of the oldest old-style brokers, Merrill Lynch, which for years has been the largest stockbroker in the world and has now joined with one of Britain's biggest banks, HSBC, to form Merrill Lynch HSBC. It will find it hard to carve out a big share of the market, but one of the attractions for customers is the ability to get investment advice, at a price, as well as access to both companies' formidable research material.

The stock market's class system also extends to the provision of information. Anyone can buy the *Financial Times*, of course, and it can and should be mined for information. But real-time share prices and other up-to-the-second market information is only available to the privileged few who will wish to purchase it, which usually means the professionals. Computer services with real-time prices and up-to-date news cost in the region of £10,000 a year, though at the time of writing, the Financial Services Authority is trying to change this (see Chapter 15). At the next level down are Internet services and television programmes such as those provided by Bloomberg, CNN and CNBC. These are free, as are services like the BBC's Ceefax, where the share prices, however, are far from current, just updated from time to time.

If you watch the football scores on Ceefax while matches are in progress, you will notice that goals are marked up almost immediately they are scored. It is strange indeed that a goal in a game of football is considered more significant than a share price movement that may affect many thousands of investors. Put another way, would viewers be prepared to accept a ruling by the Football Association that publication of scores could be delayed for fifteen minutes because the rights had been sold to British Sky Broadcasting? It is unthinkable. Yet the world's most important stock exchanges, including those in New York and London, have for years been able to get away with an insistence that publication of prices should be delayed for fifteen minutes except by those information providers that pay the exchanges a hefty fee. It is surprising that, in Europe at least, this practice has not been the subject of scrutiny by the European Competitions Commissioner, who would surely declare it anti-competitive.

In order to understand the class system of share dealing, it is worth examining in some detail the way it applies in the London market. This will also help small investors to comprehend why it is very hard for them to compete in the day-to-day marketplace, and why it is usually better for a private individual to stand back from the flurry of the trading floor and make medium-term, rather than short-term, judgements.

The Trading Systems

The principal shares traded in London are those in the companies that make up the FTSE 100 index. Since mid October 1997 these shares have been traded on the Stock Exchange's order book system, known as SETS, an acronym for Stock Exchange Electronic Trading System. This matches orders placed electronically by prospective buyers and sellers, partly replacing the quote-driven system where deals were done by telephone.

So instead of agreeing to trade at a price set by a market maker, as described later (see p. 58), buyers and sellers of large blocks of stocks can advertise through their broker the price at which they would like to deal, and then choose to wait for the market to move in their favour, or execute the deal immediately at the best price currently available. Only members of the London Stock Exchange can enter orders directly into SETS.

Under the system, investors wishing to deal will contact their broker by phone or electronic mail, and agree the price at which they are willing to buy or sell a particular stock. The broker will enter the order directly into the order book, and it will be displayed anonymously to the entire market.

For example, the broker could open his screen on the stock and find an investor wants to sell 4,000 shares at once, at the 'best price' available. At the time, the best buy order available is for 17,800 shares at 938 pence. The sell order for 4,000 shares will automatically trade against the buy order – leaving 13,800 shares at 938 pence still on the order book. The second the order is executed, the trade is automatically reported to the Exchange, and the market informed immediately.

This is only one type of share trade using the order book system. Another common deal is the limit order. Here the investor posts specific details of the proposed trade – the number of shares, the price and the date upon which the offer will close. These limit orders sit on the SETS electronic order book until either they are matched or they pass the expiry date. There is also the execute and eliminate order, which might sound like a command from the old Soviet KGB, but in fact is very similar to an 'at best' order, but with a limit price specified.

Automatic execution through the order book takes place between 08.30 and 16.30. From 08.00 there is a half-hour period during which orders can be added or deleted in readiness for the trading day. In the half-hour between the end of the trading day and 17.00 there is a housekeeping period during which orders that have not been executed may be deleted if brokers do not wish to leave them on the book overnight.

The market-making system has a much stronger human element. Market makers set the prices for all transactions other than those booked through SETS. Although the London Stock Exchange had hoped that most of the FTSE 100 trades would be conducted through SETS by the new millennium, the market makers and their spreads are still in evidence.

The job of a market maker is sedentary. They sit at their terminals all day, their only exercise swivelling in their chairs to shout across to a colleague, or taking a thirty-minute break to visit a gymnasium or squash club. Not all market makers can trade all shares; their bailiwick is those sectors in which their firm has elected and been authorised to make a market. Like the jobbers of the past, the market makers will typically specialise: for example, in media stocks, the leisure sector, industrials, banks, and so on. Once bid and offer prices have been entered, the market maker is obliged to trade at those prices, although of course he can alter his figures at any time in response to market conditions – in other words, after he has seen what competitors are doing. Shares are traded on a computer system known as SEAQ, which stands for Stock Exchange Automated Quotations System. This covers more than 3,500 securities, and is divided into three groups of stocks – alpha, beta and gamma.

As the name implies, alpha stocks are the most actively traded shares, and market makers who buy or sell them must immediately enter the trade into the SEAQ system. From SEAQ the trade details are passed instantly to the London Stock Exchange's electronic information service, which is available to traders, brokers and investors.

How it works

Take the example of an investor purchasing 500 shares in British Petroleum: how does the SEAQ system work? His broker or licensed financial intermediary will call up the BP page from the system, and see an array of offers from more than a dozen market makers, each of them identified by a code. One line will say 'ML 36–40 1 × 1'. This means that Merrill Lynch, for example, are prepared to buy BP at £10.36 and to sell at £10.40, and that their figure applies for purchases or sales of 1,000 shares or fewer. Another line might say 'DMG 36–41 1 × 2', indicating that Deutsche Morgan Grenfell will buy at the same price as Merrill Lynch, but that they will only sell BP at £10.41, and then only in units of up to 2,000.

Another page on SEAQ will reveal that ten minutes earlier there had been a large transaction of BP shares at £9.38. Assuming he wants to trade, the broker calls the dealing desk of his own or another firm and asks to buy BP at £10.40. If the broker's firm is also listed as a market maker in BP, the broker will try and keep the deal in-house by persuading his own colleagues to match the Merrill offer, which they may or may not be willing to do. When the bargain is struck, the market maker enters it into the BP SEAQ page; other market makers, noting the transaction, readjust their offers accordingly.

Deals in beta stocks are concluded in exactly the same way, except that not all trades are logged, and there are fewer market makers, perhaps only two or three, who will usually be in firms that have decided to specialise in a particular sector, such as electronics or insurance. In the case of gamma stocks, only indicative quotes are provided, so that any broker anxious to consider a purchase has to call the market maker and negotiate a price, often based on volume. Many of the market makers in the gamma section may be regional brokers, who know companies in their area well and are better placed to hold the book than a large London conglomerate.

For the technically minded, the SEAQ system operates on two dedicated mainframe computers, designed to respond to entries within one second, update information at a peak rate of twenty items per second, and handle up to 70,000 transactions an hour. In the event of a computer crash, a major fire or bomb outrage at the Stock Exchange, all the records would be saved, for parallel computers operate in another part of London and, for double protection, in the United States.

While equities represent the most interesting aspect of stock market activity, and offer the investor the greatest degree of risk and reward, it is important not to overlook gilts, as they are known in Britain, or bonds everywhere else. There is a substantial market in buying and selling these bonds, the prices of which vary according to how far out of line their fixed interest rates are with the standard rates of interest applying at the time in the economy. If interest rates are falling, then gilts with a higher rate will be sold at a premium to their basic price. As with equities, prices are set by market makers, drawn from twenty-five firms.

Indices

When listening to the radio or watching television, the one aspect of the financial markets that regularly gets reported is the ups and downs of stock market indices.

Indices reflect the overall value of all the stocks held within them, and in many cases are calculated on a minute-by-minute basis. In Britain the most popularly quoted index is the FTSE 100, known colloquially as the Footsie, which covers the hundred companies with the largest market capitalisation. The BBC often refers inaccurately to this index as the 'One Hundred index', presumably because it is reluctant to plug the *Financial Times*, although it never seems to have the same problem with the Nationwide Football League or the FA Carling Premiership.

As a company, FTSE is autonomous and independent of the London Stock Exchange, although the exchange and the *Financial Times* are co-owners. The company actually calculates thousands of indices each day, with more than a hundred of them, including the FTSE 100, being updated in real time. Many of these indices are based on mathematical values, such as the FTSE 250, the FTSE All Share or the FTSE 30. Others require value judgements as to which stock should be included. One of the most controversial is the new FTSE4Good index of 'socially responsible' companies. The selection criteria for this index covers three areas: working towards environmental sustainability; developing positive relationships with stakeholders; and upholding and supporting universal human rights. FTSE claims that 'there is no other socially responsible index quite like it. Independently defined and researched, FTSE4Good sets an objective global standard for socially responsible investment.' The company keeps adding and deleting companies according to its own criteria. New kids on the block from September 2001 were Aventis, National Australia Bank, Royal Bank of Scotland, and the oil giant Total Fina Elf. Kicked out were Compaq, Nortel Networks, and Bayerrische Hypo-Und Vereinsbank. Tesco, which had been clamouring to get in, was still excluded.

There are also FTSE international indices. The FTSE Actuaries World Indices cover all major and some smaller stock markets, expressed in terms of the local currency, dollars, sterling, the yen and the euro. There is also the FTSE Eurotrack 100, which covers major mainland European companies. British companies are included in the Eurotrack 200.

The Dow

The pre-eminent index in the United States is the Dow Jones Industrial Average, one of many indices generated by the Dow Jones Company, publishers of the *Wall Street Journal*. The DJIA is usually referred to simply as the Dow, and like the FTSE 30 in Britain it is a formula based on the stock prices of the thirty major industrial companies. The formula adds up the stocks' prices and then divides them by a certain number to derive the average. Consequently the higher-priced stocks will have a greater effect on the average. Other Dow indices include the Transportation Average (twenty airlines, trucking companies and railways), the Utility Average (fifteen gas, electric and power companies) and the Composite (all sixty-five companies in the previous three).

The S & P and the NASDAQ Composite

Another widely used index because of its greater spread across the United States economy is the Standard and Poor's 500. This comprises a broad spread of 500 companies, broken into smaller industry segments, and also includes forty financial companies. The NASDAQ Composite has an even wider spread and includes a large number of technology stocks.

The techMARK

This market was launched by the London Stock Exchange in 1999 to provide a home for high-tech companies that might otherwise have been lured to Germany's Neuer Markt or even NASDAQ in the United States. FTSE requirements that companies need a three-year trading record to list do not apply to techMARK, provided market capitalisation on launch is at least £50 million. At the time techMARK was launched, that figure was attainable by many high-flying companies, but more recently the number of those seeking a listing has dropped sharply. At the time of writing, even a good company looking for investors would be hard put to find any. Many of those in the index have struggled as the new millennium recession has struck home, with Telewest, Kingston Communications and others all seeing plunging prices. Even so, techMARK is established and its future seems assured.

The DAX

The main German stock market index is the DAX, which is based on the thirty most actively traded German blue-chip stocks. It represents over 60 per cent of the total equity capital of German exchange-listed companies, and trading in these shares accounts for three quarters of the market volume. Another index, the FAZ, operated by the leading German newspaper *Frankfurter Allgemeine Zeitung*, is also an important pointer, being more broadly based than the DAX.

For a time Germany was slow to embrace the tough regulations favoured in the Anglo-Saxon world (these are discussed later, in Chapter 15). But these days stringent rules are in place to fight corruption and encourage transparency. Based on the model of the US Securities and Investment Board, a Federal Securities Supervisory Office is tasked with uncovering and prosecuting insider traders and other miscreants, as well as supervising disclosure requirements.

Paperchase

Once shares have been bought and sold, settlement takes place. This is carried out in what is called the 'back office' of the stockbroker, reflecting the old days when dozens of clerks would huddle in the basement or another unsalubrious corner of the office and issue hand-written statements seeking payment for shares bought. Once the shares had been paid for, the clerk would inform the registrar of the company whose shares had been acquired, and he would send out a share certificate. Share certificates were and are valuable documents, like property deeds, to be kept in a safe or bank vault. Two weeks were allowed for settlement, and it often took much longer to issue updated share certificates. The amount of clerical work involved was considerable, and, in part, justified the high commissions once charged by stockbrokers.

Three developments put an end to all that. The first was the rise in volume of trading and the tendency for many shares to be sold after only a short period of ownership. This resulted in tremendous pressure on back offices, and long delays in handling the paperwork. The second was the arrival of electronic trading, and the use of sophisticated systems. It made sense to try and integrate settlement procedures into dealing systems, and to reduce what had become an almost unmanageable paperchase. Unfortunately, this proved not as easy as was first thought, and, particularly in London, caused numerous problems and headaches. The London Stock Exchange spent tens of thousands of man hours and huge sums of money developing what was called the TAURUS system, but it flopped, and was replaced by another system called CREST. Slowly, over the years, CREST was made to work.

The third development was a move amongst frequent investors away from paper certification. They became used to the concept of having their share ownership registered electronically, and those with accounts with online brokerages such as Barclayshare and Charles Schwab accepted that their holdings could be placed in electronic nominee accounts. Effectively the brokers held the shares, and in return for forfeiting the rights to certificates, investors enjoyed lower commission charges and detailed statements of all transactions. It has worked well, although from time to time some online brokerages make mistakes, and those who use them are well advised to keep their own records and check them against broker statements. The London Stock Exchange has now introduced its own scheme

whereby small shareholders can have their shares registered electronically there, rather than have a paper certificate. This excellent
scheme is free of charge to those with three stocks or fewer; after that,
there is a modest charge.

Stamp Duty

Stamp duty, a euphemism for an additional tax, is payable on all
share purchases in Britain, and the rate is 0.5 per cent. The United
Kingdom is one of the few countries where this tax is levied. Stamp
duty is also levied in the United States, but at the modest rate of 0.003
per cent.

In the year 2000, the Treasury pocketed almost £4 billion from
stamp duty, so the Government's reluctance to drop a tax collected
for it by brokers is understandable, though undesirable. It is
undesirable because it is a tax on savings, not spending, and because
it discriminates against those who trade their shares in Britain rather
than elsewhere. Wealthy investors and institutions can trade shares
in large companies in New York and avoid the tax. Speculators can
use spread betting – betting on future stock movements in the same
way one bets on racehorses – and avoid the tax. It is a strange world
where betting shops are treated much more favourably than stock
markets.

5 Global Markets

I would rather be vaguely right than precisely wrong.
Warren Buffett

Risk arbitrage is not gambling in any sense. Traditional stock investing is much closer to gambling than is risk arbitrage.
Ivan Boesky, *Merger Mania.*

The New York Stock Exchange is perhaps the most substantial and perfect financial temple in the world.
John Rodemeyer

Wall Street is the term used to describe the financial district of New York. Like the City of London, it occupies only a small area of the business capital of the United States. Wall Street is in Lower Manhattan, facing out to the Statue of Liberty, and the stock market grew up there in support of the merchants and bankers who, two centuries ago, established themselves on the tip of the island, when it was the pre-eminent business centre of America.

In those days Wall Street was the city's most important thoroughfare. Cargo ships were moored on the nearby East River, and the commodities they brought were traded in offices and warehouses on what became known as 'The Street'. As in London, everything in the area was destroyed by a Great Fire: the one in Wall Street occurred in 1835, and the damage stretched from the present site of City Hall to Battery Park.

The New York Stock Exchange, now the world's largest, with a market capitalisation of $18 trillion encompassing the stock of the most powerful companies on earth, was founded on its present site, the block bounded by Wall, Broad and New Streets and Exchange Place, in 1863. It has been rebuilt several times, culminating in the construction in 1984 of Renwick's $2 million marble-fronted building, highlighted by eight lacquered columns and a rococo cornice. The first New York Stock Exchange was more like a gentlemen's club than a business centre. There were 1,100 members, and its books and records were as closely guarded as those of a Masonic lodge. There was an honorary president, with few duties, and two salaried vice-presidents, but they had little to do except open and close trading at the morning and afternoon sessions.

The Exchange conducted its business by way of auctions, not dissimilar to those used by Sotheby's in the fine art market. Sellers would hand in their shares to the vice-president, who would guard them rather like a cloakroom attendant at a large hotel. They would be auctioned in blocks, and sold to the highest bidder. Inevitably, as with real-estate auctions, some deals took place outside the room, usually in the street, and a number of sub-exchanges grew up, often handling specialist shares.

One of these developed into an exchange of its own, operating from another building in Lower Broad Street. It was known as the Open Board, so called because access was available to anyone prepared to pay a $50 membership fee. Once inside, there was no auction, no organisation and no records kept; buyers simply met potential sellers and dealt. The Open Board operated six days a week, and stayed open as long as there were sufficient traders on the floor. Out of this chaos developed the ticker, a trail of paper printed from telegraph machines which simply listed the latest prices at which stocks were traded. As access to the ticker spread beyond Wall Street and New York to other American cities, further share trading exchanges grew up, using the ticker as a guide to prices.

This development was viewed with some alarm by the elders of the New York Stock Exchange. Although the ticker services generated more business, their activities were outside NYSE control, their prices were sometimes wrong, and they led to the proliferation of rival trading locations. So from 1885 onwards, reporters of ticker companies were barred from the floor of the exchange, and forced to purchase the information. Within five years the New York Stock Exchange had control of the ticker, and was able to insist that Western Union, the telegraph company that distributed it, should restrict its access to licensed brokerages and other approved buyers.

By this time business had grown to such a level that the auction system could not cope. What took its place was a sub-system of specialist auctions within the trading floor. Legend has it that a broker called Boyd broke his leg and, finding hobbling around the floor on crutches difficult, remained at one post to trade his shares. After his leg had mended, he discovered that this mode of operation had become hugely profitable and stuck with it, thus creating the specialist market-making auction system that still exists today.

I can find no evidence that this story is anything but apocryphal, but something like it did take place, and provided the basis for present-day trading in New York, with its unique layout of market stalls manned by specialists. These specialists form about a quarter of the professionals working on the floor of the exchange. The others are the people they deal with – the brokers and traders. Some people believe that this system is old-fashioned, and that there there is little use of technology. That is not the case. How could it be when $50 billion worth of shares is traded on an average day? In fact there are 5,000 electronic devices within the 36,000-square-foot floor area of the NYSE, as well as 8,000 telephone circuits. Electronics plays a part in every trade.

The NYSE, known as the 'Big Board', likes to claim that it is the 'world's fairest, most open, and most technologically advanced marketplace'. Only member firms who own a seat on the NYSE can trade there. These firms can be huge corporations like Merrill Lynch or small entities owned by individuals. There have been the same number of seats, 1,366, since 1953, despite the large rise in share trading. Each of the brokers who are members of the NYSE has a booth. Some orders are telephoned in by the broker's distant offices or an outside agent, but most simply appear on screens in the booth, having been keyed in from afar by the person taking the order from a customer. The orders used to be passed to the firm's floor broker by way of a paper slip, but these days it is more usual to convey the information by pager, textmail on a mobile phone, or wireless telephony. The broker will then go to one of the twenty-two trading posts, and seek out a specialist.

Each company whose shares are quoted on the NYSE is allocated to a specialist or specialists, who trade only in named stocks at a prescribed trading post on the floor. All trading in shares takes place at the designated trading post, which has a computer screen above it listing the shares in which its occupants will offer a market. These specialists act as auctioneers. At the start of each trading day they set a guide price for each stock under their remit, for both buying and selling. As market makers they are obliged to trade at these prices, though once a trade has taken place they can make changes. As soon as the ringing of the bell has signalled the start of trading, their auctioneering function begins, as the floor brokers gathered round the trading post will bid up or push down prices. Every time a bargain is struck, the prices are flashed on to the screens in the exchange and to the outside world.

The specialist's role does not end there. Some floor brokers will have been instructed by their booths that the firm's client will only buy or sell at a specific price – 'on limit' is the expression used. Fortunately for them, they do not have to wait, on a knife-edge, for the price of the stock to move to the set limit before acting. They leave their limit order with the specialist, who then will act as an agent and effect the trade if and when the limit is reached. This technique will have an important impact on the specialist's thinking, for if he knows that a large buyer is waiting in the wings for a stock to fall to a certain price, he will be more confident in his dealing.

In theory the market maker only changes his prices by notches: thus he is not supposed to react to any dramatic turn of events by radical shifts. In practice he is human, and will not want to pay over the odds for a share which is tumbling. Running for cover is not encouraged. On the other hand, when big institutions trade very large blocks of shares, it is unreasonable to expect an individual to hold out against a hurricane. The New York Stock Exchange attempts to keep market makers on track by policing price movements very carefully, and by encouraging competition.

The specialist will make his money on the difference between the buying and selling prices in the stocks in which he makes the market. But the job is not without risk. At the end of the day he has to balance his own books. If he is left with an oversupply or shortage of stock when trading ends, he has to hold it in his own account. An exposed position overnight can be highly dangerous, for example to those holding airline stocks on the day of the September 2001 calamity at the World Trade Center.

NASDAQ

In the spring of 1999 an event took place in New York which those who remember the era of Chairman Mao Tse-tung in China would have thought inconceivable. The Chinese premier, Zhu Rongji, paid a visit to the market room of NASDAQ.

The fastest-growing stock market in the world is not the Big Board but the NASDAQ, an acronym for National Association of Securities Dealers Automated Quotation System. It was the first all-electronic market, it is the only stock market that can claim to be truly global, and it is the home of over half the companies traded in America. All trading is conducted through a sophisticated computer and tele-communications network – a network that transmits critical invest-ment data at lightning speed to more than 400,000 computer screens around the globe.

But back to 1999, and the Chinese premier's visit. The tour over, he presented Frank Zarb, chairman of the National Association of Securities Dealers (NASD), with a red bull, symbolising the hope that the buoyant United States market would continue to see a rising market for ever. Zarb replied with the announcement that he intended to open an office in Shanghai, China's business capital, as the 'beginning of a process to create for China a way to bring investors' capital to growing companies'.

NASDAQ has done precisely that for the United States, raising money for some of the nation's hottest stocks – Microsoft, Intel, Cisco, MCI WorldCom, Dell, Sun Microsystems, Oracle and Yahoo. Nine out of ten companies making initial public offerings do so on the NASDAQ, which now claims more securities listed than all the other American markets combined. It was set up in 1971 as the first ever specialist technology market, and led the way in electronic trading. Most of the world's leading technology companies list on NASDAQ, and some of the biggest, like Microsoft, choose to list only there, despite the greater pull of the NYSE. NASDAQ now has a market capitalisation of just under $2,500 billion, and all trades are transacted electronically. Visitors to Times Square in New York cannot fail to be impressed by Nasdaq's Market Site tower, seven storeys high, and the largest video screen in the world, updating itself in real time twenty-four hours a day.

No trading takes place inside this building, though visitors can see financial television programming from Bloomberg and CNBC going out live from studios there. However, there is a public exhibition, which, this being the United States, is called an 'experience' and gives visitors thirty minutes of exposure to a multimedia presentation of the stock market of the future. This is fun for both adults and children, and is an excellent attempt to give passers-by the feeling of how markets work. When I stopped by I could not help but contrast the efforts made by NASDAQ with the grey and unwelcome portals of the London Stock Exchange and its sullen security guards, whose inclination is to pounce on you the moment you have shuffled through the door. If you do not have proof of an appointment you will be sent straight back out into Throgmorton Street without so much as a brochure to study.

Like Britain's SEAQ, for which it provided a model, NASDAQ uses computers and telecommunications to bring securities firms together electronically, enabling them to compete with each other over networks rather than on a trading floor in a single location. All the information needed for trading is in the open, on the NASDAQ computer screen, available at the click of a mouse.

The fundamental difference is that while a traditional floor-based exchange centralises people in a single location, where trading takes place face-to-face, NASDAQ centralises the information, but then makes it available to those who need it, wherever they are. It is open to non-American approved brokers, so most major British firms have direct access to its market makers and can save administrative costs for themselves and their clients.

The central computer system for NASDAQ is in Trumbull, Connecticut, but there is a full back-up facility in Rockville, near Washington, in case of failure. Trumbull and Rockville are connected by 80,000 miles of leased telephone lines to 3,400 securities houses, which use them to display the prices at which they are willing to trade, as well as to report sales and purchases, and other market data. The NASDAQ system is always being refined and updated and is considerably superior to SEAQ. There is plenty of competition; a typical NASDAQ stock has eleven market makers hungry for business.

NASDAQ market makers, which include large national full-service firms, regional firms, local firms, and wholesale market makers – are based in thirty-eight states. Securities dealers in over 6,000 offices have at their fingertips an exact, instantaneous wholesale national price system, available in San Francisco, Chicago or Dallas at the same time as Wall Street. Indeed, it goes beyond that. There are over 8,500 quotation terminals outside the United States, most of them, about 5,000, in Europe, and NASDAQ plans to extend this.

NASDAQ information is also as accessible to the woman in the stockbroker's coffee lounge in Austin, Texas, as it is to the Barclay-share member in Liverpool who might want facts about the American market. There is nothing to stop individual investors subscribing. Those who pay a small subscription have access to the system through a dumb terminal and a black and white monitor. By using a word code on the terminal keyboard, they can obtain on the screen a representative bid and a representative ask price on the stock; for example, if dealers or market makers have quoted bids on a particular stock of 40, 40.25, 40.5 40.75, and 41, the representative bid would be 40.5. If those with a terminal wish to buy or sell – or if their customer so wishes – all they have to do is phone their broker and seek a real quote, asking that it should be close to the representative figure on the screen, and stipulating, if they wish, how far from the figure they are prepared to trade.

All deals in securities that are traded regularly and in large volume – a list of about 3,000 stocks – must be reported within ninety seconds of the trade taking place. There are safeguards built into the NASDAQ system to attempt to prevent malpractice, and to seek to provide the investor with the same security that he has under the London jobbing system. Once registered in a stock, a NASDAQ dealer must be prepared to buy or sell at any time, in much the same way as a jobber is obliged to stand behind his price. There must be at least two market makers for each stock quoted.

A market maker whose spread – the difference between his buy and sell quotations – is more than double that of the representative or average spread will be warned by the computer that it is excessive. The computer warning also finds its way into the directories of the National Association of Securities Dealers, which will almost certainly call for an explanation, and may take disciplinary action.

Another safety measure is a provision in the NASDAQ rules that when a member dealer buys on his own account and not on behalf of a client, he should do so at a price which is fair in relation to the prices being made by the market makers. The factors which should be taken into account by both members and disciplinary committees in determining the fairness of such deals are set out in the Association's Rules of Fair Practice, and include the type of security and its availability in the market.

All members of NASD must be members of the Securities Investor Protection Corporation (SIPC), established by Congress in 1970; this means that those who buy and sell through the system have exactly the same protection as they would if they were dealing on the New York Stock Exchange. If an investor, or anyone else, feels he has been maltreated, or that there has been malpractice, the SIPC will contact the Association, which maintains a three-year computer file record of every price movement in a stock, and may trace the history of the stock second by second, identifying when changes took place, who initiated them, and what the root cause was. With such a complete audit trail, investigations are relatively easy to conduct.

LIVERPOOL JOHN MOORES UNIVERSITY
LEARNING SERVICES

Images and Reality

There is nothing like a good Hollywood movie to create a false impression, and Wall Street has had its share, with the film of the same name and another based on Tom Wolfe's book *Bonfire of the Vanities*. There are doubtless dozens of Gordon Geckos on Wall Street, though some of the worst offenders have gone to prison. There are also some very rich people in the Street, though most of them are not inclined to ostentation, preferring a sandwich lunch at their desk to anything more pretentious. It surprises many to discover that on summer weekends some of the Street's wealthiest choose to travel up to their weekenders in the Hamptons on Long Island not by helicopter or light aircraft, but by the standard bus service.

Wall Street has its carers too. I invited a friend from Merrill Lynch to lunch one Saturday only to find that he was spending the day with an unemployed teenager from the Bronx. He was one of many in Merrill's mentoring scheme, wherein high-salaried executives gave one of their most precious commodities, spare time, to try to help those at the bottom of the heap. For every success story there was a failure, but at least they cared.

Perhaps the greatest test for Wall Street came on 11 September 2001 when two passenger airlines were flown directly into the upper floors of Wall Street's tallest buildings, the twin towers of the World Trade Center. Several thousand Wall Street professionals either died instantly or perished as they tried to leave the burning, tottering wreckage. They, and hundreds of valiant firefighters who lost their lives trying to save them, will go down in history as the victims of the worst terrorist attack the world has ever known. Some got out, but it was not a case of the rich looking after themselves. The *New York Times* told the story of John Paul DeVito and Harry Ramos, the senior officers of investment bank May Davis. DeVito managed to coax his twelve terrified employees down eighty-seven floors to safety. Ramos, meanwhile, stopped on the thirty-sixth floor to help a complete stranger. He was never seen again. His partner told the *Times*:

> If you had seen what it was like in the stairway you would be proud. There was no gender, no race, no religion. It was everyone unequivocally helping each other. I am sick and tired of hearing on Wall Street that the good guy always finishes last.[1]

---

[1] *New York Times*, 16 September 2001.

Although loss of human life was the most tragic consequence of the acts of barbarism perpetrated that day, there was no doubt that the goal of the terrorists was to wreck Wall Street, the premier fortress of capitalism.

The next morning it looked as if they had succeeded. Several major finance houses had lost many of their staff, their offices and their computer systems. Those in adjoining buildings, like Merrill Lynch, Lehman Brothers, American Express and scores of others, were spared loss of life, but their buildings were uninhabitable and, in some cases, unsafe. The Millennium Hilton, a favourite of visitors to Wall Street, looked set to topple in the first strong wind. The whole of the Street – indeed, the whole area of Manhattan below Greenwich Village – was declared a no-go area for all but rescue and recovery teams. Trading on the New York Stock Exchange, the smaller American Stock Exchange and the NASDAQ was suspended indefinitely.

After three working days and a weekend, Wall Street was up and running again, after a truly remarkable effort. Merrill Lynch regrouped its top executives at the home of its head of com-munications in Chelsea Village, and then set up a command centre in an empty warehouse in Greenwich Village. Next day it phoned its staff and ordered them to other offices across the Hudson River in New Jersey. In the process it had to install new computers and new telecommunications, and draw back all its records from a back-up centre outside New York City. In this same period, Lehman Brothers took 665 rooms at the New York Sheraton in Seventh Avenue, and refurbished them as offices for 1,500 brokers and analysts

During the chaos that followed the disaster, the actual systems held up well. NASDAQ, whose headquarters are at One Liberty Plaza, directly across the street from the World Trade Center, evacuated its building as a precautionary measure, but switched its operations to its other centres and could have resumed operations on the morning after the disaster. Because there are more than twenty NASDAQ connection centres throughout the United States, with plenty of back-up, there was no technical reason for it not to open. Those trading rooms that could not connect were offered twenty-four-hour support as they established themselves in other locations. The reason why it did not open on 12 September was explained by NASDAQ's chief executive:

It was a textbook example of effective cooperation among the government, markets and private industry. Telecommunication, power and employee access problems created enormous complications and risks in reopening the market. In addition there was unanimity among all participants that the equity markets should open as quickly as possible, but only when we could ensure that they could operate efficiently with proper liquidity available, without additional constraints and with universal access for investors. We also believed that, given the uncertainties, it was important for investor confidence that all equity markets open simultaneously.[2]

And so they did, although there were those who pointed out that a quicker reopening would have been possible and desirable but for the physical location of the trading floor of the NYSE and the need for people to be present there.

At the time of writing, it is impossible to know how Wall Street will recreate itself, but it is a fair bet that many large dealing rooms will migrate away from Manhattan to the leafier corners of Connecticut and New Jersey. The terrorists may have delivered an unintended benefit to the new economy, because it has now been proved beyond doubt that it is no longer necessary for those who work on the stock markets and in financial services to cluster together in one narrowly defined location which provides an obvious and easy target for terrorists.

NASDAQ has ambitions to become the global stock market, and has already set up subsidiary operations in many locations outside America, including Canada, Europe, Japan and Hong Kong. In most of these centres it is in stiff competition with long-established stock markets that have also adopted electronic trading, but inevitably there will be mergers and consolidation. Now that the London Stock Exchange is a publicly quoted company, it must be vulnerable to takeover unless it can itself link up with another large market.

Europe Takes to Shares

Although there is evidence that a stock market flourished in Amsterdam at about the same time as London began share trading, the Europeans lagged far behind the Anglo-Saxons in developing equity finance. No one should be surprised by this: the mayhem

---

[2] Hardwick Simmons, CEO of NASDAQ, in testimony to the Senate Committee on Banking, 20 September 2001.

caused to business and trade by two world wars meant that most people holding shares would have seen their values wiped out. Either the businesses or industries were obliterated or they were taken over by the state. Many thousands fled to America; others with savings put them under their beds or in the bank. Those Russians who owned shares prior to the Revolution had them confiscated.

Stock markets, known in Europe as bourses, were reopened after the end of World War II, but they could not be said to play a central role either in people's saving or in the financing of industry. Those functions were dominated by the banks, which, as one writer explains, re-established their earlier pre-eminence.

> The big continental banks evoke a much deeper dread than the British, partly because they have embraced industry with a closer hug. Their power goes back to the nineteenth century. The French Rothschilds helped to finance the railways in France and beyond, and their rivals the Pereires set a pattern for the 'universal bank', collecting savings from small savers and deploying the capital for the development and control of industry, which was followed elsewhere on the Continent. The French banks soon fell behind the German banks, who played a key part in the new industries, and used their deposits, and their customers' proxies, to establish controlling shares in the big companies. A German bank, as the saying went, accompanied an industrial enterprise from the cradle to the grave, from establishment to liquidation throughout all the vicissitudes of its existence.[3]

It was not until the winter of 1990, when the Berlin Wall came tumbling down, symbolising the end of the Cold War, that Europe began to rebuild its stock markets. Now they are growing very rapidly. In 1993 the combined market capitalisation of all the European exchanges was little more than half that of London. By 1997 Germany's market had risen from one tenth of the value of London to a third, while France's bourse was a quarter the size of London. And for the first time ever, the total size of Europe's bourses exceeded London's market capitalisation.

Fuelling these changes has been a wave of privatisations, as aggressive as that in Britain in the Thatcher years, with Germany the prime mover. The biggest of these, Deutsche Telekom, raised DM 20 billion in December 1996, with 690 million shares sold at DM 28.50 each. Deutsche Telekom is now an aggressive global company.

---

[3] Anthony Sampson, *The New Europeans*. NY Hodder, USA, 1968.

Also energising the interest in Europe's stock markets has been a wave of mergers and acquisitions, a phenomenon little in evidence in the eighties and the early part of the nineties. The arrival of European Monetary Union and the introduction of a single currency has been the prime motivating force, but another equally powerful catalyst has been the trend towards globalisation in business.

One of the most remarkable days for the European markets was 13 October 1997, when news of five major cross-border mergers hit the screens, involving capital of around $100 million. These were:

- a move by the Swiss Zurich Group to take over BAT's financial services company to create a new group worth $35.7 billion
- a merger between Britain's Guinness and Grand Met, with France's LVMH having a 10 per cent stake in the new $39 billion entity
- a merger between the Anglo-Dutch group Reed Elsevier and Holland's Wolters Kluwer to create the world's largest scientific and technical publisher, worth $10.6 billion
- a hostile $7 billion bid by Italy's Generali insurance company for AGF of France
- a hostile $2.8 billion bid by Lafarge of France for Redland of Britain

European countries have now created high-tech stock markets to match the new mood. The largest is the Deutsche Borse (DB), which replaced the federation of eight regional stock markets that used to comprise the German market. The regional pattern has, however, been retained, as DB operates through a series of city exchanges, the largest of which is the Frankfurt Wertpapierborse, or Frankfurt Stock Exchange, based in Germany's financial capital. The DB is the fourth largest exchange in the world.

Despite these changes, the German financial services industry is still conservative. The exchange continues to be controlled by the banks, who are very reluctant to loosen their grip on any aspect of the capital markets. It is run by a council of twenty-four members, elected for a three-year term. Besides bankers, council members include official exchange brokers, independent brokers, insurance companies and other issuers and investors.

The family firm
It is the structure of European industry, and its hangover from the

past, that limits the activities of the continental bourses in a way that will still take many years to unravel. The main influence is family ownership of large companies, with many interlocking directorships, something that simply is not a major factor in America and Britain. Rupert Murdoch's News Corporation is one of the very few Anglo-Saxon mega-corporations that is dominated by family interests, but neither it or Murdoch himself owns a substantial stake in a bank or a large non-media company. In Europe, such cross-ownership is commonplace. It is not unusual to find a major family controlling several industrial companies while also holding down a seat on a bank board. One academic study found that:

> The United Kingdom and the United States have 'outsider systems' of corporate control. There are large equity markets, dispersed ownership and active markets in corporate control. By contrast a majority of Continental European markets have 'insider systems' with small numbers of quoted companies, concentrated share ownership, and comparatively low levels of takeover activity. Germany is a good example of an 'insider' system. It has less than 800 quoted companies, compared with nearly 3,000 in the UK, and 85 per cent of the largest quoted companies have a single shareholder owning more than 25 per cent of voting shares.[4]

What this means is that there is substantial pyramid ownership. In half of Germany's companies one single shareholder owns 50 per cent of the stock, which gives them control of the company. The company they control then often owns 50 per cent of a second company. Work that out and you will see that it is possible to control the second company from on high by buying only 25 per cent of the equity, or 12.5 per cent if you go one further step down the pyramid. This could not happen in Britain, first because institutions, rather than operating companies, hold most stock in big corporations, and secondly because British law provides that once you hold 30 per cent of the stock of a company, you must bid for the remainder at the highest price you paid for the earlier share purchases.

There is a misapprehension that the banks hold large blocks of shares in German companies. They do not. Only 6 per cent of shareholdings in excess of 25 per cent are held by banks.[5] What

---

[4] Julian Franks and Colin Mayer, *Ownership and Control of German Corporations*, September 2000.
[5] Ibid.

banks do have are proxy votes, often entrusted to them by family companies, which represent more than one fifth of holdings over 25 per cent. That is where they wield their power, particularly through blocking resolutions that might be damaging to their friends and clients.

German companies, and those in some other European countries, are controlled by a two-tier strucuture. The first tier is what is called the supervisory board, which is composed of shareholder, employee and stakeholder representatives. Then there is the management board which consists of full-time executives, headed by the chief executive. The supervisory board appoints the management board, approves the accounts and long-term strategy, and can intervene when there is a serious deterioration in the company's fortunes. The chief executive is not a member of the supervisory board, and does not normally attend its meetings. What is interesting here is that representation on the supervisory board goes hand in hand with ownership; in three out of four German companies, where the shareholder is another company, the shareholder appoints the chairman of the board and one in four of all remaining members.[6]

One interesting initiative, which would also work well in London, is the German Equity Forum. One of the services it provides is to give enterprises seeking capital a low-cost medium to profile themselves or to set out financing needs and offer investment opportunities. The Deutsche Borse does not act as an adviser or mediator and does not take any responsibility for the accuracy of the information. What it has done is to run a forum, the first of which took place in Leipzig in September 1996. It also now has an Internet site which enables companies and investors to publish bids and offers (htpp://www.exchange.de). This is a useful way of putting venture capitalists together with ventures which, later in their development, may wish to obtain a listing on the Borse.

Deutsche Borse also provides an Internet share market database which provides online price and volume data for all shares, bonds, indices, derivatives and foreign exchange instruments traded on German exchanges. This means that for the first time private investors will be able to access directly data, including real-time prices, that was previously available only to market professionals.

Another initiative has been the Neuer Markt, which provides a framework for companies to meet disclosure requirements and gives

---

[6] Franks and Mayer, op. cit.

investors direct access to company information. Members must agree to meet the most rigorous international standards of disclosure (as well as the German ones), must issue quarterly and annual reports in English as well as German, and provide regular events for analysts and investors.

Despite these strong advances in recent years, there is still much work to be done, particularly amongst the medium-sized companies that care little about their global financial image and often disregard the regulations.

Mainland Europe's second largest exchange, the Paris Bourse, has also radically transformed itself in recent years. Its fine historical building on Rue de la Bourse belies the fact that, operationally, France now has one of the most modern and efficient stock exchanges in the world, with both screen and floor trading, a modern transactions system known as Relit, and deregulated commissions for brokers. But it is still perceived to be over-regulated by the French Government.

One interesting innovation from France has been the Nouveau Marché. This was specially constructed for small but fast-growing companies in 1996. By its first anniversary in March 1997, it had twenty-three listed companies with a total market capitalisation of almost FF9 billion. In that time it raised FF1.87 billion of new capital. The Nouveau Marché has many similarities with the US NASDAQ. It requires the publication of quarterly results, and investors are obliged to retain their shares in the company after quotation and cannot just sell out to make a quick profit.

The six million Swiss are perhaps the most heavily banked people on earth, and once had seven stock exchanges. But the big three banks – Union de Banque Suisse, Swiss Banking Corporation and Credit Suisse – decided to put a stop to this, and withdrew their support from the four smallest exchanges. Switzerland may well end up with only the Zurich Bourse, controlled by the banks. In Zurich there are no market makers and no brokers: virtually all the work is done by the bankers' representatives, who only abolished fixed commissions because the Swiss Cartel Office forced them to do so. Institutional investors are not particularly active: Swiss pension funds have only about 5 per cent in local equities, though this is expected to increase. Despite its strong role as a banking centre, Zurich is not an important bourse. The twelve major Swiss stocks are also traded in London, which handles a fifth of total Swiss trading volume.

Tokyo

Not long ago trading on the Tokyo Stock Market resembled the crowd at a Premiership soccer match. The surging mass of dealers swayed to and fro pulling faces and shaking their fists, sometimes shouting hysterically as they raised their hands in a kind of salute to capitalism. From time to time those involved in the mêlée were punched, pushed and kicked as 330 million shares changed hands on a daily basis.

Those days are gone. Since 1999 Tokyo, and the other lesser Japanese exchanges, has become becalmed in electronic systems similar to those deployed by NASDAQ in the United States and by exchanges in London. The Japanese economy has also been embroiled in deep recession, and the markets have been depressed and are likely to be so for some time.

Tokyo's recent history has not been helped by a series of scandals, ranging from simple market rigging and insider trading to the fall from grace of Nomura, Japan's largest securities house. Nomura, founded as a small money changer in the back streets of Osaka in 1872, was once the world's biggest stockbroker, and was forecast to swallow up both American and European rivals. While it is still a giant, it has spent much of the last five years restoring a reputation tarnished when it was forced to admit making illegal payments, totalling $50 million, to *sokaiya*, mob gangsters who made a good living from threatening to disrupt companies' annual meetings. It was ordered to stop trading for a month as punishment, and lost $36 million in revenue. Its revenues fell further when long-standing customers moved their business elsewhere.

The Ministry of Finance in Tokyo had threatened an even tougher penalty – a ban on trading for six months – but withdrew the threat when Nomura's president, Hideo Sakamaki, resigned in disgrace and was replaced by Junichi Ujiie, who undertook to clean up the company. Ujiie was untarnished because he had been out of the country running the United States operation when the crimes were committed. He immediately sacked twenty of Nomura's forty-three directors, including everyone at the rank of senior managing director or above, in doing so reducing the average age of the Nomura board from fifty-five to forty-eight. It was the biggest purge ever at any Japanese company.

Nomura and the two other leading Japanese financial houses, Daiwa and Nikko, are the main brokers in Japan, accounting for three quarters of the underwriting business and half of all trade on the Tokyo Stock Exchange. The TES is organised in four sections. The first section is for the largest and most successful companies, the second comprises smaller companies with much lower trading volumes, the third is for international companies like Barclays Group, IBM, Volkswagen and Merrill Lynch, and the fourth for emerging and growth stocks. Of the thirty-eight foreign companies listed, fourteen are from the United States and seven from Germany.

Despite its problems, Nomura has sought to recruit English staff from across the globe. Its London office has been a very active investor in the British leisure market, at one stage buying up a number of the country's public houses. It has also been one of the largest recruiters of Oxbridge graduates, taking them to Tokyo for months of intensive training before posting them round the world.

I met a group of Nomura recruits on a visit to Tokyo a few years ago, and here is what they said:

> **Christopher:** I joined Nomura because I think their global expansion programme is absolutely phenomenal. I am sure they are going to come up as number one ahead of the others.
> **Catherine:** They are going to be very, very big. They are very ambitious, and the togetherness and the spirit really is obvious.
> **James:** They really believe in team work. I am also amazed at the degree of responsibility that last year's graduates have been given. (James held up a white Nomura carrier bag.) I have brought this to show you because it sums up Nomura's attitude. It says: 'Nomura makes money make money'. Now a British institution would probably have had a Latin ode.

6   The Share Buyers

Have I made thee more profits than other princes can.
                                        Shakespeare, *The Tempest*

The power to make money is a gift of God.
                                        John D. Rockefeller

What a wonderful time it is to be a boss of a big company.
Money pours into your lap.
                                        The Economist, August 1999

Almost everyone owns shares, either directly or through third parties investing on their behalf in pension schemes, life assurance, unit trusts, mutual funds or other pooled investments. In recent years there has been a conspicuous rise in the number of individuals who have chosen to buy and sell their own stocks, instead of or in addition to collective investments. In Britain and Europe the number of private shareholders rose sharply after the great privatisations of the eighties and nineties, and they now form a substantial portion of the pool of investors, though not the largest. That category is reserved for institutional investors, who, according to the most recent credible survey, own just over half of the £1,545 billion worth of shares in the market.[1] Private shareholders, however, are the most active group accounting for 60 per cent of all trades in London.

There are now around twelve million private shareholders in Britain, which represents 25 per cent of the adult population, compared with just 9 per cent in 1979. Between them they own 16.5 per cent of all equities.[2] Given that private share ownership had been all but wiped out by the disastrous policies of the early post-war Labour governments, these figures are remarkable. While the initial take-off occurred during the privatisations of the Thatcher government in the early 1980s, a further surge occurred at about the time

---

[1] The actual figure is 50.9% (Office for National Statistics).
[2] Shares and Share Ownership, Proshare, November 2000.

when Tony Blair's New Labour administration moved into Downing Street. The main reason for the second wave, though, is more likely to be the large number of mutual insurance groups turning themselves into corporations, providing windfall shares for their policy holders in the process.

Although the percentage of shareholders in many other countries is much greater, Britain is sixth in the league table. The United States comes top, with 48 per cent of the adult population owning shares, followed by Australia, with 40 per cent. Then come Sweden and Switzerland, with 36% each, the Netherlands (30%) and Russia (27%). Canada is at the same level as Britain with Japan at a very low 9%.[3]

In Britain the share-owning society is not, as some pundits have suggested, restricted to affluent Londoners, for a greater percentage, more than one in four, comes from the north of England. The place where the highest percentage of the population are shareholders is the Grampian Television region of Scotland. Nor is share ownership the preserve of the highest socio-economic group. In June 2000, 59 per cent of share owners were in the C or D socio-economic group.[4] Finally, share ownership does not seem to appeal to singles, for 89 per cent of private investors are married. This is curious, for you might expect single people to be more ready to take a punt on the markets. The explanation, perhaps, is that they have other preoccupations.

It used to be the case that most individuals held shares in only one, or at the most two companies, usually from the early privatisations like British Gas and British Telecom. Not any more. Over two thirds of individual holders have shares in two or more companies. By far the most popular has been Halifax, with 3.4 million individual holders, followed by another former building society, Abbey National, with 2.5 million.[5] By the year 2000, the top ten included only three privatised industries. Unfortunately for the people concerned, some of the best-supported companies have been those whose managements have been disappointing – BT, Railtrack, British Airways, Marks and Spencer, Marconi and Vodafone. Size does not always mean success.

Some private shareholders have been very successful, and ended up in the league tables of the super-rich. There are people like Bill Gates

[3] AKTIEN Forum, Vienna, quoted in Proshare 2000 study.
[4] Ibid.
[5] Ibid.

and Rupert Murdoch who are at or near the top of the Forbes 1000 list of the world's richest people because of their personal holdings in businesses they have built themselves from scratch. There are others who have achieved wealth by using their judgement and astuteness in trading shares in other people's enterprises.

A relatively new phenomenon in individual share ownership has been the rise in the wealth of senior executives in business, who increasingly are rewarded with paper in their companies as well as pound or dollar notes. High-profile executive directors and managers of major corporations expect to receive considerably in excess of their agreed annual salaries as a matter of routine, and in most cases this is achieved through the issue to them of free executive share options in the company for which they work.

The stories in the newspapers about exalted earnings for chairmen and chief executives – or multimillion-pound pay-offs when they are forced out or 'retired due to ill health' – usually fail to report that share options are now an important ingredient of any manager's employment package. The theory is simple: the better the company does, the more the manager gets. And the better the long-term reward, the less likely he or she will be to resign to join up with a competitor. The level of remuneration that chief executives earn has now become a political issue.

These kinds of share options are not to be confused with those you can buy and sell on the markets, which are also discussed elsewhere (see p. 121). They are awarded by the employing corporation, and those lucky enough to be given them get a certificate entitling them to buy up to a specified number of the company's shares at an agreed price after an agreed length of time. Normally, but not necessarily, the price is set close to today's price, and the right to exercise the option kicks in after a period of between three and five years. If, during that time, the price falls, the options are worthless, and are not exercised. The executive gains nothing, but has lost nothing. If the shares rise sharply, there is a handsome paper profit, and tax is not normally payable on the capital gain until the shares are sold. So if you live in a country where there are capital gains taxes and you do not need the money, you can hold the shares until you have moved to a tax haven, or until you reach retirement age and pay lower taxes. Or you can sell a sufficient number each year to stay within the limit of disposals without facing a tax liability.

Thus executive share options can be very lucrative, even if you are not responsible for the success of the company. Take the case of a senior executive in Pearson receiving 10,000 share options at the start of the 1990s, with the right to exercise them any time between 1995 and 2000. In 1990 the shares languished around the £2 mark, partly because the British market was still recovering from the 1987–8 crash and also because the company's management at the time was regarded as limp and lacking ambition. By 1998 the old management had gone, and a lively American, Marjorie Scardino, was brought in to refocus the company, whose shares had come out of the doldrums and risen to around the £6 mark. Mrs Scardino pledged to double shareholder value, and by 1999 had done better than that, with a valuation above £13. The executive with the 10,000 1990s options could exercise his rights and increase his wealth by £110,000. However, by the autumn of 2001, the shares had fallen back to just above the £6 mark, and for those hanging on to them the result was disappointing.

While the use of executive share options in senior management compensation has grown in Britain, their significance is small when compared to what has happened in the United States, where awards have increased to astonishing levels. Since America tends to set the trend in management rewards, it may be expected that the practice will become universal. According to an executive compensation company, Pearl Meyer and Partners, the 200 biggest United States companies had by 1998 granted shares and share options worth about $1.1 trillion – that is, over 13 per cent of corporate equity. Fifteen of these companies have committed a quarter of their equity to such schemes. They include household-name firms like Merrill Lynch and Apple Computer. The same firm named some high-profile individuals who had made large gains on exercising options: Jack Welch of General Electric, $31.8 million; Tony O'Reilly of Heinz, $34.8 million; Andy Grove of Intel, $49 million; and Sandy Weill of Citicorp, $220 million.

There are problems with these kind of mega rewards. One is that the rise in share prices may not be the result of individual effort, but rather be due to a general rise. The spectacular growth of information superhighways is down to brilliant innovations from Silicon Valley and a sympathetic and sensible White House. Another factor has been sound economic management by the Federal Reserve Board and the United States Treasury, both public bodies, which have allowed interest rates to fall to low levels. Equally, good corporate management may be blighted by a general downturn in economic activity.

Another concern is that the incentives on offer from share options may be so great as to encourage top managers into policies that may not be in the company's long-term best interests. Cutting costs goes straight to the bottom line, thereby improving immediate performance, but it may handicap the opportunities for growth if there are not sufficient trained and skilled workers when you need them. Measures designed to build short-term share value can demoralise employees and damage service levels, as evidenced by British Airways' recent experience.

It is also likely that chief executives will become predatory in acquiring rival corporations because of the share benefits that will accrue to them if they can swallow another large company and downsize it. The fact that their corporation may have to borrow heavily to do this is overlooked or even ignored. Against this it is argued that a motivated chief executive is less likely to go in for wasteful corporate extravagances if his reward package depends on shareholder value, and certainly some leaders make a point of practising frugality in headquarters buildings and corporate travel. Others, however, do not, and still display a lust for the trappings of power. There seems to be no clear pattern.

One curious aspect of executive share options – and an attraction for boards using them as incentives – is that in some countries they do not end up as a cost on company balance sheets. In America there were moves to include them on the balance sheet, but corporate bosses mounted a furious lobby and defeated them. Had their protests been unsuccessful, corporate profits would not have been what they were, and perhaps share prices might not have risen so much. According to a London research company, Smithers and Co., quoted by *The Economist*, leaving out options from the balance sheet means that the US companies issuing them have understated profits by a half.

The famous global investor Warren Buffett had this to say about this curious practice in the annual report of his company, Berkshire Hathaway:

> Accounting principles offer management a choice: pay employees one way, and count the cost, or pay them in another form and ignore the cost. If options aren't a form of compensation, what are they? If compensation isn't an expense, what is it? And if expenses shouldn't go into the calculation of earnings, where in the world should they go?[6]

---

[6] Berkshire Hathaway annual report, 1998.

He has a point.

The feel good factor that these men must experience is not necessarily shared by all of those who have to get out of bed each morning to go to work for them, especially as it appears that real average earnings have fallen in the United States during the period of these grandees' enrichment.

Still, many ordinary employees do enjoy similar benefits to their bosses, albeit on a much less grand scale. Employee share ownership has been growing rapidly in Britain. According to the Inland Revenue, there are more than 2.5 million Britons participating in employee share schemes.[7] In the United States there are 10 million workers involved in company share plans, and 16 million people also save money to buy shares at cheap rates in the companies for whom they work. None of these schemes are obligatory. France seems to be the only country, at least in Europe, to have passed a law which dictates that every firm with at least fifty employees must establish a company savings scheme. The law is obligatory on employers, not employees, who have the right to choose not to save in this way, although it appears that almost one in four do so. Perhaps the most lucrative example of company share generosity is Microsoft, which from its early days has had a policy of offering share packages in exchange for lower salaries. In 1996 the shares rose ninety-fold, and this astonishing increase made many employees very rich. A more modest scheme came from the Asda supermarket chain, but it is one of the largest, with over 26,000 members.

In Britain not all workers are in the type of scheme enjoyed by their bosses, though some are. These favoured schemes allow companies to provide selected employees with the right to buy shares within three and ten years of options being granted at the price prevailing at the time the option was granted, usually referred to as the strike price.

Most employees, however, are in what are called profit-sharing schemes, better known as free shares plans. Under these ingenious plans, companies can reduce their taxable profits by subscribing to a trust fund whose trustees buy shares in the company and distribute them to employees. There are rules, the most important being that membership of such schemes must be open to all employees, both full- and part-time, who have been with the company for at least five years, though many firms accept those with shorter service. Another

---

[7] Inland Revenue Statistics, 1999, Table 6.1.

rule is that employees must be given shares on similar terms. This does not necessary mean an equal number of shares for all, though it can do. More likely is an allocation arrangement based on a percentage of salary.

Less popular but still generous are save-as-you-earn schemes. Here employees are given the right to buy at a future date a limited number of shares in their company at a price fixed when the option is granted. They are then obliged to commit to saving a fixed amount per month with a recognised financial institution such as a building society, and have to do this for a period of either three years or five years. The least that can be saved is £5 per month and the most £250. At the end of the period employees then have the choice of keeping their savings plus interest, or using them to exercise the options and buy the shares. No tax is payable on the benefit of being able to buy the shares cheap. As with free share schemes, the save-as-you-earn schemes must be open to all employees with five years' service.

Table 6.1: Percentage of shareholders by age in employee share schemes

Age group	Percentage
16–34	45
35–44	28
45–54	24
55–64	15
65+	10

Source: Mintel Share Ownership Survey, 1999

Those in employee schemes, however, are overshadowed by private individuals who make their own decisions. I knew of an old man who lived extremely modestly in a caravan in the small Norfolk market town of Fakenham. By appearance he was shabby and poor, as befits the image of a district reporter for the local paper. But each day he bought and studied the *Financial Times*, and spent half an hour on the phone to his broker buying and selling shares. By the time he had retired from the *Dereham and Fakenham Times* he had made much more money from the stock market than from his modest pay as a newsman.

Most individual investors are soloists, making their decisions daily, weekly or monthly based on their own hunches and beliefs. Many take advice from stockbrokers or other financial professionals.

Increasingly, though, investors are seeking out like-minded individuals and working together in investment clubs.

Table 6.2: Percentages of private shareholders

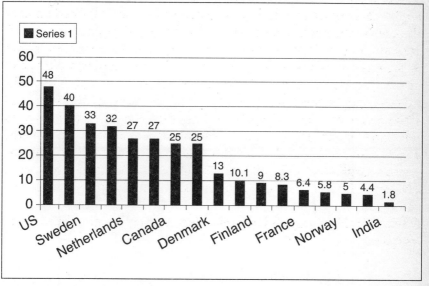

Source: Proshare

Day Traders

Day trading has emerged as a much publicised if not particularly significant phenomenon in Britain since the last edition of this book. A day trader is a speculator or gambler, not an investor, since as the name implies, shares are bought and sold with a view to making a profit within the trading day. By definition you will never keep any of the shares you have bought.

Many people who call themselves day traders because they buy and sell stocks regularly do not fit the description. A number of people have written regular newspaper columns on day trading, but what they are doing is more like week-by-week trading, in which you attempt to spot an undervalued stock with a view not to keeping it for the long term but to selling it after it has seen a rise of perhaps 10 per cent. If your judgement is wrong and the price falls, you will probably put a stop-loss on it if it drops 10 per cent below the purchase price. A stop-loss is a standing instruction to your stockbroker to sell your

Table 6.3

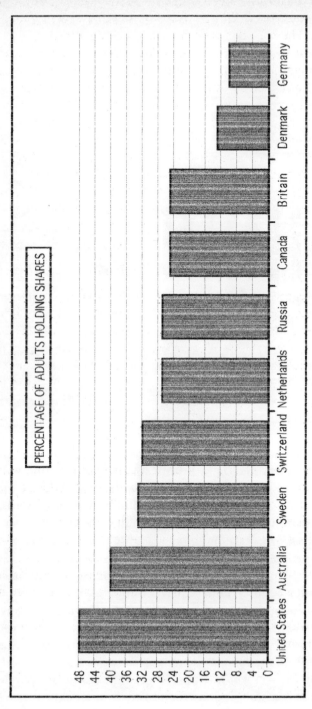

PERCENTAGE OF ADULTS HOLDING SHARES

Source: Proshare

shares once they have fallen to a predetermined amount. Using this technique, you will hope to make money by having more gains than losses. The accurate description for this activity is frequent trading. Frequent traders benefit from much lower dealing costs from online brokerages, although they still have to pay the same stamp duty.

Real day trading is an altogether riskier proposition. For starters you will be pitting your wits against professional traders in London, New York and elsewhere. They will almost certainly have much more sophisticated systems than most individuals can afford. These differences can be overcome if you have the ability to undertake detailed technical analysis and an iron discipline that gives you the will to take profits when they are there without being greedy for more, and to accept losses before they grow larger. At the end of your day's trading during which you will have bought and sold many stocks or derivatives – sometimes buying and selling the stock several times in large volumes – you will close out your positions and take your profits or losses.

There are people who have exchanged well-salaried jobs with guaranteed pensions and company Mercedes to sit at home, wearing jeans and sweater, day trading at a computer terminal. It may beat wearing a suit or commuting on the London Underground, but it can be gruelling in other respects. You need to be able to think mathematically and work systematically. It requires total concentration, an ability to grasp fast-changing situations, and, if you have a relationship, an understanding partner. You cannot go out and walk the dog or attend your child's school concert when you have exposed positions on the markets. The core skill is to understand the trend for the day in any given stock or derivative you are following, and then to be able to quantify the degree of resistance to the trend. How much could it rise or fall in the remainder of the trading day? This assessment is made all the harder in that most share price movements take place within minutes of the markets opening, often meaning that the scope for further gain or loss is minimal.

Advice is not hard to come by, and there have been many books devoted to day trading, and related activities such as technical analysis and charting. None of them are much of a substitute for hard experience, which should be gained by attention to detail rather than instinct. According to one expert:

> One certainty exists. If you allow your trading decisions to be driven by intuition or gut feelings, then losses will result. Day

trading can really be very consuming. You will need to follow the markets on a minute-by-minute basis. As a day trader you will be making trading decisions on your assessment of technical issues, rather than fundamentals that are more relevant to the longer-term investor. Also never lose sight of the fact that you will be competing with professional traders in securities firms and investment banks who will be trading with a greater degree of market information than is available to most other participants, and that electronic trading means you will be devoid of any nuances, feel or flavour of the market.[8]

Long-term day traders say they often buy and sell within a four-minute time span. The most active day traders in the United States deal between 200 and 300 times a day. So those with slow Internet access, or no Internet access at all, should forget it. Anyone serious about starting as a day trader should experiment first before giving up his or her salaried job. A good way of finding out whether you have the ability to make money this way is to conduct notional trades first. You can do this in the evenings using US stocks and derivatives if you have an online account which allows the buying and selling of American stocks. Remember though not to process the trade once you have got the market quotes. Remember also that in the long run it will not be possible to make money using the average online broker for day trading.

Effectively you will need a mini dealing room in your home office. That means investing in a Bloomberg terminal or equivalent that will allow you real-time prices, and access to what is called Level II information. This is the same information the professionals have, an immediate read on how markets in each stock are moving, and an indication of the weight of buyers versus sellers and the prices they are prepared to pay. For those reluctant to invest the £12,000 a year or more that may be necessary, try advfn.com's professional service, which costs a mere £25 a month.

Some day traders do not like the idea of working in isolation, or surfing the web with a noisy toddler biting their ankles. There is an alternative, but it means a return to commuting. For the gregarious enterprising frequent trader, brokers like Carllin Securities and InvestIN Securities have opened day-trading centres in the City. A seat and a terminal can cost as much as £500 a month, but you will get the feel that you are working in a real dealing room, great for those who may be dealers who have been made redundant. If the day

---

[8] John Newman, head of business development, Sweden UK Ltd, 11 May 2001.

trader executes more than 350 trades in a month, then InvestIN Securities will refund the rent. There is, however, a snag. Before being allowed to sign on, customers will have to go through an interview to establish their competence.

Frequent Traders and Short Sellers

As explained earlier, many who describe themselves as day traders are in fact frequent traders. Frequent trading can be fun and profitable, and the expansion of online brokerages on the Internet has made this activity a possibility in any household equipped with an average computer with Internet access. It is possible to be a frequent trader through telephone dealing, but the charges are higher, and the services slower and less user-friendly.

Frequent trading would be more popular still if online brokers permitted or encouraged short selling, because this would mean that traders could bet on the price of shares falling as well as rising. Short selling is a technical term that describes the practice of selling a share in the belief that it will fall in price in the near future. When it does fall you buy the stock back at a lower price, thereby gathering a profit. Since many people seem to find the concept of selling something they do not already own hard to grasp, let me explain with an example.

We are in a prolonged period of bad news for British Telecom. (When weren't we!) Jill believes strongly that BT shares are set to fall further, so she sells 2,000 at the quoted price of £4. If she actually owned the shares she would send the certificates to her broker, and within a week would receive a cheque for £8,000 less brokerage commission. But she does not own them, and cannot produce certificates. If, within the three-day settlement period, BT shares fulfil her predictions and fall by 50 pence to £3.50, she will buy the shares back at a cost of £7,000, thereby closing out the contract. She will have made £1,000 profit less commission and stamp duty, and her only cost will be these deductions. Expressed in percentage terms, her profit will be just below 1,000 per cent in less than a week. However, if she is wrong, and the price of BT rises, she will have to buy the shares she does not own in the marketplace, pay for them, and deliver the certificates. Assuming the price goes up by a similar amount to the previous example of a price fall, she will have lost £1,000 plus commission and stamp duty. In percentage terms the loss, including opportunity costs, will, however, only be about 30 per cent.

When investors trading stocks in Britain had just under two weeks to settle, the risks involved in short selling were significantly less than they are now, with only three days allowed for settlement. Short selling today is a very risky proposition, and one that is increasingly being discouraged by most brokers catering for the private investor.

7   The Big Institutions

In the world we now face, an ever-higher premium is likely to be placed on efficiency and flexibility. Our present structures fall short on both counts. Savers' money is too often being invested in ways that do not maximise their interests. It is likely to follow too that capital is being inefficiently allocated in the economy . . .

Report to the Treasury by Paul Myners, 2001

However strong the rise of private share ownership, most people's stake in world stock markets is indirect. Most of them have no idea what they own. If they bothered to find out, or if anyone cared to tell them, they might be surprised to learn that a tiny proportion of their weekly pay packet or monthly savings was invested in giant oil companies, cigarette manufacturers, or the design and construction of highly sophisticated technological weapons. There will be families who shop weekly at Sainsbury's but whose pension fund supports Tesco. Some whose search for value for money leads them to support Ryan Air or the Egg bank might be surprised to learn that their savings are in British Airways or Lloyds TSB.

Almost everyone owns shares, either directly or through third parties investing on their behalf in pension schemes, life assurance, unit trusts, mutual funds or other pooled investments. These institutional investors, as they are called, operate from the financial capitals of the world, or from cities where historically there has been a tradition of investment management, such as Edinburgh and Norwich in Britain and Boston in the United States. In Britain this tradition grew out of the development of the insurance industry, where the millions of pounds garnered from insurance premiums had to be invested prudently against the day when claims had to be paid.

Insurance companies and pension funds form by far the biggest sector amongst institutional investors. Their holdings of £652 billion in September 1999 amounted to about 42 per cent of the total of

£1,545 billion.[1] This is not as great a percentage of the total market as they held nine years earlier, in 1990 when it was nearly 49 per cent, or in 1995 when it rose to over half the total British market capitalisation at more than 52 per cent. One reason their portion has been pushed lower is the impact of globalisation. At £487 billion, overseas holders now own almost one third of Britain's publicly quoted companies, whereas ten years earlier, their ownership represented only about 15 per cent.

In the United States, the proportion of the market controlled by institutions is much the same as in Britain, and the total amount under their control is huge. The top money managers in America manage over $12.9 trillion dollars for third parties, with pension funds and mutual funds representing the greatest slice.[2]

Some of the pension funds are huge. The largest in Britain is that of BT, with assets of £29.7 billion, and all of those in the top ten are valued at more than £10 billion apiece.[3] One of the biggest is the Universities Superannuation Scheme, with £22 billion. Almost all of these and other major pension funds do not manage their own schemes, but contract out to professional fund managers (see p. 101).

Most pension funds are organised as trusts – legal vehicles which are independent of the company whose pensions they manage. Trustees are part-timers and often have no experience whatever of investment matters; therefore they are not usually competent to make a judgement on the quality of the fund managers they have contracted. In 2001 Paul Myners completed a study into the way institutional investors work, particularly their decision-making process. He was asked by Gordon Brown, the Chancellor of the Exchequer, specifically to address the government's concern that the big institutions may have an overwhelming focus on quoted equities and bonds, and avoid investing in small and medium size businesses. The results of the study are outlined in the Myners Report which is well worth reading, as it points out many flaws in the savings industry. As Myners said when delivering the report:

> 'In the world we now face, an ever-higher premium is likely to be placed on efficiency and flexibility. The review's conclusion is that our present structures fall short on both counts.[4]

---

[1] Office of National Statistics, February 2000, Table 12.1.
[2] New York Stock Exchange Factbook, 2000.
[3] National Association of Pension Funds Yearbook, 2001.
[4] Letter from Paul Myners to Chancellor of the Exchequer, 6 March 2001.

A survey conducted for the Myners inquiry came up with these worrying conclusions:

> Many trustees currently bring very limited time and expertise to their investment responsibilities. 62 per cent of those surveyed had no investment qualifications; 26 per cent received less than one day's training when they first became trustees, and 69 per cent received two days or less. 54 per cent said they had no investment committee or in-house professionals to help them in investment matters; and 49 per cent of trustees spend three hours or less preparing for pension investment matters before a trustee meeting.
>
> The results also suggest that most trustees do not have extensive knowledge of investment issues, and in particular do not have detailed knowledge of issues relating to their own funds. Of funds with a scheme-specific benchmark, 23 per cent of trustees said they did not know what their benchmark was.[5]

In other words, the people who are charged with looking after the future incomes of tens of thousands of British people do not have much of a clue as to what they are doing! Amateurism appears in various guises in British life, but when so many people's future incomes are dependent on their pensions, it is surprising that the Myners report did not produce a great outcry.

A great percentage of Britons' personal wealth is looked after by life assurance companies; they own over 20 per cent of all United Kingdom equities on behalf of individual investors and pension schemes.[6]

Insurance companies and pensions funds have interesting characteristics, for a large number of them are not themselves publicly quoted corporations seeking to make profits for their shareholders, but mutual societies, owned and apparently operated for the benefit of policy holders; in other words, the customers. An even greater number used to be mutuals, but have opted to change their status in recent years: examples include Norwich Union, now CGNU, Standard Life, Clerical Medical, and Legal and General, now owned by Lloyds TSB.

---

[5] Report to the Treasury by Paul Myners, 2001.
[6] Association of British Insurers Yearbook, 1989–99.

Table 7.1: Top ten life companies in Britain

Rank	Name of group	Premium income £ billions	Market share
1	Legal and General	18.8	15.4%
2	Barclays	12.9	11.8%
3	Prudential	9.5	8.7%
4	Standard Life	5.2	4.8%
5	AXA	4.2	3.9%
6	CGU*	3.8	3.5%
7	Norwich Union	3.8	3.5%
8	Equitable Life	3.5	3.2%
9	Friends Provident	3.4	3.1%
10	Halifax	3.4	3.1%

* CGU and Norwich Union have now merged to form CGNU

Insurers receive an income from premiums for taking on risks (insurance) or from payments against a future inevitability, such as death or reaching pensionable age (assurance). Thus although by law they have to maintain high reserves to protect themselves against a rush of claims, their main business is investing the premiums to gain a high but reliable return.

Pension funds have the paramount objective of providing a retirement income in old age to those who have contributed either through their own payments or through payments made by employers. Thus risky investments must be avoided, or limited to a small proportion of the funds under management.

Generally there are two types of pension scheme – those that offer a pension amounting to a proportion of final salary based on years of service, and those that build up a money fund which is reinvested at retirement time to provide income. In the event of the first type of pension fund failing to provide the percentages of income pledged by employers, the employer has to make up the difference, so will obviously look for a pensions provider that can perform well and therefore avoid this unhappy eventuality. In recent years many big companies have abandoned final salary schemes because of the costs involved.

In money-based funds, it is the contributor, or future pensioner, who bears the risk of poor performance, and his or her plight is made much worse by outmoded rules which usually require that the greater proportion of the fund be invested in an annuity upon retirement. With an annuity the value of a fund is handed over to a life assurance company, which pockets it and pays out a taxable annual income until death, at which point the capital becomes the property of the assurer, not the family of the deceased. Annuities tend to be very poor investments, as discussed in Chapter 9.

In the last two decades, there has been a shift to money-based schemes, even though they are less advantageous to employees likely to stick with one company. The argument for money-based schemes is that they are more portable, and in an age when lifetime employment in one company has become improbable, it is not surprising that employers prefer a system which for them provides a much lower-cost alternative.

Because of the need for prudence, most pension funds, including those run purely for the benefit of trades unions, allocate their investments across a broad spectrum, preferring a diversified port-folio to excessive concentration in one or two stocks, or venturing into speculative projects or companies based in countries with weak or unsuccessful economies. Almost all portfolios include investments in the United States, Europe and the Asia-Pacific region.

Life assurance companies have a similar outlook. Their principal concern is to see that the premium incomes received are invested adequately to meet the eventual pay-out upon death or the end of a term. It is necessary for these huge investors to match their known obligations, calculated through actuarial tables, with investments maturing at the same time. For this reason assurance companies invest heavily in long-dated gilt-edged securities or bonds. Some governments actually insist that institutions like life assurance companies and pension funds, which so often are the beneficiaries of generous tax treatment, allocate a substantial proportion of their investments to government bonds. There is, however, a trend away from such rules. Australia, for instance, has abolished what was known as the 20/30 rule whereby for every $30 invested elsewhere, $20 had to be invested in government bonds. Japan, whose pension funds have colossal clout, has gradually been easing the restrictions which made it difficult for large sums of money to be invested in anything other than Japanese industry.

Most products sold to individuals by life assurance companies are savings schemes of one sort or another, except for term assurance, which pays out if a policy holder dies within a fixed span of time. These schemes break into two types – linked, or non-linked. Your eyes may begin to glaze over at this point, but linked life investments are important because they are directly related to the stock markets. That means that they carry a greater degree of risk than non-linked investments. Individuals who buy linked products have their investments pooled together with those of other savers. Index-linked funds are tied to the performance of a specific index, such as the FTSE 100 or the FTSE 250. Others might be linked to a group of managed investments, which will be pre-defined, or to property, a description that will include commercial and perhaps residential property as well as a range of property companies.

With non-linked life policies and investments there is in theory at least no immediate or direct link between the investment performance of the pooled funds and the return to investors. Non-linked policies and other schemes include what are called with-profit policies. Under these, instead of receiving investment growth based on the performance of the pooled funds, as in linked investments, the individual receives an annual bonus which, once given, can never be taken away. This bonus is derived not from the actual performance of the funds under management, but from the life office's perception of how things are going – two totally different things – and includes a measure of the profitability of the life company itself. With-profits policies also carry a terminal bonus – a discretionary amount payable at the end of the term. Thus a with-profits policy will build up bonuses during good years, and is less risky than one that depends on the value of shares at the actual time of maturity.

However, life is never that simple. Many people have been persuaded to buy with-profits endowment policies to cover the capital cost of a house purchase, so that during the period of a twenty- or twenty-five-year loan their payments have comprised two parts – interest on the loan, and the premium on the endowment assurance. The big inducement to sign up to these policies has been that since the sum assured might be well below the value of the loan, the 'profits' will be sufficient to make up the difference when the time comes to pay the money back. However this is an expensive way to buy property, because you pay interest on the full amount borrowed throughout the term instead of on the amount outstanding. And sometimes the 'profits' are not sufficient, leaving the policy holder with a nasty shortfall when full repayment is due. The result is the much-publicised mis-selling scandal, which has resulted in household name companies like the Prudential being fined millions of pounds for duping customers.

Because life assurance companies tend towards very high market-ing budgets, large sales staffs or commission agents, extravagant premises and inflated management costs, their investment teams would need to be star performers to match investors without such encumbrances, even allowing for the weight they can wield because of the size of funds under their control. But life companies have a whole set of other burdens placed on them by the Government. Some of these are sensible, such as the requirement that they maintain a minimum margin of solvency. They are also required to have assets 'adequately diversified and reasonably spread to avoid excessive reliance on one particular category of asset, investment market, or investment'.[7]

Unit Trusts and Investment Trusts

Also under the heading of institutional investors are mutual funds (known in Britain as unit trusts), investment trusts, and other managed funds. The way these work was described in Chapter 3. In Britain there are more than 150 separate unit trust groups, but despite this and their high visibility through advertising and editorial exposure in the financial press, they account for only 2.7 per cent of total market capitalisation. Investment trusts have an even smaller slice, at 1.9 per cent, and the big institutions account for two thirds of their activity.

The Fund Managers

Fund managers are the men and women who look after other people's assets – mostly those of the pensions and life assurance industry, but also other large chunks of money belonging to corporations, rich individuals, or national institutions like the Kuwait Investment Office. Some of them work directly for the com-panies whose assets they manage, but increasingly fund management has become a separate industry, working under contract to clients like pension funds, life assurance companies and other institutions with spare cash. Perhaps the main reason for this is that the range of investments available are so complex that it has become

---

[7] Insurance Company Regulations, 1994.

mical and counter-productive to run them in-house. Another
s an increased emphasis on performance. As the Myners
report put it, it was not 'simply about finding a safe pair of hands to
look after pension contributions: institutions focused increasingly on
the ability of managers to "beat the market".'[8]

The greatest centre for fund management is New York, where the
United States fund management industry is responsible for $18.5
trillion. Britain comes second, with by far the largest asset management industry in Europe. Switzerland is about half this size, and the
total of the rest of Europe's fund management is less than that run in
the United Kingdom. Within the industry there is considerable
globalisation. For example, one of Britain's most significant fund
managers, Mercury Asset Management, was sold by S.G Warburg to
Swiss Bank Corporation, who passed it on to the American giant
Merrill Lynch. Deutsche Bank owns the UK company Morgan
Grenfell. Gartmore has been bought by Nationwide Mutual of the
United States.

The industry employs over 25,000 people in Britain alone, with
about one in five of these directly involved in managing investments.[9]
The number could be much higher because the figure quoted applies
only to the large firms; 40,000 seems a more accurate figure.[10] Fund
management has become one of the country's more important
industries, and is a big export earner.

Yet there is cause for considerable concern about the future of fund
management. Although there are some outstanding fund managers
with immense reputations, many of those in the trade are not all that
good. This is an industry where success is measured by performance,
and in the long bull market which ended in 2000, many fund
managers were achieving significantly lower returns for their clients
than the rise in the main index, the FTSE 100. Another concern is
that fund management is becoming significantly more expensive,
with the inevitable result that those at the retail end of the business
have to charge more for financial products, making them less
attractive. The main reason for the higher costs is the very high
salaries paid to fund managers, often out of all proportion both to
the value they bring and also to those with similar skills working
elsewhere. The Myners report found that 'rewards for fund managers

---

[8] Report to the Treasury by Paul Myners, 2001.
[9] Fund Management Survey, Fund Management Association, 1999.
[10] British Invisibles, Fund Management.

have risen at a rate well ahead of that for many other professions, even though profit margins have remained flat'. Other reasons for higher costs include the burden of additional regulation, and better corporate governance (see p. 219).[11]

A combination of these higher costs and less than brilliant performance has led many pensions trustees and other institutional investors to opt for what is called passive management, broadly meaning that computers do many of the jobs of the fund manager. Instead of picking stocks and exercising judgement on when to sell them, passive managers set a goal – for example, tracking the FTSE 100 index or the Dow Jones Industrial Average. They do this by buying every share in the index they are tracking, weighted exactly to each share's position. This is done through software solutions, so the computer takes over, and since there is no need for chartists, analysts, or other highly paid specialists, costs are much lower. This style of investment management has become popular, accounting for just under one in four institutional funds. As the Myners report noted:

> Although there is a substantive question as to what index a manager tracks for a given market – and increasingly complex methods of execution have been developed – passive investing is essentially a commodity. Its most significant impact on the market for active investment management has been on fees, because active managers have had to compete against the availability of the cheap passive product.[12]

But are not the movements in these indices themselves largely the result of the decisions of the active fund managers? Myners agrees there is a concern here.

> As an investment strategy passive investing seeks to free-ride off the more or less efficient capital allocation of active fund managers. As such, it could in principle lead to odd pricing effects. However it would not be legitimate to argue on that basis that institutions should not use it. Their concern is not with the efficiency of the capital markets as a whole, except in so far as this may affect the interests of their beneficiaries. Passive investing is a legitimate strategy for an investor who values its tangible cost advantages over the possibility of achieving additional return through superior stock selection.[13]

---

[11] PricewaterhouseCoopers, Fire on the Horizon, 2000.
[12] Report to the Treasury by Paul Myners, 2001.
[13] Ibid.

Tracker funds built on passive management lost some of their appeal in the bear market that developed at the turn of the millennium, although, of course, for those not invested in them the lower value of the major indices could be seen as a tremendous buying opportunity. It seems likely that fund management charges are likely to fall towards those levied by passive investment groups, probably to be replaced by a system of basic fees plus sizeable bonuses based on performance. However, experience in the United States, where high fees for outperformance have been tried, has not been wholly successful.

The issue that has to be confronted in Britain is the period of time over which performance is measured. While it is right that the management of a company should receive rewards based on their company's profits, it does not follow that this should be applied to fund managers. If the fund's objective is ten-year growth, then any reward should come when and if this aim is achieved, not if the first year proves to be a good one. Short-term success, while the prevailing paradigm of the City of London, should not enter into it. Unfortunately, many financial institutions treat their fund managers in exactly the same way as Britain's soccer club owners behave towards their team managers: sacking them at an early stage for poor performance.

Significant and important though these issues are, they pale beside the question that surrounds the role institutional investors and their fund managers can and should play in the operation of the companies into which they have channelled investments.

Most fund managers or their institutional investor masters have never worked in manufacturing industry, managed a company, hustled for business in an overseas market, or designed a robot, a machine tool or a new building. Whether based in London, New York, Tokyo or a handful of other financial centres, they wear grey suits and the introverted look of those who have spent too long staring at spreadsheets and annual reports. They take themselves, and their jobs, seriously. Hardly a working day passes when they are not meeting with directors or managers of companies in which they have invested. Although they deny that they have a day-to-day influence on managers, they do sometimes step in and wield their power when things go wrong.

Because they can sack boards, determine the outcome of takeover bids, and make or break corporations, they have to exercise this power judiciously. They are courted assiduously by corporations anxious for them to maintain or increase their holdings. When Granada mounted a hostile takeover bid for the Trusthouse Forte hotel group in the mid nineties, Rocco Forte, son of the founder of the group, Lord Forte, ran a huge campaign to attempt to persuade the institutions not to accept the Granada offer. Simultaneously, Granada's Gerry Robinson and his team conducted their own battle for the hearts and minds of the same groups. At the end of the day the vote was close, with one key institution, Mercury Asset Management (now Merrill Lynch), holding sufficient shares to have the casting vote. MAM's fund manager, Carol Galley, cast it in favour of Robinson, sealing the fate of a great family business and ensuring that famous hotels like London's Grosvenor House and the King George V in Paris would lose the individual Forte touch. The unfortunate Rocco gained plenty of cash but lost his business, and had to start from scratch again.

Questions have repeatedly been asked as to whether hard-headed individuals like Galley should have this kind of power, but it is difficult to see an alternative that would work. And there are many who believe that the investment institutions ought to be more interventionist. When it was revealed that some of the management of British Airways had been involved in a shoddy dirty-tricks operation against competitor Virgin Atlantic, some fund management groups complained to the airline's directors. But none of BA's institutional investors went so far as to call for changes in top management, even though there were demands in the media that senior directors should resign.

But this begs the question of who runs companies, and for whose benefit? The British Government of Tony Blair has suggested that business should be run for the benefit of stakeholders. This definition includes shareholders, but also customers and employees. This in itself has raised considerable debate, but also begs the question of who runs businesses – the management or the owners? And if it is, ultimately, the latter, how well equipped are institutional investors to throw their weight around? This will be discussed later, in Chapter 16.

8   Investment Clubs

*The message is clear. Ignore the ups and downs of the markets
and pick individual winners. Do your homework; ferret out
companies that will continue to make first class profits no
matter what happens in the big world outside.*
   Terry Bond, development director, Proshare Investment Clubs

*Women like to gossip. They like to swap ideas and to speculate
– that's why they make good investors.*
   Margaret Lee, secretary of the investment club, The Optimists

It might be an episode of *The Vicar of Dibley*, or the village fête
committee ruefully considering an annual event that has been washed
out by the summer rains. Yet the flickering screen of a laptop, and
spreadsheets strewn across the table in the back bar of an Essex
alehouse show that something much more serious is on the agenda.

It is mid evening, and the regular meeting of the Dirty Harry
Investment Club is underway at the Harry public house in Leigh-on-
Sea, a suburb at the tip of the Thames estuary. Dirty Harry is one of
more than 10,000 clubs in Britain alone, and it is fairly typical in that
it meets monthly on licensed premises, has twenty members, and
mixes investment with pleasure, while taking the former seriously.

On this particular evening the monthly performance presentation
from the honorary treasurer is decidedly downbeat. A portfolio that
cost the twenty members just over £20,000 one year earlier has
almost halved in value, with some stocks shedding 90 per cent of
their purchase price.

Not that the atmosphere is glum. In the face of adversity, Essex
man's humour can be characteristically defiant. Barry Lake, the
treasurer, better known as Bazza, hands round his analysis, which
shows a minus on almost every line. 'We've lost another £245 today,
boys,' he says. 'I am thinking of putting in expenses for red ink.'

However one of the securities has actually risen a few pence
because previous profits forecasts turned out to be too pessimistic.
'It's a very sad indication when profit warnings are good news,'

comments Tony drily; like other members, he has seen his losses rise to above the £500 mark.

The Dirty Harry Investment Club was formed in late 1999 with a limited life of five years and a defined goal, maximum capital growth. Its members, most of them men, nearly all come from the Southend area, with a wide variety of occupations represented. There is a banker, a money broker, a company director, a retired chief executive, and a probate lawyer. There is also an electrician, two truck drivers, two policemen, a quantity surveyor, an insurance man and a customs officer.

At this meeting several absentees are noted, which does not please the chairman, Mark, who wants their non-appearance recorded in the minutes. Perhaps when markets fall, members lose interest, I ponder, as we turn to a detailed examination of the portfolio. First, Baltimore Technologies, the rising star with which the club kicked off their investments two years earlier, buying 186 shares at £5.35 each. Tonight Baltimore shares stand at 44 pence, less than a tenth of the purchase value. 'Not worth selling,' says Bazza. 'It will all go in brokers' commission.' He adds: 'Let's face it, we put too much into technology. We have been looking at the wrong sectors; other sectors have risen. And anyone who says "I told you so" gets beaten up.'

A cheer goes up as the landlord arrives with more pints of beer and bags of crisps, along with soft drinks for those whose turn it is to drive. The twenty members put in about £10 a week, and the club has £750 in the bank which it could invest after this meeting, after detailed discussion and deliberation.

How it works
Individual members keep watch for buying opportunities, and at the monthly meetings suggest additions to the portfolio. They table the proposed acquisitions, and then present the case for each of them, backed up by their own research. After discussion and regular reference to web sites like adfin.com, the members reduce the suggested acquisitions to a short list of three by a paper vote. At this stage the assumption is made that the club will buy stocks. Once the short list has been selected, it is open for any member to make a formal proposal for action. Assuming no one does this, the portfolio will remain intact. It may be that a proposal is tabled for certain shares to be sold, and one or more of those on the short list bought. All proposals are put to a majority vote, and acted upon the next morning.

Six stocks are now put forward for debate. Bazza nominates Canary Wharf. It is one of those ventures which 'began like the Channel Tunnel', but two of the three new towers were topped out (that is to say, fabricated to its highest point, though not necessarily completely finished) and the company is now running on a 55 per cent profit margin and buying back its own shares. 'They are solid and are going to climb within the lifetime of our club,' says Barry.

Mark likes Shell. 'They are also aggressively buying back their shares; as a result the earnings per share are rising.' He reminds us that Shell pay solid dividends, and that a third of the company's turnover is in America. 'I think Shell will be considerably higher than they are now,' he says, adding cautiously: 'I do not see any reason why they should dive.'

Bazza puts the case for Manganese Bronze, the manufacturer of London taxicabs. 'They forecast a loss this year, but an improvement next year,' he says, pointing out that net asset value is about twice the present share value, and that this could mean they are ripe for takeover.

As discussion continues late into the evening, other stocks debated include Land Securities ('running a 69 per cent profit margin'), Halma ('a 700 per cent rise since 1975'), and Jarvis, a facilities management company ('lots of infrastructure work to be done for Railtrack'). Mark, though, thinks the club should lift its stake in Biocompatibles International, which has lost 47 per cent of its value since it was first acquired at the top of the market in the starting portfolio. 'There is nothing wrong with the company,' he argues. 'Everything we bought it for is still there.' He explains how he believes the company's growth strategy is still intact, despite a recent profit warning, and points out that the US Food and Drug Administration has just approved one of its key products. A United States company has also just invested heavily in convertible loan stock.

It is time to vote, and at the count Biocompatibles gets the most crosses on the ballot papers. Tony puts forward a motion proposing that the club liquidate three of its worst-performing tech stocks, BATM, Parthus and Reflec, and invest a further £1,000 into Biocompatibles. The members agree they will wait until next month before considering further purchases. The vote is carried by a narrow majority.

They close the meeting reflecting on a successful summer barbeque and passing a warm vote of thanks to the member whose home was used as the venue. The Dirty Harry Investment Club enjoys its social side too. Some members move off to an Indian restaurant for a curry, and I head for the last train to London reflecting that there must be few clubs where it is possible to derive so much enjoyment from losing money. But then there is always the hope that one day there will be a crock of gold at the end of the rainbow.

Investment clubs do not operate in isolation, though there is nothing to stop them doing so if they wish. When the first edition of this book was published in 1986, there appeared to be only five clubs. One of these was at West Houghton in the Lancashire industrial belt, where a group of women had decided to get out of British Telecom shares to buy Marks and Spencer, because 'it's always busy'.

The 10,000 clubs that have sprung up across the country since then are well organised and meet regularly, with over half of them having assets of more than £5,000. Research shows that these assets have grown rather more than money under the management of professionals. In the year 2000, the average club portfolio grew by £7,100 to £18,400.[1] The average club meets monthly, usually on a weekday evening in the first half of the week. Half of them meet in public houses and wine bars, though there is also a partiality for ethnic restaurants. Many important share purchases have been hatched up over a curry and a beer.

Every few months, members of registered clubs have the opportunity to meet each other at a series of investment seminars organised in the regions by Proshare, the not-for-profit body that has done much to build up interest in private share ownership and is the driving force behind Britain's investment clubs. It was established in 1992 with a remit to provide both formal and informal education in personal financial management. It has the support of all the main British political parties, and is funded by the London Stock Exchange, the Gatsby Charitable Foundation, the John Templeton Foundation, and over 200 leading companies.

It is interesting to analyse the list of those who have given positive support to an organisation designed to promote private share ownership. Most of the major banks are there, but not the Royal Bank of Scotland. Charles Schwab, Barclayshare, and almost every online brokerage make their contribution, but not Merrill Lynch, the world's biggest. Sainsbury's are there but Tesco could not spare the

---

[1] Proshare, 2001

cash. The Corporation of London, whom one might expect to support an educational initiative, is conspicuous by its absence. Many large legal firms have contributed but not Freshfields, one of the richest of City solicitors. Through its owner, Pearson, the *Financial Times* is the only national newspaper contributor, though the Norwich-based *Eastern Daily Press* is a sponsor.

After some quiet and ineffective early years, when it encountered opposition from both the educational establishment and the more staid and complacent elements of the City, Proshare has blossomed into a significant force for the encouragement of private investors. It has done this by concentrating on three sectors – youth education, investor clubs, and assisting companies with employee share ownership schemes.

I enjoyed the company of a large number of investor club members at one of Proshare's weekends in Bournemouth, the manicured south coast resort. The enthusiasm was palpable. Why else would several hundred people forsake the spring sunshine for a basement conference hall of a three-star hotel? But there they were, early on a Sunday morning, staring at a big screen which proclaimed: 'Time is the Great Healer'. The audience, predominantly greying and middle-aged and beyond, heaved a collective sigh, and for a moment I imagined I had gatecrashed a diocesan retreat.

Here, though, the God is Mammon, and the preacher is Ross Greenwood, the perky editor-in-chief of *Shares* magazine. He is at full throttle. 'When you are at your most frightened, you should be optimistic,' he intones, 'and when you are euphoric, you should be scared.'

The 250 members of the audience scribble this down, for they are scared, and these are words of wisdom. Most of them have seen previous profits in share trading eroded, many have lost money in the dotcom crash of 2001, and some are what Greenwood terms 'ninety per centers', investors who have lost all but one tenth of their original investment capital.

Meeting club members, I was struck by their diversity and knowledge. There was a most impressive ethnic group from south London who had formed their club six months earlier, making regular monthly contributions but deciding not to commit to their first purchase 'until we have learnt enough to be confident we know what we are doing'. How different from so many people who are bulldozed into bad money decisions by commission salesmen.

The variety of backgrounds is what is most impressive about share clubs. Some clubs are based in the workplace. The thirteen members of Aeroshare work for British Aerospace in Blackburn, mostly in supervisory jobs or on the shop floor of the Eurofighter project. By mid 2001 they were looking at losses on their £50-a-month investments, with a chunk of the losses coming from their first and largest holding, the company for which they work.

Many are young groups, like the Stab in the Dark (SID) club, which meets monthly in the Black Horse public house in Denshaw, near Oldham in Lancashire. The average age is just above twenty-one, and the group has a varied portfolio which until the time of writing was outperforming the FTSE index. The club uses what it calls a share champion system whereby each of its members takes on the obligation to become an expert in one of the stocks held. The champion has to report to the other members weekly on the web, as well as at the monthly meetings.

SID also operates a carefully thought-out stop-loss system to limit the impact of bad decisions or sudden shocks. A stop-loss is a price which an investor sets to limit the fall he is prepared to take in a share's value. It is an essential tool for any investor, particularly for a person who does not follow the markets on a daily basis. Each share's champion sets a danger mark halfway between the price paid and the stop-loss, at which the future of the stock in the portfolio is discussed. Here is how they make it work:

> The mechanism that we have agreed on at Stab in the Dark comes in two parts:
>
> 1. We calculate the initial stop-loss at 80% of our investment plus £12 to cover disposal costs (spread over the number of shares held). For example, if we buy 500 shares in Company X at 100p each and the cost of purchase is £15, the investment is £515. The initial stop-loss would be set at $((£515 \times 80\%) + £12)/500 = 85p$. I accept that it is a little mechanical, but it does reflect the initial risk we are prepared to accept in share-price fluctuation.
> 2. We also set an 'alarm' price which is set somewhere between the stop-loss and the current price of the share. This price is set by that shares champion through discussion with other members. The reason for the alarm price is to prompt some discussion on reasons why a given share has fallen to, or below, the alarm price. A sale of the stock could therefore occur well before it reaches the stop-loss if we consider the future looks bleak for that particular share.
>
> To sum up, we have the stop-loss, which means that if a share

drops below this figure the share must be sold. We also have the alarm price that is designed to force discussion on a share if the price drops below this figure. It is then the responsibility of the share champion to propose the stop-loss and alarm prices at the monthly meetings. Normally if the price is falling below our original purchase price the stop-loss will stand at its original level (unless extreme specific circumstances justify considering a review). However, when the price is increasing and we are in a profit situation, which is where it gets interesting . . .

An intriguing feature of the club scene is that there are many all-female clubs, and often they outperform those that are exclusively for men. In Campsie, near Londonderry in Northern Ireland, The Optimists have lived up to their name and won a major award at the end of their first year of operation. The club was established by a group of women who decided they wanted to learn more about finance, and the twenty members discovered they had a natural aptitude for investing. According to secretary Margaret Lee: 'For the first six months we simply tracked various shares and watched the market until we had a good understanding of how things worked. The fact that we were cautious seemed to pay off.'[2]

The club meets over a meal and drinks at the White Horse pub in Campsie once a month. The women each contributed £250 to set up the portfolio, and the monthly subscription is £20. Each member is expected to come up with a share recommendation every month, and then they all vote on which to buy. They have had success with penny shares and with big-ticket stocks like Vodafone, but lost money on Tottenham Hotspur. Says Margaret:

> Women tend to be very thorough and the level of information that comes into our meetings is really quite astonishing. We are good listeners, so everyone gets their turn. And that means we have twenty brains all putting forward different investment ideas. We all get a real buzz out of it.

Another all-women club, The Giddy Aunts, was established because the members felt they needed 'a workout for their brains'. This group consists of British Airways staff charged with looking after unaccompanied children travelling with the airline. One of the advantages of being airline employees is access to discounted travel, and The Giddy Aunts have visited Hong Kong and its stock market

---

[2] *Mail on Sunday*, 2 May 1999.

to look at prospects in Asia, while in 2001 they were planning a trip to Wall Street. Their travels have already led the Aunts to adopt an international perspective. Publishing their own predictions, they say that many goods that are now sold at a variety of prices will soon be reduced to a commodity arrangement.

> The markets of Chicago and Rotterdam are superbly efficient, where oil, pork bellies and RAM are traded. Virtual auctions are starting to boom in the wired world, Sotheby's and Amazon are now on the same web site! More and more products will become commodities just as computer chips have in the last few years. Pricing will have to be efficient; otherwise the manufacturer will be swept away on the global competition tide. New opportunities for source of supply and new direct markets will offer the plus side. The efficient will quickly thrive, the dinosaurs quickly die.

The Giddy Aunts are among a number of clubs that have very effective web sites, with a variety of web tools and hyperlinks that would be of use to any investor. On their site they expound their philosophy:

> A guru recently forecast that only 10% of the Fortune 500 would survive the next 10 years because of their slow rate of adopting new technology. Surely it's not just the technology that they have to adapt to but also all the changes in the marketplace and customer service that go with the revolution. Our philosophy is to adapt to those changes, think more globally and research thoroughly before investing.

Some of the clubs seem to operate in a permanent cloud of self-deprecating humour. The Hairy Pies Investment Club says it was created to fill a niche in the investment advice industry. 'It was noted that far too much research was being used to determine investment advice, and not enough random guessing. All of our tips are based on firm, well-established gambling techniques. The club's manual contains this nice disclaimer:

> Always remember that shares can go down as well as up and can collapse completely. Only invest with money that you can afford to lose or money that belongs to a friend who is smaller than you. The information within Hairy Pies is NOT FSA regulated, percolated or elongated and you should do your own research and get advice from a registered financial consultant or some strange bloke down the pub before making any investment.

LIVERPOOL JOHN MOORES UNIVERSITY
Aldham Roberts L.R.C.
TEL. 051 231 3701/3634

Some aficionados belong to several clubs. At the Bournemouth weekend, I ran across Barry (Bazza) Lake from Dirty Harry's, but found him talking about the Brass Monkeys, the H and G Club, and the St Leger Club. The St Leger turned out to be a group that meets only once a year, on the day of the St Leger race, and picks just one stock on which it will gamble for a year. And the Brass Monkey? According to Bazza:

> It started with the suggestion 'Monkey and Pony' as we all started with a 'monkey' (£500) and were putting in a 'pony' (£25) a month. Sally thought that was silly, and suggested 'Brass Monkey', as we were hoping to make some brass out of the deal. Quite honestly, we were getting bored by this time and the £10,000 we had to spend was burning a hole in our pockets, so 'Brass Monkey' it was.

Schools and Investment Clubs

Schools too have investments clubs, mainly as a result of work by Proshare in introducing shares to the classroom. The leading pioneer in schools has been Peter Hogan, now the principal of Llandovery College in mid Wales, and previously a teacher at schools in Leeds, Sunderland and Derby.

In Leeds he took an approach which is not dissimilar to *The Times* Portfolio game. Pupils were given a notional amount of cash, with which they could 'buy' shares quoted on the London Stock Exchange. They could buy and sell on a daily basis, using the prices quoted in the *Financial Times* as the guide price. After a period their portfolios were valued, and the pupil who had made the most gains was declared the winner. However, Hogan found that the novelty of a game that was not for real soon wore off, and believes that games that mimic the stock market have limited benefits. 'It's a bit like dressing up in the football kit of a Premiership team, and then going and having a shower.'

Hogan's real chance to bring influence to bear came when he heard of the establishment of the Wider Share Ownership Task Force to look at teaching children about the stock markets. Although he was concerned about its approach, he was co-opted on to the group, and was at the heart of a pilot project which ran at eighteen schools in the Midlands. The project consisted of a series of challenges to sixteen-year-olds in participating schools. In the green challenge, the students were asked to put together a portfolio of shares in environmentally friendly companies. This meant that they had to research a number of companies from a substantial list, make a judgement on those likely to perform well, and list reasons for their choice. The blue challenge required them to do the same with blue-chip companies, while a third project involved looking at companies with operations within twenty-five miles of their schools.

The scheme was beneficial because it forced children to think and to find out more about companies. Teachers were also cooperative because they were provided with teaching packs and could play their full part, even if their own knowledge of the stock market was limited. It contrasted with previous schemes which allowed outsiders like local bank managers and financial advisers to visit schools and provide a barely disguised sales pitch.

After the pilot scheme, a new body, the Personal Finance Education Group, was set up to promote and facilitate the education of all schoolchildren. Rather than being just an industry body, it was based on Hogan's advice that teachers, government, consumer groups and the regulators should be included.

Within this group the lead was taken by Proshare, with its National Investment Programme, in which 3,500 teams of pupils competed in 2001 as a voluntary part of the National Curriculum. Teams of up to four students were given a notional £100,000 to invest, creating a portfolio using a fully interactive web site. Over the two-month period of the contest, three out of four of the teams made a profit, and more than four out of ten beat the FTSE All Share Index. The exercise was supported by sponsors which included the Department of Trade and Industry, the London Stock Exchange, and Charles Schwab.

The competition was designed to be as realistic a simulation of actual investment as possible, rather than just a share portfolio game. Substantial back-up was provided for teachers with a series of worksheets, available online and in hard copy. One of these introduced pupils to the process of raising money on the stock markets, and was based on the fictional case study of the Birmingham-based Interactive Broadcasting Company, which was set up so listeners could hear it over the Internet nationwide as well on local radio receivers. Students were asked to look at various ways in which the company might finance a new station in Manchester, and to consider the advantages and disadvantages of each method. The teachers' version provided a step-by-step guide to the answers. The next task for pupils was to look at the changes that would become apparent when the company became a plc quoted on the stock market, and to answer the question as to why the price of IBC's shares might fluctuate. The exercise also involved looking at the web sites of the London Stock Exchange, and other exchanges, all adding to the learning process.

A second worksheet studied ways of assessing investment opportunities, outlining concepts that could be used to reveal information about companies, and questions that would help in making investment decisions. There were also worksheets on unit trusts and investment trusts, with the case study on the latter using the web site of Chase Fleming to support the tasks. The need to understand annual reports was addressed in a further worksheet by comparing these to school reports. Students were asked to telephone or write off for reports from companies of their own choosing, and then to answer a series of questions. It has always seemed strange to me that annual reports from some of Britain's best-known companies are not sent to school libraries, as they would be a useful reference tool.

From 2002, Proshare will take control of the operation and change its name to Proshare's Student Investor 2002. The same teaching materials and online resources will be provided to all schools and sixth-form colleges, and the portfolio challenge goes on, along with another contest for younger children in which they are expected to make an educated guess at the future prices of certain stocks, and state their reasons.

So teaching children about the stock markets has come some distance since Hogan's first efforts, but there is obviously still a long way to go. This latest initiative is to start an investment trust for pupils and their parents, at Llandovery College. The trust is effectively run by children, though strict corporate governance has had to be put in place to meet the requirements of the regulators. The Arian Trust – *arian* is the Welsh word for gold – has a cautious, low-risk approach to investment, and so far has managed to outperform the FTSE index.

Hogan has had to struggle at every stage to persuade bankers, brokers and the regulators to allow him to establish this trust. The result is that the children running it have to act as unpaid advisers to a three-strong board of directors of the holding company, Arian Investments Ltd. These unpaid advisers were all selected by interview for their roles. There are five fund managers, who recommend to the board which shares to buy and sell, as well as accountants, a marketing team, and a sponsorship manager.

The team meet for tea and biscuits once a fortnight to review the portfolio, and consider ways of growing the company, which has a share base of 1,000 shares available at £100 each. Anyone in the school can attend the meetings, and once decisions have been made, corporate actions are taken by one of the directors.

9 Specialised Investors

Saving for Old Age

Young people find saving for old age a yawn, and many of them do not do it, unless persuaded or forced into a company pension scheme. Things tend to change at middle age, when long-term partners and families become a basic part of everyday life. Those with aged parents living in penury because they saved little and became dependent on a government pension collected weekly from the post office have come to realise what retirement might mean, especially if it is forced upon them prematurely through redundancy.

The result has been a rapid growth in personal savings and pension schemes, with most of the monthly savings ending up in a pool of money invested in equities, bonds and unit trusts. Most people have chosen to leave the management of these schemes to professional fund managers, but some manage their own portfolios within tax-efficient mechanisms created by the Government to encourage thrift.

These are ISAs (Individual Savings Accounts), which at the time of writing allow a saver to put away up to £7,000 a year in a savings plan, which is shielded from tax. Equities, bonds or unit trusts sheltered within an ISA are not subject to capital gains tax provided the plan is kept in being for at least five years. Nor is any income tax payable on the dividend or interest generated by the investments, and this revenue may be reinvested in the plan.

Personal pensions are a different concept, although money put into them also ends up being invested on the markets or in property. There are several kinds of personal pensions, but the two most important in recent years have been AVCs and personal money schemes. From April 2001, Britain's Labour government added a totally new concept: stakeholder pensions. I will consider these in turn.

AVCs
Additional voluntary contributions (AVCs) are mostly for employees who are already in company pension schemes, and who wish to top

up their contributions to receive more upon retirement. Most of these schemes are run by company pensions departments, but it is possible to take an AVC independently. Contributions are fully deductible against tax, although the percentage of salary that can be shielded from income tax is limited. However, if you are a higher-rate taxpayer, deductions are allowed against the highest rate of tax. So, at present tax rates, £10,000 a year contributed to an AVC will mean a tax saving of £4,000. Put another way, if you save £6,000 into an AVC, you will be getting £10,000 of contribution value.

The problem with AVCs comes on retirement day. First some AVCs perform poorly, and if the hard-earned money you put away has been managed badly then the fund created will not be as large as you had hoped. Worse still, at the time of writing British law requires that you invest your whole retirement fund in a poor financial instrument known as an annuity. The company providing the annuity will take the pool of money saved under the AVC and pay you an income for life. If you live to be a hundred, then you may feel the benefit, although the life company will normally pocket all the money generated by way of dividends, interest or capital gains. If you die young, perhaps at three score years and ten, then the money remains with the insurance company, and will not be passed on to your heirs. A simple example will serve to reveal the iniquity of annuities.

Your AVC fund on maturity is £100,000 when you retire at sixty. A company offers you a taxable annuity of £7,560 a year. This is 7.5 per cent return on your savings. You would get 5.5 per cent by putting the money on deposit at the nearest Tesco store, slightly less than the annuity, but upon your death the £100,000 would form part of your estate rather than vanishing into the coffers of the life assurer faster than your coffin is conveyed into the fiery furnace. Had you been able to put your money into a respectable corporate bond fund, you would be getting an income of £7,000+, with your capital intact.

The Conservative government of John Major planned to abolish the inequitable law compelling those with AVCs to buy annuities, but never got round to it. The Blair government has considered abolition, but the Chancellor, Gordon Brown, under considerable pressure, one suspects, from his friends in the large Edinburgh-based life assurance industry, has decided to refer the issue to a committee of inquiry. An argument for annuities, often repeated in the financial press, whose publishers gain huge revenues from life assurance companies, is that, left to their own devices, AVC holders might become reckless and spend all the money on extravagant living, travel or foreign property. Having enjoyed tax relief on their savings, it is argued, pensioners should use their AVC's with prudence, a word much in favour with the present Chancellor. However, if that were truly the argument, then people should be given the choice of putting the money into national savings, an ISA, or an alternative long-term investment vehicle. The reality is that annuities are an additional form of death duty, except that the beneficiary is not the state but the life assurance industry.

Many people who have made additional savings through AVCs would have been better served by paying the tax on their incomes and buying property to rent. For them it is too late. However, those now faced with the option of subscribing to an AVC should read the small print, study annuity rates, and hope that before their fund reaches maturity date, the law has been changed.

Personal money schemes are mostly used by high wealth individuals or the self-employed, and work in two ways. Traditionally individuals have signed up with a life assurance company as the pension provider, and contributed premiums every month or every quarter, leaving the institution to invest the money at their discretion where it thinks fit. An alternative is to instruct the institution to act as your pensions provider, but to create and manage your own portfolio of stocks, bonds and unit trusts within it. With the financial service industries love of acronyms these schemes have become known as SIPPs, or self-invested pension plans. The trouble with SIPPs is that most assurance companies expect you to invest at least £25,000, and the charges for the minimal amount of work the assurer has to do are high.

Stakeholder pensions

In contrast to the 'mother knows best' attitude towards annuities, where reasonably well-off retirees are not thought capable of looking after their own savings, the Treasury and its political masters have recently introduced the concept of stakeholder pensions, which are designed to encourage Britons to take more responsibility for funding their old age. Just why the politicians and Whitehall mandarins believe that those on low or modest incomes are more likely to be able to manage their savings better than those who had the wit to put aside additional chunks of their earnings has never been satisfactorily explained. It is all the more perplexing since by introducing stake-holder pensions the Government is forcing the pensions and life assurance industry to lower charges to consumers, while at the same time permitting these same institutions to rip off retirees who have no choice but to buy annuities.

It remains to be seen whether stakeholder pensions take off. An immediate advantage is that they have no initial charge, and the buying and selling price for acquiring or disposing of units has to be the same: there is no bid-offer spread such as ordinary investors suffer.

Riskier Investments

Options

Options are as old as history itself, and mean exactly what the name implies. Phoenician merchants bidding for the opportunity to buy the cargoes of the first ships to arrive in port used to purchase an option to acquire a vessel's contents – in other words, the right to be first in the queue. If the cargo turned out to contain little of any interest or value, the merchant would not exercise the option. Today, a family interested in a new house being built but unable to sell their own property might advance a small sum of money as a three-month option to buy at an agreed value. This would both prevent the developer from selling to anyone else during that period, and also assure the price. But if the option was not exercised, the purchaser would lose the cost of the option.

Options are now highly developed on global stock markets, and for those prepared to risk a little money on speculation, they offer an attractive prospect. Many people have been heard to say: 'I would like to be able to buy shares in BP, ICI, or Microsoft, but their prices are so high I could not possibly afford them.' Leaving aside the loose logic of that statement – for an individual can always buy fifty or even twenty-five shares if he wishes – it is true that the chances of a major capital gain on one of the large and better-known shares are slim.

Options increase opportunity, but at a known cost and defined risk. For example, let us say that just before Christmas an individual thinks that a retail group is going to achieve record sales over the holiday, and that the margins on this extra volume will be such as to generate handsome profits for the full year. He fancies risking £5,000 on his theory that the shares will rise. But at 642 pence each his £5,000 will only buy him 778 shares. Even if the shares rise by £1 to 742 pence, he will only have made a profit of £778, less the broker's commission on both the sale and the purchase, which would bring the profit down to about £650.

By using his £5,000 to buy options he would have done much better. At a cost of 30 pence each, his £5,000 would have bought him 16,666 three-month call options – giving him the right to buy the shares at any time during the next three months for the original 642 pence price. If the shares do not go up he does not exercise the option – and loses his £5,000. That's the risk. But if they do in fact rise by £1, as in the previous scenario, he will have made a capital gain of £11,666, (£16,666 less the £5,000 spent for the options).

If the stock is one in which the Stock Exchange runs a traded options market, then the investor has another possibility open to him, and that is to sell the option to another investor. The price of a traded option is decided by two factors: the underlying price of the share itself, and the market's expectations as to which way it will move in the weeks or months ahead. Obviously those operating in the traded options market expect to make a profit, so there is a premium to be paid for selling the unexpired portion of an option rather than sitting it out. But where an investor fears he has made a major misjudgement he can, to some extent, cover a big position by using the traded options market.

Another form of option is the put option, which is the opposite of a call option. A put option is taken out in anticipation of a fall in the value of the relevant share, and gives the owner the option to sell a quantity of shares at a given price. A put option can act as insurance against an investment in ordinary shares falling in value. The profit on a put option could offset any loss in the value of the underlying share.

Information about the prices at which you can buy or sell both call and put options is readily available in the daily newspapers that take investment seriously, such as the *Daily Telegraph* or the *Financial Times* in Britain, or the *Wall Street Journal*. Reproduced below is part of a table from the *Financial Times*. The column on the left lists some of the better known securities in which options are traded. The first numbers column shows the price at which the holder of the option can buy or sell the underlying share at the given dates, listed at the top of the remaining columns. The prices in these columns are the amount that has to be paid per share to obtain the options.

Table 9.1 A Typical Option Price Selection from the *Financial Times*

		CALLS			PUTS		
Option		Oct	Jan	–	Oct	Jan	–
ASDA	200	20	20	–	–	–	–
(*220)	220	1	1	–	–	–	–
Option		Oct	Jan	Apr	Oct	Jan	Apr
Abbey National	1100	34½	107½	139	19½	77	116½
(*1114)	1150	13	82½	111	48	101½	139
Allied Domecq	550	33	58	74½	1½	19½	29½
(*581)	600	4	31	49	22½	43	53½
Ald Dom ex	330	16	35	47	3½	18	25½
(*342)	360	2½	21½	32½	20	34	41½
Allied Zurich	700	22	60	83	4½	40	51½
(*711½)	750	3½	36½	57½	38½	65½	76½
Astra Zeneca	2800	61½	206	275	32	142	193
(*2827)	2900	18½	156	224	89½	192	241½
BAA	420	34	48	60	½	14½	21½
(*453)	460	6	26	39	12½	33	40
BAT Industries	460	17	45	57½	4½	27	43
(*472)	500	1½	27	39½	29½	49	66½
Barclays	1800	73½	186½	236½	19½	111½	164
(*1851)	1900	23	134	188	69	159	214
Bass	700	30	57½	75½	5	40½	53½
(*724)	750	5½	34	53	31	69	81½
Boots	600	40½	61	80½	1	21	33
(*639)	650	7	34	54½	17½	44½	56
British Airways	300	17½	31	41½	1	16	22
(*316)	530	2	17	27½	15½	32½	37½
BP Amoco	550	20	50	68	5½	30½	46½
(*563)	575	7	37	55	18	42	58½

Taking the example of British Airways, the table shows that a call option to buy 1,000 shares at 300 pence in the airline any time between 14 October 1999 and January 2000 may be bought for 31 pence per share. If a longer call option period were required to buy BA at the same price, the option cost per share would be 41.5 pence. A put option for the same dates would, however, cost less – 16 pence and 22 pence per share respectively. These figures indicate that those writing the option – in other words taking the risk – expect BA shares to rise marginally rather than fall.

Writing an option contract – as distinct from buying traded options – is a job for a professional. It reverses the risk of buying and selling an option. Essentially the option writer is taking a gamble that the option will expire worthless, and that he will garner his profit from receiving the put or call money for taking the risk. The job is not unlike that of an insurance underwriter, who charges a premium in the hope that you never make a claim, or not one that is anywhere near the value of the premiums. Just like a risk underwriter, those offering options need a thorough knowledge of the markets and companies concerned. Those who do write options have to deposit cash, called margin money, with their broker as security for the performance of their obligations.

In Britain the concept of investing in options has been slow to catch on among general investors, although it plays a major part in the lives of the professionals. There is no reason for this, other than lack of education about the markets. In the United States, where attitudes are very different, options are booming.

The Chicago Board Options Exchange is the third largest securities market in the United States, after the New York Stock Exchange and NASDAQ, and more than two thirds of those who use it are private investors. It is helped by the attitude of the US regulatory authorities, who are strong supporters of options trading, with the Securities and Exchange Commission arguing that it significantly enhances liquidity and makes for better and more accurate markets.

Europe is catching up. In 1978 there were only two equity options markets in Europe, one in Britain and the other in Holland. Today they are either established or being set up in every advanced country.

In Britain, futures and options are traded on LIFFE, the London International Financial Futures and Options Exchange. Until a few years ago, LIFFE's dealing room underneath the platform of Cannon Street railway station was one of the City's most interesting spectacles, as young men and women dressed in brightly coloured blazers in the livery of their firm traded by shouting and yelling under an auction system. Alas, like the London Stock Exchange, the trading floor is no more, and LIFFE operates through a state-of-the-art electronic dealing platform called LIFFE Connect, accessible from anywhere in the world.

In equities, LIFFE offers option contracts on about one hundred British companies, as well as a number of indices.

If you imagine that by buying options you are sure to win a fortune, be warned by the following remark from Stephen Figlewski, the Associate Professor of Finance at New York University: 'Small investors lose because they believe their information is better than it really is. They take positions that aren't any better than their beliefs, and their beliefs aren't any better than throwing darts.'

As with other risky investments, it is as well to experiment with notional or paper money before taking the plunge and opening an account with a broker. Another way of trying your hand without getting burnt is to use the trading simulation game thoughtfully provided by LIFFE on its web site (www.liffe.com/usf). This enables you to practise trading in real time, exposing yourself only to ridicule rather than real financial loss.

A more frequent use for options is as insurance. An investor may believe that a share will rise, but wants to protect himself against a potential fall, so cushions this risk with an option. Or you may have a large bundle of shares that you do not want to unload because of liability to capital gains tax, but fear that they will fall. So you buy options as an insurance against this happening, using a put spread.

There are other forms of share options that are much more familiar to members of the public, those that are available to employees of public companies. These are often, though not exclusively, reserved for executives, and usually allow the employee the right to buy a limited number of shares in the company for which he works once he has completed five years' service. These options are available for nothing, and the price is normally set at a discount of the price at the start of the option period.

Another options scheme involves employees putting their own money into the company they work for through savings for shares. Some far-sighted employers in Britain encourage all employees to join a government-backed scheme that gives tax incentives to companies who promote a long-term saving plan with a building society or bank where the final amount saved is used to buy shares at a low-cost pre-set option price. Unless you work for a company that is on the slide, these are the best form of savings plan available, combining the benefit of regular commitments via a building society with the chance of cashing in on long-term capital appreciation. It is perhaps the only risk-free route to the stock markets. Unfortunately many companies fail to explain these schemes adequately to their workforces; if they did, there would be a much higher percentage of the workforce owning shares.

Futures

If trading in options sounds a little like a casino, it is dull by comparison with the activities on the futures markets. There are futures in everything – commodities like cocoa, coffee, wheat, lead, zinc and gold; meats like beef and pork; currencies like the dollar, the yen, the euro and the pound; and of course, shares.

Buying futures is speculation, and some people make and lose millions doing it. It requires knowledge of changing circumstances, as well as intuition as to the way events will turn out. If you think that there will be a severe frost in Brazil – or are prepared to bet that this will be so – you may buy six-month coffee futures, in the belief that by the time your coffee, is delivered at the end of the period, it will be worth a lot more. Of course you have no intention of taking delivery of the coffee for you would not know where to put it; if the frost comes, the price of your futures contract will rise sharply, and you will sell, and make a profit. If the price falls, you will still sell the coffee delivery to someone who needs it, but at a lower price.

There are, of course, good reasons for buying futures other than speculation. If you are a coffee wholesaler and you fear a cold snap in Brazil, you will buy futures to protect yourself, regarding the extra cost of the contract as an insurance premium. The same is true of the manufacturing industry. If you have ordered an expensive set of machine tools from Germany, due to be delivered in six months' time, you will not want to pay for them until delivery. But supposing the pound falls against the mark in the mean time? You cover yourself by buying the required amount of euro futures. This process is called 'hedging'.

There are futures markets in all the major financial centres, while Chicago has assumed pre-eminence in the trading of commodities.

There has been considerable growth in bond futures, for the increase in the number of gilt-edged market makers has placed a premium on hedging contracts. For instance, a fund manager may know that in three months he will receive cash for investment in gilts, and he has picked long gilts – those maturing in fifteen years' time. Rather than waiting to see what the interest rate will be at that time, he can lock into today's rate by buying LIFFE's long gilts futures contracts for delivery in three months' time. If gilt yields then decline, the investor will have to pay a higher price, but the price of the long gilts futures contracts will have risen, and the fund manager's profits will reduce the effective cost of buying the stock.

There are also futures contracts on most stock market indices. The FTSE 100 futures contract is priced by taking one tenth of the value of the FTSE 100 Share Index published throughout each business day. It may be used by an investment manager concerned that the market will rise before he can place funds becoming available to him.

Dabbling in futures carries a greater risk for private investors than do options. This is because of the greater leverage involved. Investing in commodity futures, in particular, has proved a fatal attraction for many speculators who have wrongly assumed that they can pit their wits against the experts: I do not recommend it. Let me give you an example of how a commodity futures contract works. Suppose coffee for delivery three months from now is trading in London at $900 per tonne. A speculator buying ten tonnes will have coffee worth $9,000, but will have to pay only a 10 per cent deposit for a contract providing for delivery at the end of the quarter. The speculator does not, of course, take delivery. If the price goes up to $1,000 a tonne, he sells the contract and takes a handsome profit of $1,000. Although the coffee price has gone up only a little over 10 per cent, his return on capital is well over 100 per cent. But if coffee goes down to $810, he will be obliged to buy the coffee at the agreed price of $900, and then sell it again before delivery at its lower market rate. The loss would probably more than wipe out his deposit; in other words, he would have lost his bet.

Many people imagine that they can follow stories in newspapers and on the wires and second-guess what tropical storms or frost will do to coffee prices. They are much mistaken. The professional buyers, working for companies like Nestlé, Costa and Starbucks, have agents on the plantations and know exactly what the crop will be. My guess is that anyone seriously interested in trading futures will probably not be reading this book.

Hedge Funds

Most people associate hedge funds with high risk, but in fact the concept of hedging is to reduce risk. Hedging usually involves an investor taking an opposite position in the futures market to the one held in the ordinary market, so that if share prices fall the loss will be offset by a gain from the futures contract. On the other hand, if prices rise the investor will gain, only to see the gains cut back by losses from the related futures contract.

Not all investors use hedge funds for protection; many see them as a finely tuned gamble to get a better return than in the ordinary equity markets. It is a form of gambling, but in the first quarter of 2001 net inflows to hedge funds was nearly $7 billion.[1]

---

[1] *The Economist*, 2 June 2001.

10   Getting a Listing and Using the Stock Markets to Raise Money

Continuing obligations form an essential part of maintaining orderly markets and ensuring an acceptable level of investor protection . . .

FSA Handbook, 2001

Almost every entrepreneur has a dream that he will be able to build up his own business as a private company, and then, because of its success and opportunity for further growth, be able to sell it to the market. For many the happiest solution is to find large numbers of individuals prepared to buy a total stake of, say, 47 per cent, so that the original founder and his family may retain control, while pocketing the cash generated by the sale. The lucky ones who do this become instant multi-millionaires, and are still able to hold on to the businesses they started and to run them in much the same way as before.

So how can an entrepreneur use the stock markets for his own benefit? The cardinal rule is that there should be some other reason for turning a private company into a listed one rather than simply to obtain a personal fortune. It would not be easy to bring a company to the markets if that were seen as the prime purpose. The most obvious attraction of going public is that obtaining a listing on any major stock exchange improves the standing of the concern and its products. There are not that many manufacturers of branded products or household names that are not public companies or corporations.

Apart from the benefit of obtaining a better image, becoming listed on a stock exchange also makes it easier, in normal times, to raise finance for expansion and development. Both investors and lenders have a strong preference for an enterprise that is not the play thing of an individual, or a group of individuals. Even though it is still possible for one man to hold the reins of a large public company, there are many more checks and balances than on private companies, where clever accountants can play interesting games with the balance sheet. The accounts, and other indicators of performance, of public companies are closely scrutinised by meticulous analysts, who are always prepared to publish adverse comment where they believe it to be deserved. Thus most public companies are assessed with one objective – are they good investments? By contrast, the potential of private companies is not easy to assess, even when they are open to scrutiny.

Private company accounts are freely available only at Companies' House, and, for a small fee, from the web, but they are usually at least one year in arrears. This alone explains why both institutional and private investors are reluctant to commit large sums to unquoted companies. What happens when the leading figures in a private company die? Their heirs may be hopeless businessmen, or may be forced to sell up part of their holding at an inopportune time in order to pay capital transfer tax. Father may drop dead just as the next recession is approaching; subsequent family feuding and a forced sale could leave the outside investors with little to show for their years of support.

Another strong advantage for an expanding business of being publicly listed on an exchange is that it helps in takeovers. Instead of paying cash for an acquisition, a company can often meet at least a part of the cost by offering a share swap, as in the summer of 1985, when Guinness offered shareholders in Bell, the whisky distiller, paper worth considerably more than the market price of their own scrip. When an efficient company is taking over a dull one, shareholders of the latter are often only too glad of the chance of just such an easy escape route.

A further advantage of obtaining a listing is that the company attracts unsolicited funds. If they think you are doing well, any number of investors will buy your shares. Regular mention in the financial pages is useful publicity and, in the case of well-run companies, makes for easier relations with customers and helps when attempting to attract executive staff.

Going Public

When a company decides it would like to go public, it does this through an IPO, an initial public offering. First it normally approaches a firm of investment bankers or a securities house through its accountants or trading bank. There is then usually a lunch or dinner, a getting-to-know-you session at which little more will be achieved than a general understanding of the nature of the business, and its goals and aspirations. The directors of the company considering a listing will also obtain some idea of how the operation, which is almost certainly a lengthy one, is to be planned.

The investment banker will also give an opinion as to whether the company will be able to meet the listing requirements of the Financial Services Authority. Once the job of the London Stock Exchange, the role of governing admissions is now carried out through a unit of the FSA, the United Kingdom Listing Authority, universally known as the UKLA.

The UKLA works from a thick rulebook that has become thicker as the European Community adds to listing requirements. A copy may be obtained from the FSA for £50, and does not appear to be downloadable on the web. The rules govern admission, the continuing obligations of issuers, the enforcement of those obligations, as well as draconian measures such as suspension or cancellation of a listing. However, the organisation is more user-friendly than the Stock Exchange, which used to send out frosty letters demanding an explanation if the rules were broken, always supposing its officials were alert enough to spot them. These days the UKLA staff tend to be younger, and work on the telephone.

If an issuing company or its representatives have a problem, there are numerous specialised help teams waiting to provide an answer. If UKLA officials think that a company may be breaking or bending the rules they will call up the person responsible and discuss it with them, trying to put right or resolve the problem swiftly, before resorting to the prosecutor's office.

While this may be an improvement, the new process is more legalistic – and therefore more onerous – than it used to be. The FSA is particularly hot on its disclosure obligations, where it states the defining principle as 'to ensure that the information emanating from a company, its advisers or agents is given to the market as a whole, is timely, sufficient and relevant'.[1]

If directors on the board of a non-listed company thought they had an easy time, they will change their minds once they come to grips with the requirements for a full listing. Each one of them will have to sign an undertaking confirming that all the information the UKLA

---

[1] UKLA Principles, Financial Services Authority, March 2001.

requires has been provided, and once the business is listed, all their earnings and share dealings will have to be recorded.

How the UKLA works

Once the formal application for a listing is made, the UKLA ticks off a huge checklist, seeking to satisfy itself that the company has met all its conditions. It will approve or reject listing particulars, and closely examine the prospectus drawn up by the company's investment banker, watching particularly for any statements that might lure an investor into an over-optimistic outlook. Don't expect the UKLA to accept at face value all of the information provided to it, even if a well-known City banker has signed it off. UKLA officials will be on the phone asking questions, or requesting a meeting at which a more thorough interrogation may take place. They will not be playing at being policemen, and don't have the capability or mandate to go out and carry out detective work. The role is more like that of an investigating magistrate, asking questions and expecting the supplicant to come up with the right answers. The UKLA also attaches considerable importance to the role of the applicant company's sponsor, and to other professional advisers, who will have to provide the assurance that the listing rules will be met.

Once the company is listed, it will join the ranks of all those scrutinised on a daily basis by the UKLA's monitoring and compliance group. People in this team will be on the look-out for breaches of the rules on price-sensitive information, and will not hesitate to call in directors or senior executives if they spot such a breach.

At this stage, there is likely to be some discussion on the identity of a sponsor. In Britain it is now a legal obligation for new entrants to the higher level of the stock market to have a sponsor, who may be either a company or a partnership, and who will guide the application through the regulatory hurdles discussed below. A sponsor is expected to have considerable experience of corporate finance, as demonstrated by its employment of senior staff with relevant backgrounds. It will have to show that at least four of its executives have been involved previously in providing advice to companies on a listing over a three-year period. It also cannot act for any organisation with which it might already have connections, for example as an investment or merchant bank, or stockbroker.

Preparing the Prospectus

Once contact has been established, and a decision made in principle, a partner in the Securities house originally approached will seek a total brief on the company – particularly its management structure, strengths and weaknesses, labour force, present shareholders, competitors – and, of course, will also undertake a detailed study of full sets of accounts for the previous five years. Quite often this study will show that a listing is out of the question. In Britain, investors and fund managers are spoilt for choice, and with governments the world over offloading billions of pounds' worth of assets in state enterprises, any company that does not offer first-class prospects will not attract support. To go down the road towards a listing and issue a prospectus and then have to withdraw it would be a costly mistake.

Assuming, however, that the feasibility study shows a good prospect of success, the next stage for the stockbroker is to visit the company and its major plants or operations and to see it at work. This will usually be carried out by a senior member of the firm, under the supervision of a partner. The staff member will also try to visit competitors of the company, to seek another assessment, although the need for strict confidentiality makes this aspect of the study difficult. A firm of accountants, not the company's own auditors, will also be commissioned to carry out a thorough investigation.

All this will have to be done within three months, if a reasonable target for a listing is to be achieved. The next step is for the brokers to prepare a detailed proposal for the flotation, which will, in effect, form the blueprint for the day-by-day progress towards the listing. The broker will suggest a price band within which shares might be offered – the decision on a firm price will come much later. He will set out a list of financial requirements which will have to be met and propose underwriters who, at a substantial discount on price, will agree to purchase any shares if the float is undersubscribed.

The company will usually be asked to pay off all major loans – for no investor is keen on picking up a load of debt – and to revalue all its properties. This stage completed, the next step is to decide how the capital of the company is to be made available to the public. In most cases, this will be through the issue of a prospectus, offering the shares at a price expected to be lower than the price at which the company will start its life on the exchanges. In the main European markets, such a prospectus is published in full in the *Financial Times*, and occasionally in other newspapers. The prospectus is, in fact, an offer for sale. It will detail the price at which shares will be available, and name any proposed restrictions on voting rights. The terms of sale will be set out, as well as the names and addresses of the company's auditors, stockbrokers, bankers, solicitors and directors. There will be a full description of the company's products or services.

Isotron, a company providing the only independent gamma radiation service in Britain, published just such a prospectus. It devoted thousands of words to an extremely detailed description of its technological processes, and its business prospects. A large part of the prospectus was devoted to the curricula vitae of the directors and senior employees, right down to site managers. There was a chapter on safety procedures, while over a page of closely spaced print was devoted to publication of the independent report by accountants KPMG Peat Marwick. The reader was spared no detail, and the prospectus constituted an extremely thorough insight into the company.

Once the prospectus has been written, usually by the merchant bankers advising the company in association with the stockbrokers, the approval of the local exchange where the shares are to be listed must be sought. This is much more than a formality, and it is quite normal for questions to be raised on matters of detail. For instance in London the most pressing concern of the LSE's quotations department is to see that the prospectus gives as full and accurate a picture as possible of the company and its prospects, and it is unlikely that a document will pass through unamended.

The terms of sale vary widely. Sometimes an underwriting firm of brokers will agree to buy all the share capital to be offered for sale on a given day, and then do their best to dispose of the shares to investors at a sufficiently high price to offer them a profit. Sometimes the shares will be offered directly to the public by advertisement; where this happens the underwriters will only have to take on the shares left unsold, and if the issue is a success may end up with no commitment and a useful underwriting fee.

Finding an underwriter is usually not a major problem, for all brokers have a list of those they can call upon, whether institutions, investment banks or other financial groups. Underwriters do count, however, on the integrity and accuracy of a broker's recommendation.

No securities house can consider accepting the job of arranging a flotation unless it is convinced it is a sound investment.

An increasingly popular way of raising the cash is through public tender – used by bankers J. Henry Schroder Wagg and Co. in the Isotron case mentioned earlier. Here 3,290,088 ordinary 25 pence shares were offered at a minimum tender price of 120 pence a share, the principle being that those prepared to offer a higher rate would receive the biggest allocation. Having received all the applications, Schroder's were left with the task of setting a 'striking price', not exceeding the highest price at which sufficient applications were received to cover the total number of shares offered. A public tender was also used by Schroder's and UBS Phillips and Drew in bringing Andrew Lloyd Webber's Really Useful Group to a full London listing.

Obviously public tender is a system favoured by highly successful, confident and relatively well-known companies. It is not to be recommended if oversubscription is thought unlikely. Since the price has been fixed beforehand, it also avoids 'stagging' – a stag being the individual who buys new issues in the confident belief that over-subscription will lead to the price rising sharply on the day of listing.

Whether stagging occurs in the majority of cases when the tender system is not used depends, of course, very much upon the price at which the shares are fixed for sale. Pricing can be the key to the whole issue. If prices are pitched too low, there will be a huge over-subscription, involving vast amounts of extra paperwork, the return of cheques, and the difficult job of selecting the lucky applicants to receive shares. Where there is oversubscription, those applicants who are left out, or awarded derisory holdings, feel aggrieved, even bitter, while the stags will reap rich rewards. If, at the other extreme, the price is pitched too high, the issue will be a disaster, and months, even years, of work will be wasted.

Fixing the price is not easy, however, because most companies are the prisoners of current events. A series of air crashes, for instance, could damage the price of the shares of a manufacturer of jet engines. Inevitably, setting the price is left to the last possible moment, with brokers and bankers using their experience to judge market con-ditions as D-Day approaches. The forty days and nights before and after the day of flotation are the busiest, especially in the offices of those directly participating. It is not unusual for the major people involved to camp in their offices during much of this period, and certainly holidays are out of the question. While the final offer documents are away at the printers, they just hope that they have got it right.

Whether a company goes public through a full float or sale by tender, it is a costly business. The experts needed – lawyers, investment bankers, accountants, brokers and financial public relations men – do not come cheap, especially in the City of London. There are few ways of doing it cheaper, but one of them is to arrange what is called a placement. In this case, the stockbroking firm buys all the shares and sells them direct to its clients, avoiding the cost of dealing. This method is used in small new issues in London or where there is unlikely to be much public interest. But even here, the Stock Exchange regulations stipulate that at least 35 per cent of the company's issued capital must be in the placement, thereby preventing directors from using the system as a ploy to pick up some useful cash while still totally dominating the company. At least one quarter of the shares must also be sold to the public on the stock markets, which helps when open dealings start. A placement is considerably cheaper because the costs of advertising, printing and professional services will be much less, and there is no need for underwriters.

There is also the alternative of arranging an introduction, but this method of obtaining a quotation in London is only available to those companies that already have a wide distribution of shareholders, and where there is no immediate intention of anyone selling out. No capital is offered prior to listing, and it is therefore not necessary for the company to go through the procedures described earlier, or to issue a prospectus, although it is required to take out an advertisement to publicise the move. This method is most commonly used when a large foreign company decides to have its shares listed in London as well as on its home exchange.

The number of listings in any given period depends very much on the state of the market. When shares are falling, there will be fewer enthusiastic takers than during a bull market, though good issues will almost certainly get away unless things are really bad. Successful issues in 2000 included Carphone Warehouse, and Egg, the bank launched by Prudential.

Raising More Money

The stock markets were founded to raise money for industry and to provide finance for great national projects such as railways and canals. They did so with great success until the Second World War, and in the early post-war years it was where companies went for extra funds if they wanted to expand. Borrowing from the banks was, in Britain at least, considered expedient only for short-term finance. Borrowing from overseas – through instruments such as eurobonds, and more recently euro notes – was not even in the minds of those few City types who supported Jean Monnet's post World War II vision of an integrated European Economic Community. Raising money was the job of the Stock Exchange. Why go further than Throgmorton Street?

Things began to go badly wrong with the capital-raising function of the Stock Exchange when successive governments in the middle years of this century decided that the best way of paying for expensive public programmes was to tax the rich, which, to them, included almost everyone who did not belong to a trade union and pick up his wages in a brown envelope once a week. Income from share ownership was 'unearned income', and somehow thought of as less decent than interest obtained from a building society. Making a capital gain by selling one's own shares at a profit in order to pay for old age, school fees, or even a trip to the Bahamas was regarded as sinful, and therefore had to be discouraged through extra taxation. Company taxes were raised, making it harder for businesses to fund expansion. And in order to justify an ill-judged attempt to curb a free market for wages, 'dividend restraint' was imposed. With little point in investing either for capital growth or for income, investors followed the example of the trade union movement, and went on strike. In other words, they ceased buying shares.

The effect of the political onslaught on the investor in the 1960s and 1970s was to bring to an almost complete halt a stock exchange system which allowed development capital to be raised, pluralistically, by a large number of individuals and institutions, and to replace it with a more costly system of finance through banks. It seems unlikely that the trend will ever be completely reversed, but in recent years there has been an encouraging revival of capital-raising on stock exchanges, to the benefit of both saver and entrepreneur.

Today, business school studies by Nobel Prize winners Professor Franco Modigliani and Professor Merton Miller show that the costs of debt and equity financing are comparable. The cost of debt – of course – is easiest to measure: it is the interest paid by the company on its bank loan or bond. Assuming the company is a highly credible and successful one, it will pay a premium of about 2 per cent over a bond issued by a creditworthy country like Britain or Germany.

The cost of equity is the dividend yield, which should be cheaper, but often is not. Dividends often depend on taxation policy. Raising money through the share markets from rights issues also strengthens balance sheets and prevents the kind of over-borrowing that has forced many large companies into difficulty.

Sometimes companies will want to use both methods. For instance, a British company may use a rights issue to fund a UK acquisition, but, if seeking to take over a European company, could use a foreign currency bond to match the currency of the target company's country.

What happens with a rights issue is that the holders of ordinary shares in a company are offered further shares at a discount, usually substantial enough to make it attractive. Under British rules, such new shares must be offered to existing stockholders in quantities proportionate to their holdings. This is known as a pre-emption right, which has been abandoned in the United States. A lively debate has been taking place in Britain over whether this rule is sensible. In many cases not all shareholders are willing, or even able, to take up the rights offer. So under the present system, underwriters have to be found who will. As with new issues, pitching the price is crucial. If a rights issue is undersubscribed, there is a danger that the share price will fall, even if underwriters have been appointed, and this will defeat part of the objective of the exercise, which is to raise more capital.

The most important question for a company making a rights issue is to decide on the terms at which it will offer new shares. Normally this is done by offering the shareholders the right to buy a number of shares at a special price for each share they own. So, for example, in 1990 the British brewing group Bass sought to raise £558 million by giving its equity holders the right to buy one new share for every five they already owned. This is known as a one-for-five issue. In order to persuade shareholders to subscribe to a rights issue, the price has to be a worthwhile discount to the prevailing market price. But this does not mean that rights issues present shareholders with a bargain – an offer they cannot refuse. As soon as a rights issue has been completed, the price of the existing shares usually falls to reflect their dilution as a result of new stock on the register.

The small shareholder offered a rights issue is often in a Catch-22 situation. If he takes up the offer, he has to dip into his savings and increase his risk exposure to the company concerned; in other words an additional investment is forced upon him. If he does not take up his rights, he may sell them to a stockbroker for the difference between the rights price and the market price, but unless there is a substantial volume of shares involved, the commission is likely to be prohibitive. If, as often is the case, he does nothing at all, the company will automatically sell his rights for him, and pay him the proceeds.

Rights offers are usually contained in a long and arcane document preceded with the suggestion that if you do not understand it you should see a stockbroker. Many people, particularly those who have not paid close attention to their investments, or who have inherited equities, mistakenly throw these documents into the rubbish bin, and lose out.

After the deregulation of Britain's financial markets at the time of Big Bang in 1986, many people believed that companies would move across to the American system of placements, described earlier. The British Government was supporting a change in the rules, which would have allowed companies to raise additional capital directly from new shareholders, but they reckoned without the big pension funds and life assurance companies which dominate the British markets. These institutional investors, sensitive to the threat to their automatic right to get a slice of anything new, formed a cosy cartel, which called itself the Pre-emption Group, with the goal of protecting at all costs the right of existing shareholders to get first refusal of any new shares.

The Pre-emption Group introduced a rulebook binding on all its members. One of the guidelines was that in any issue of more than five per cent of a company's capital, the existing shareholders had to be given first call. Of course, as long as the institutions stuck to their own rules, their dominance in the market was such that nobody would be able to change matters. And, in Britain at least, so it has proved.

A rights issue is not cheap, which is one of the main arguments against this form of raising additional capital. First there are under-writing fees, paid by the company seeking to raise the money to the merchant bank or securities house managing the issue, and to those who have undertaken to buy any unwanted shares. These fees come to about 2 per cent of the amount of money raised. Then there is the paperwork – fees to lawyers, accountants and public relations consultants, plus the actual cost of printing and distributing the substantial amount of documentation necessary. Add to this the discount which must be offered to make the rights issue attractive – a figure of around 20 per cent is common practice – and it is easy to see why many a corporate financial director would rather go to see the company's bankers, or, if it were possible, arrange a placement.

An alternative to a rights issue is loan capital, which may be raised on the Stock Exchange through either unsecured loan stock or convertible stock. Loan stock is usually issued only by blue-chip companies. It might offer the additional inducement of convertibility to enable the holder to convert all or some of the loan stock at a later stage to equities. A company without a top rating would not find investors ready to buy it even at very high interest rates.

If a company is planning to modernise its plant to increase output and productivity, loan capital can be a particularly attractive vehicle. The interest paid is deductible before corporation tax is payable, so the company's tax bill is reduced. And as output, and hopefully profits, rise, so does the company's share price, making it beneficial for the shareholders to make the conversion.

As with new issues, there are several ways in which a stockbroker can obtain loan capital for his clients. He can arrange for a full prospectus detailing the offer to be prepared, published and advertised, and wait for the response, usually stipulating preferential treatment to existing shareholders. He may, if he chooses, place the loan stock with institutions direct – unlike placements with new issues, where a proportion has to be offered on the Stock Exchange. Or he may limit the offer to existing shareholders, an unlikely course because especially attractive terms are usually necessary to get full support. A placement is usually much more efficient.

Then there is the bond market, of which the eurobond market is the best known. Not long ago, only governments of stable and prosperous democracies and large international institutions such as the World Bank and the European Investment Bank would raise funds from the bond market, by issuing securities at good interest rates with maturity dates between ten and twenty years away. Mostly denominated in dollars, these securities offered large institutional investors an attractive hedge against the fall of sterling and against inflation. The introduction of the single European currency has brought a spate of euro-dominated corporate bonds to the market as companies begin to exploit a new capital-raising opportunity.

Taking AIM

Money can also be raised for small and medium-sized go-ahead businesses through the junior stock exchange, better known as AIM, an acronym for Alternative Investment Market. Similar markets have evolved in Europe and the United States, and the concept has widespread political support because small businesses have proved to be major sources of job creation, technological innovation and entrepreneurship.

AIM offers most of the benefits of the stock market, such as the opportunity for a higher public profile, and access to new capital and investors, but with a much simpler entry structure than going for a full listing. For instance, there are no restrictions on the size or location of companies who join, the length of time they have been operating, or the percentage of shares to be placed in public hands. AIM offers those who have a business case and can present it well the chance not only of raising capital for expansion, but also of becoming rich in the process. If the company does well, it will inevitably lead to an enhanced status with both customers and suppliers, though the reverse will be the case if things go badly.

The regulatory regime within AIM is less stringent and less bureaucratic than seeking a full listing on the London Stock Exchange through UKLA. There are a number of tax benefits, and soon there may be more. It is also much easier for a company on AIM to go for expansion via acquisition than would be the case if it were fully listed.

AIM was founded in 1995 as the successor to the Unlisted Securities Market, the London Stock Exchange's earnest but less than successful attempt to find a way of embracing start-up businesses, whose only previous recourse to funding had been to the banks or venture capitalists.

There were only thirteen companies in AIM's first list. Now there are just under 900, with a market capitalisation of £13.3 billion. Of the thirteen founder companies, six graduated to a full listing, while four remain in AIM. Two were taken over, and one was wound up. One failure from thirteen over six years is not a bad record. Share price performance has been mixed. One of the founders, Brancote, a minerals explorer, saw its share price almost quadruple before slipping back to offer a 250 per cent gain over six years. Others have fared less well.

The kind of companies that are listed on AIM are rich and varied.

There are leading-edge technology companies. Many of the businesses are in the leisure industries, with quite a few football clubs, such as Charlton Athletic and Birmingham City, who over recent years have struggled between the television rich Premier League and the less well-endowed Division One. There are Internet firms, privatised railways, recruitment consultants, wine importers and many restaurant groups, to name just a few of the sectors.

How it works

Companies seeking to list and raise money on AIM do not have to be British. Nor do they have to be of a certain size, or prove a lengthy trading history. But they must be public companies, registered under the laws of their country, and have published accounts which conform to internationally accepted accounting standards.

A company does have to show that it is 'appropriate' for it to come to the market and be publicly traded. It would be inappropriate, and disallowed, if the company's owners wanted to run it as a closed book, or as a relatives-only family business. Shares in an AIM company have to be freely transferable.

So before a company decides to join AIM, its owners must be prepared to accept the disciplines that go with being a quoted company, and be prepared to take into account the interests of outside shareholders. Directors must realise that a company's share price might be affected by factors beyond their control, and that flotation will inevitably lead to closer scrutiny of the company. This scrutiny will involve the media and share market analysts, who will run a slide rule over the company's performance and not hesitate to put a 'sell' recommendation out if they believe it is being badly run. This alone could dent an owner's worth. And if directors buy or sell shares, the transaction will have to be made public. These new disciplines will force boards to look at their public, media and investor relations, and hiring staff or consultants to do this can be very costly. The AIM company may not need to commit itself to road shows which take up the time of chairmen, chief executives and finance directors for a total of about three to four weeks a year, but even a minimalist effort in this area is expensive. A consultant working in this field does not come much cheaper than £750 a day, which is almost as expensive as a City lawyer.

In making the decision to list on AIM, a company needs to tick off the following points.

❏ Do we need access to capital for growth, or can we achieve the kind of development we need with financing from our bankers or our own resources?

❏ Do we wish to create a public market for our company's shares, allowing anyone to buy at the market price?

❏ Do we want to realise cash for ourselves at this particular time, acknowledging there will be tax liabilities?

❏ Do we expect our company to have a high value?

❏ Are we prepared to face up to a heightened public profile, and critical comment, which may come at a time when we least want it?

If the answer to these questions is an unqualified 'yes', then it is time to proceed. Yet it should be said that there are many growing businesses that have decided to eschew any kind of listing, preferring to continue as private companies. One such group is Eastern Counties Newspapers, which has a near-monopoly of the print media in East Anglia, owning, amongst others, the *Eastern Daily Press*, Britain's best-selling provincial newspaper. Over forty years its owners have resisted generous offers for the company, preferring to maintain control and run it (successfully) in their own way. Whenever they have needed money for expansion or acquisition, they have found it themselves. The result is that the cities of Norwich and Ipswich are among the few places in Britain to enjoy the benefits of a strong local press not owned by a national or international conglomerate.

Once a decision is made to join AIM, the first step is to appoint two key individuals. One is called a nominated adviser and the other a nominated broker, and both must be approved by the London Stock Exchange. These appointments are mandatory. The nominated adviser, who could be a stockbroker, accountant or banker drawn from a list of about seventy people, has the responsibility for deciding whether a company is suitable for the market, and for making sure it conforms to the AIM rules. Once listed, the company must retain the adviser to keep it on track and to make sure it fulfils its obligations, which include disclosing all material information to investors. The nominated adviser has to undertake to be available at all times to advise and guide the company's directors on the AIM rules. The nominated broker has to be a member of the Exchange, and, in the absence of a market maker, provides a means for investors to buy and sell the company's shares.

The next step is to produce an admission document – effectively a slimmed-down prospectus. It must include a full description of the company and its principal activities, the company's financial history and performance, details of the management, the directors and their personal business histories, and the names of substantial shareholders. This must be made available to all prospective investors without any kind of discrimination.

The cost of joining AIM is much less than a full listing, but can still be expensive. The modest annual listing fees are the least of the expense: the highest cost will come in the engagement of the nominated adviser and the other City of London professionals needed to keep the operation on track. Further details may be obtained from the London Stock Exchange.

AIM is clearly designed for professional, rather than amateur investors, and is for the risk-taker who accepts that not all young and growing companies succeed. It is of particular appeal to the large number of fund management groups that specialise in investing in smaller companies.

AIM shares are bought and sold on what is called SEATS PLUS, which enables investors to trade with each other through the LSE. They can do this either through a market maker, if there is enough of a market to justify one, or by an order board, which publicly displays orders to buy and sell shares, and enables trades to be executed automatically. The service also allows financial information about each company to be entered by the nominated broker, thus helping investors to evaluate the shares.

A comparable operation exists across the Channel in France, where the Nouveau Marché was set up in 1996 to cater for small and fast-growing businesses. This also has relaxed joining rules so that, for example, new companies do not have to provide three-year financial projections, but must provide quarterly results. At the time of writing, the number of companies listed on the Nouveau Marché was measured in tens rather than hundreds, but since its launch the index has grown by more than 50 per cent.

The problems of raising money for small companies in Britain are not confined to the equity sector; banks have also often failed to provide adequate funds at a reasonable price and on reasonable conditions. Despite attention-grabbing advertisements proclaiming their support for small business, the banks have been severely criticised in this area. Under pressure to improve their margins and the quality of their loans following the mistakes of the 1980s, the high street banks have demanded interest rate margins and levels of security that make it very difficult for a small business to establish itself. HSBC as good as admitted this when its chief executive suggested that the best way for the small business sector to move forward would be if there were some kind of government support or guarantee for small business loans. He has a point, but the British Government had its fingers badly burnt with the ill-fated Business Expansion Scheme, largely used for property-backed ventures, many of which collapsed in the early 1990s.

Across the Atlantic, the NASDAQ market discussed earlier (see p. 68) has provided the capital support for some of the most dynamic and innovative companies in the United States – Microsoft was founded in this way. A company seeking an IPO (initial public offering) in America will normally be advised by its investment bankers to offer its stock at 10 to 15 per cent below trading expectation in order to attract suitable support. The bankers will produce a highly detailed prospectus, with considerable attention paid to competitive advantages compared with other listed companies operating in the same field. The Securities and Exchange Commission (SEC) has a complex set of rules governing the issue of a prospectus, the foundation stone of which is full disclosure of anything likely to be relevant to an investor. But this rigorous attitude pays off; it gives the investor more confidence. In the United States a prospectus must include information about products and services, manufacturing facilities, competition, and possible risks – apart from full financials – and omission of information, or inclusion of misleading information, can provide a valid cause for a class action lawsuit. Once a prospectus has been filed with the SEC, the officials review it, and come back with comments, suggestions and criticisms.

Once a public offering has been made and the company is trading, it is subject to strict rules on corporate governance and the provision of information. There must be a minimum of two independent directors on its board. There is a total ban on the issuing of any preferential shares, or taking any action that would restrict or reduce the voting rights of ordinary shareholders. The company must also complete SEC documents 10-Q and 10-K, which require disclosure of a wide range of information, including executive compensation, and securities ownership of certain beneficial owners and managers.

For small companies, the route to a listing is usually the NASDAQ

Small-Cap Market, which has about 1,200 smaller companies listed. The requirements for listing on this market are substantially less than those for NASDAQ itself, and it is used as a conduit to the main exchange.

Another new market in Britain is OFEX, which is for companies that are not yet ready to join AIM. OFEX is short for 'off the exchange' and is a low-cost trading company which enables investors to buy and sell shares in companies that are not listed. Technically it is not a market, even though it is frequently referred to as one. It is really just a dealing facility in which OFEX's owner, J.P. Jenkins Ltd, is the market maker. Most members are seeking to raise between £250,000 and £500,000 in capital, and want their backers to have an opportunity to trade their shares rather than being locked in. The requirements for joining OFEX are nowhere near as onerous as those for joining AIM.

Once listed, whether on AIM or on the full market, the company's obligations have only just begun. Nor is the UKLA the only authority or institution with which companies have to deal. There is the Accounting Standards Board, the Panel on Takeovers and Mergers, the London Stock Exchange, and a number of others.

One of the most onerous of the rules that have to be obeyed to the letter involves the dissemination of information. The lax and carefree ways in which companies could leak or publish stories about their activities are gone for ever. So are many of the practices once beloved of company public relations people and financial journalists. The editors of the well-padded business sections of Britain's Sunday newspapers love to get exclusive stories, partly for competitive reasons but also because there is very little financial news around on a Saturday. This led to the practice of the 'Friday night drop', whereby a financial public relations firm would deliver a brown envelope to a favoured business editor containing the elements of a story about a client company or one of its competitors. Almost inevitably the story was market price-sensitive, in other words it would move the company's share price the following Monday.

When it was the regulator, the London Stock Exchange turned a blind eye to this practice, even though it clearly broke the code that said that price-sensitive information should first be disclosed to the exchange itself so that all investors were treated equally. The FSA is made of sterner stuff, and has become determined to put a stop to the Friday night drop.

It is now a legal requirement for listed companies that all price-sensitive information be distributed only to authorised and approved media outlets, and these outlets, which include Bloomberg, Reuters, and other agencies, are obliged to make it publicly available in short order. These approved agencies are called PIPS, or primary information providers, and have replaced the monopoly once enjoyed by the London Stock Exchange's own Regulatory News Service. (RNS).

Companies have also to watch for unusual price movements in their own shares, and report these to the London Stock Exchange and the UK Listing Authority, whose supervisory unit will investigate, if need be. The disclosure rules also have a number of implications for a company's everyday contact with analysts, brokers and the media. Companies talking to analysts can only brief them on information that is not price-sensitive or is already in the public domain.

So what does a company do when it feels that the market itself, or one particular analyst, has misjudged its share price? It is possible to 'send out signals' through investor relations specialists to correct matters, but any semaphoring of this kind needs to be handled extremely carefully. Here is what the London Stock Exchange advises:

> Because analysts' forecasts are such a central determinant of the market's expectations, and are aggregated to form a 'consensus forecast', the finance director will sometimes find it necessary to call up when an analyst's forecasts get dangerously wide of the mark, and steer him or her the right way by reaffirming some of the company's previous public statements. This delicate process is made easier by the fact that analysts will generally send their note through for the company to check for factual errors on matters already in the public domain. However a company must not allow itself to be drawn into correcting any incorrect price-sensitive information or assumptions. If the company decides it does need to speak to the analyst on factual corrections, then the call should be made quickly, because the analyst will not wait long before publishing.[2]

Sometimes unexpected circumstances can trigger an announcement requiring you, in the Stock Exchange's words, 'to move very fast indeed':

> If a company's share price does move sharply for no apparent reason, then that company and its brokers are likely to receive a

[2] *A Practical Guide to Investor Relations*, London Stock Exchange, April 2000.

call from the regulatory authorities to establish whether a leak of price-sensitive information may have occurred. If this may be the case, or there is a risk of a disorderly market, then your company will be required to make an announcement to the market. Similarly you could find yourself woken in the small hours of the morning by a call from your advisers telling you that the press is carrying a speculative story about your company. Much of the article may be wide of the mark – but it could contain just enough truth about your commercially sensitive negotiations to force you to make a rapid announcement.

A particular problem with newly quoted companies is that they drown in the hype that they have created, or has been created around them by publicists and over-enthusiastic media. This was particularly the case when lastminute.com was floated in a huge bubble of publicity, much of it surrounding one of its founders, Martha Lane Fox, a fetching twenty-something-year-old with a good repertoire of one-line quotes. *Fortune* magazine added to the hype by emblazoning a rather sexy picture of Ms Lane Fox on its cover. Lastminute.com was slow to dampen down the hype with doses of realism, and investors deserted the stock in droves, plunging it to earth.

Biting the bullet can be difficult too. Some companies hold back on releasing bad news in the forlorn hope that it will get better. They get a lashing from the LSE:

> An early and full announcement of both the problem and the corrective action is not just a regulatory requirement. While obviously negative for the share price in the short-term it means the company can ensure the issue is aired on its own terms and in the right context. The alternative is a potential drip feed of bad press, with the company placed on the defensive and appearing indecisive and not in control of the agenda. Announcing a bit of bad news one week, and a bit more the week after, gives the impression – quite rightly – that the management is floundering.[3]

Raising money through a listing is arguably the most interesting stage in the growth of a business. While many small companies choose, rightly in most cases, not to take this course, the step of listing is an essential move towards joining the big league. It is also a process that is fraught with difficulty and expense, and should never be undertaken lightly.

---

[3] *A Practical Guide to Investor Relations*, op. cit.

11   Mergers and Acquisitions: the Takeover Trail

That's what a dawn raid is – you hit at dawn.
Robert Holmes à Court

Hardly a day goes by without a major story about a takeover. Usually it is one large company bidding a multi-billion dollar sum for another, such as America Online's epoch-making purchase of Time Warner, a corporation which itself was the product of a merger and had also just swallowed up another corporation, CNN. These were agreed takeovers, but often the bid is unwelcome: that is, the directors and management of the targeted company would rather be left alone to run the business undistracted by the prospect of working for new owners.

What normally happens is that the firm of investment bankers working for the corporation that plans a takeover sends a printed letter, known as an offer document, to all shareholders of the target company, proposing to purchase their shares for cash or for stock in their own business, or a mixture of the two. Cash is usually more attractive because predators' share prices have a nasty propensity to fall sharply after acceptances have been returned, as in the case of America Online, where acceptance of that company's offer became more an act of faith in the new group's future than a quick profit.

This inevitably poses the biggest question that arises with any takeover – value. How do you value a public company? One simple answer is market capitalisation: the price of each share on the stock markets on a given day multiplied by the number of shares issued. Then all a bidder has to do is to pitch his offer sufficiently higher than the current price in order to persuade shareholders to give up their long-term prospects with the existing board of directors.

But is the stock market price the right one? As discussed earlier, in Chapter 3, prices of shares are fixed not by any measure of assets or even current profits, but by the market's perception of value based on all the information that might affect a company's future cash flow.

All the company's financial statements are digested and assessed against competitive forces by scores of analysts. Their collective wisdom is added to the judgement of traders and distilled into a share price. This sounds entirely plausible, but how can you then account for the fact that the world stock market as a whole on 19 October 1987 was worth only four fifths of what it had been the previous day? Or that on the same day ten years later the FTSE index was three times higher? Share prices can only really be the best guess at a value. An acquirer is not really buying the buildings, machinery and workforce – he is getting what he thinks these are capable of producing.

As the Wall Street arbitrageur Ivan Boesky, later to be convicted of and imprisoned for insider trading, put it in 1985:

> An analyst may fully understand a company he is following, may even be able to forecast its future earnings with unmatched precision. Does that mean he can forecast its future stock price with any precision at all? Of course not. Price-earnings multiples averaged as high as 25 or so in the heyday of stock trading in the 1960s. In the mid-seventies these multiples had fallen to 6 and 7. Any stock market price is buffeted by sweeping market forces that are virtually impossible to predict with any reliability. These forces are often important: the growth rate of the economy, the course of interest rates, the international value of the dollar, the inflation rate, an overseas war, a presidential election. They also can be distressingly unimportant: this week's change in money supply, the Federal Reserve Board's sale of securities, its reversal of that sale the next day.
>
> Nevertheless many large and significant public corporations have changed hands on the simple basis of share values. The predators have got what they wanted. The shareholders, presumably, were satisfied because they were able to take a profit and re-invest their money elsewhere. But the companies and their staffs that found themselves with new owners were not necessarily better companies for the transformation. In some cases new blood made them more efficient, and more effective use was made of their assets. 'Making assets sweat' is one of the main justifications for takeovers. In many others the acquiring company, its costs swollen by the expense of its own acquisition, has fallen apart.[1]

Not all of those carrying out takeovers continue to run the businesses they have bought. In many cases they sell the assets for

---

[1] Ivan Boesky, *Merger Mania*, Bodley Head, 1985.

cash. Asset-stripping became fashionable in the eighties and is a popular occupation of those who believe that the stock markets often underestimate the true value of companies. These people put their beliefs to the test by acquiring businesses and then breaking them up. This has frequently happened in the past when a company has a number of assets on its books – particularly property – which have not been revalued to reflect higher property prices. By disposing of the property, or by coming to a leaseback arrangement with a finance company, an asset-stripper can acquire huge sums of cash. By the 1990s the activities of two generations of asset-strippers had sharpened up directors to the risk, though there is still a hard core of professionals on every continent who make money by spotting companies that are undervalued.

Despite the asset-strippers and the ordinary everyday risks in mergers, such evidence as there is shows that takeovers often succeed in their objective of achieving real growth for the acquiring company. A study published by McKinsey, the management consultancy, found that even cross-border acquisitions had achieved a high rate of success compared with other forms of corporate expansion.

McKinsey reviewed the overseas acquisition programmes of the top fifty companies in Europe, Japan and the United States – and found that 57 per cent were judged a success. However, almost all the success stories related to a company merging with another in the same business. Most of those involving moving into non-core businesses failed.

Legal Background and Takeover Rules

Before considering takeover tactics and planning, it is important to look at the legal background to mergers and acquisitions. In each country there are rules that govern takeovers. In some cases these rules are enshrined in legislation; in others they form part of a code, written or unwritten. In Britain there is a fudge between the two, with the further complication of intervention by the European Commission. Commentators – particularly those with no knowledge of the financial services industry – tend to assume that it is a free-for-all, with no rules and regulations, but this is far from the case in Britain, elsewhere.

The first point of reference in Britain is still the City Takeover Panel, a group of twelve City elders with a modest secretariat. Half of them are appointed by the Governor of the Bank of England, and the rest come from institutions like the British Bankers' Association, the Institute of Chartered Accountants, the National Association of Pension Funds, and the Confederation of British Industry. There is a director-general, with two deputies, a secretary and a few other executives. The permanent staff provide interpretations of the rules, but contested decisions and disciplinary cases are considered by the Panel itself, with the right of appeal to the Appeals Committee, which sits under the chairmanship of a retired Lord of Appeal. The Panel operates under the watchful eye of the Bank of England; it is usual for the majority of its staff to be on secondment from the Bank, hopefully providing a constant flow of fresh ideas.

The Panel's most important contribution is the Takeover Code, and the interesting thing about this is that it contains a number of features designed to protect the small shareholder from the avarice of big companies. One of these features is the 30 per cent rule, which provides that once either a company or an individual has 30 per cent of the equity of another listed company, an offer must be made for all the remaining shares. Moreover this offer must be made at the highest price paid per share during the initial acquisition. To quote from Rule 9:

> Except with the consent of the Panel, when: (a) any person acquires, whether by a series of transactions over a period of time or not, shares which (taken together with shares held or acquired by persons **acting in concert** with him) carry 30% or more of the **voting rights** of a company; or (b) any person who, together with persons **acting in concert** with him, holds not less than 30% but not more than 50% of the **voting rights** and such person, or any person **acting in concert** with him, acquires additional shares which increase his percentage of the **voting rights**, such person shall extend offers . . . to the holders of any class of equity share capital whether voting or non-voting and also to the holders of any class of voting non-equity share capital in which such person or persons **acting in concert** with him hold shares. Offers for different classes of equity share capital must be comparable; the Panel should be consulted in advance in such cases.

Note the words 'acting in concert'. In the media you often hear of 'concert parties', which refers not to an expensive night out at Glyndebourne or the Royal Opera House, but to a group of like-minded investors clubbing together to win control of another business. The Takeover Code makes it clear that where this happens they are to be treated collectively as a single predator.

The object of Rule 9 is to prevent a predator buying a company on the cheap, especially where there is a wide spread of share ownership. Unfortunately, such rules do not apply universally. In many countries of the European Union, including Germany, France and Italy, it is possible to buy 50 per cent of a company without making an offer to all shareholders. This has created the network of pyramid companies discussed earlier (see p. 77).

Another rule in the Takeover Code provides that before an offer is announced, no one privy to the preliminary takeover or merger discussions is allowed to deal in the shares of either the bidding or the target company. Once an offer is announced, the share transactions in all the companies involved must be reported by all parties to the City Takeover Panel, the Stock Exchange and the press. Companies defending a bid must not do anything without shareholder approval. For those who wish to know more, it is worth obtaining a full copy of the Code.[2]

How it works

When launching a bid, those making the offer will make contact with the City Takeover Panel under conditions of strict secrecy. The bidders will almost certainly be advised by investment bankers, who are fully conversant with the rules, but the full-time staff of the Panel will also offer guidance. The staff work closely with the surveillance unit at the Stock Exchange to investigate dealings in advance of publication of bid proposals, the aim being to establish whether there has been any breach of the rules governing secrecy and abuse of privileged information.

As the bid proceeds, the Panel's executive monitors closely all developments. They check, for example, all documents and announcements issued, to make sure that they comply with the Code. They have access to the Stock Exchange's computer systems so can monitor and reveal suspicious share dealings. They give rulings and interpretations both before and during transactions.

Sometimes the Panel itself is convened – often at very short notice – during a takeover, usually to deal with an appeal against a ruling made by one of the full-time staff. What would have happened is that if there appears to have been a breach of the code, the Panel staff

---

[2] City Takeover Code, obtainable for £15 from the Panel on Takeovers and Mergers, The Stock Exchange Building, London EC2P 2JX.

invite the chairman of the company involved, or other directors, to appear before them. He or she is informed by letter of the nature of the alleged breach, and of the matters which the director-general will present to the hearing. These hearings are informal, there are no rules of evidence, and, although notes are taken, no permanent records are kept. The principal against whom the complaint has been made is expected to appear in person, although he may bring his lawyer with him. At the hearing he is expected to set out his reply, normally based on a document which should already have been produced in reply to the director-general's letter. If the Panel finds there has been a breach, the offender may be reprimanded there and then, or may be subjected to public censure with a press release distributed to the media, setting out the Panel's conclusions and its reasons for them. In a bad case, where the Panel feels that the offender should no longer be able to use the Stock Exchange, either temporarily or permanently, the case may be referred to a professional association, the Stock Exchange, the Department of Trade and Industry, or the City Fraud Squad.

In disciplinary cases – where the Panel is applying sanctions against an individual or company in serious breach of the Code – there is the right of appeal to a committee chaired by a judge. Panel rulings are subject to a judicial review, but only after a takeover is completed, not during its process, thus avoiding the possibility of litigation being called into play as a delaying tactic.

This system has the advantage of being relatively informal and flexible, but it has not been without its critics. Like so much self-regulation, its success rests on the credibility of those chosen to implement the code, and their willingness to shame wrongdoers through bad publicity. But does it protect shareholders sufficiently? The Takeover Panel does not go public with all guns blazing very often, and even when it does, the resultant press release is unlikely to make the BBC Ten O'Clock News. Not every shareholder reads the *Financial Times*, and therefore the belief that shareholders are warned off by Takeover Panel actions may be false.

The Takeover Panel has also been criticised for not following its own credo by allowing stalking, a practice where predators canvass widely a proposed acquisition without making the financial commitment necessary to activate it. Money battles between rival predators have also been permitted, as in the bidding war in 2000 between Lloyds TSB and Abbey National for Bank of Scotland.

I suspect that in future most of those involved in takeovers will make a polite call on the Panel, and then troop off to Docklands, where the Financial Services Authority has established its own bailiwick. It is no coincidence that many of the City of London's law firms most active in merger and acquisition activity have also moved their headquarters to the environs of Canary Wharf. Although the FSA has paid generous lip-service to the City Takeover Panel and its activities, and has said that it will not intervene until the Panel's appeals procedures have been exhausted, and then 'only in exceptional circumstances',[3] it seems unlikely that Britain's leading regulator will be so inactive.

The FSA has statutory powers to monitor all market activity in Britain, and to turn over to an independent tribunal those firms and individuals it believes are guilty of market abuse. It has itself taken over the Takeover Panel's code by endorsing it. The principal effect of this endorsement, it says, will be that 'if a firm fails to comply with the Code, or a requirement or a ruling by the Takeover Panel, the Panel can request the FSA to take enforcement action against that firm.'[4] It adds that it also reserves the right to take action of its own volition.

The powers and plans of the FSA are covered in Chapter 15, on regulation, but it seems inevitable that there will be overlap with the Takeover Panel. At the time of writing, the FSA is in a protracted consultancy about a much tougher set of rules, which one of its progenitors has called a 'very proactive and complicated regulatory regime'.

There is also the European Union. Its Competitions Commission can and does block mergers, even those between companies that are headquartered elsewhere but have subsidiaries in Europe. It set the precedent in the summer of 2001 when it blocked the takeover by General Electric, one of the world's largest companies, of another American company, Honeywell. The merger had not created a problem for United States regulators. One wonders what might have happened if circumstances were reversed. Had the Americans blocked a takeover of a European company by another European company there would have been howls of rage in Brussels and Strasburg about American interference.

European takeover rules are in a mess. Proposed new pan-European rules are way behind schedule. Well before the new

---

[3] Philip Remnant, director-general of the Panel on Mergers and Acquisitions, interviewed by the *Financial Times*, 27 June 2001.
[4] Consultation document from the FSA, 2001.

millennium, the Union was supposed to have agreed an official directive to create equality on merger activity, but it took ten years for the Brussels bureaucrats to draw up and agree a draft document, and another two to get it to final approval stage. By 2001, fourteen out of the fifteen member governments said they favoured the legislation, but it foundered when Germany used its muscle to persuade members of the European Parliament to block it.

The document is on file in Brussels, gathering dust, creating another problem for the future. How can there be a truly common market without a common policy on takeovers? If French water companies are allowed to buy British firms, but the reverse is not possible, where is the justice? If governments can stop denationalised corporations being taken over by using their 'golden share', how will European industry be restructured?

Making an Acquisition

Before considering how a takeover works, it is perhaps worth analysing some of the many and varied reasons for making an acquisition. The most obvious is that it is often much easier and cheaper than to start a new venture, except in the case of a product or service that is exclusive enough to depend for its success on the professional drive and energy of the entrepreneur and his team. If you have a product that will put your rivals out of business, you will usually be best served by generic growth.

But a takeover can be a useful route to expansion, particularly as it often enables you to use other people's money to achieve your ambition. A takeover can enable you to swallow up the competition, and thereby to increase profit margins. This is what happened with many of the large takeovers in the early part of the 20th century. Several of these were designed to set up large monopolies able to raise prices in basic industries such as steel, power and transport. Some of them were brought about by the legendary New York financier J. Pierpont Morgan. His biggest deal, in 1901, brought together eleven companies, accounting for half of America's steel industry, to form US Steel.

These days there are regulations designed to prevent monopolies being created by merger. In the United States there are strong anti-trust laws. The European Commission is also vigilant against the development of new monopolies. Mergers are subjected to

Commission scrutiny where the combined worldwide turnover of the undertakings involved is more than 5 billion ECU, and where the Community-wide turnover of at least two of the undertakings is above 250 million ECU. Additionally, Britain has a Monopolies and Mergers Commission, which is often called in to investigate whether or not a merger would be in the public interest.

In many cases, a takeover may be the only way to fulfil ambitions of growth. Often it may be the result of egomania on the part of the chairman or controlling shareholder; there never seems to be a shortage of new owners for Britain's national newspapers, however precarious their finances may be. Prestigious department stores and breweries also seem popular targets. Sometimes the thrust of a takeover effort is to achieve a lifetime ambition.

Whatever the reason, there are usually only two forms of takeover: those that are uncontested, and those that involve a fight. But it is never as simple as that. There have been many occasions when a board of directors has decided to open merger discussions with a potential target rather than to proceed by stealth, only to find that the opposition is so great that all they have achieved is to give the other side advance warning to prepare for an assault. And there have been occasions when a contested battle has been so fierce and the cost of the operation so high that it might have been better to attempt to achieve the same result through negotiation.

Some takeovers are solicited. Many a company, for lack of progress or good management, feels that it would be better served if it were to be incorporated into a better-run, and perhaps larger, business.

With any takeover there are two stages: the preliminaries, which may take weeks or even months; and the active stage, when the bid is made and the offer digested and voted upon by the shareholders. Very few takeovers are the result of a whim; the vast majority are usually considered only after painstaking research involving the company's solicitors, accountants and merchant banks, or other financial advisers.

Takeover specialists are at a premium in the City, and are paid enormous salaries. A senior director in the corporate finance department of one of the better-known British merchant banks may expect to earn about £350,000 a year in salary and bonuses, while a junior director, who could be in his late twenties or early thirties, might receive £100,000 upwards. American companies pay more, but offer marginally less job security. For this, the specialists advise those either making or subject to a takeover on strategy and tactics, capital-raising where necessary, and public relations, often calling in outside specialists to assist.

When the pressure is on, most advisers would expect to work fourteen hours a day, as well as attending meetings at weekends. If their homes are outside central London, they would be lucky to see their families except at the weekend, and would almost certainly have to have a flat close to the City. One merchant bank maintains an apartment for its directors above an expensive West End restaurant. However, if you are seen dining with a new client, word soon gets out. Takeover advisers have to work under conditions of great secrecy, for an essential part of the takeover game is to anticipate your opponent's next move, and to outwit him.

However, for the merchant bank that can grab the lion's share of the business, the rewards are great, with takeovers in the European markets earning the largest portion of income.

Tricks of the Takeover Trade

In planning a takeover, it is essential to work out a strategy before making any announcement. This usually means weeks closeted with financial advisers, and it is a time when security is all-important. A stray document left in a photocopying machine, a loose word dropped to a friend in a bar, or even a minor indiscretion at lunch can lead to a leak. One paragraph in a newspaper can be enough to set the takeover target's shares racing ahead on the Stock Exchange, which could rule out a bid, alert rivals to the possibility, or create problems with the regulators.

Directors know full well that takeover strategy is not just a matter of obtaining enough shares in the targeted concern. In almost every case, politics and public relations come to the fore.

The predator in a takeover enjoys one major advantage: it can always count on the full support of its management team, which usually has much to gain from taking charge of a combined larger organisation. By contrast, the management of a target company often finds itself in a difficult, even ambivalent, position; its loyalties are to its present board of directors, but its future, as likely as not, will lie elsewhere. It also has the burden of dealing with worried employees, not to mention suppliers, distributors, and others with whom the company has close connections. And it has to continue to run the business. It used to be the case that shareholders would usually stand by a business that had done well for them, unless those making the bid put up an irrefutable case. But in 1996, when Rocco Forte tried to persuade Trust House Forte shareholders to stick with him, they rejected his pleas and fell for the Irish charms of Gerry Robinson and his Granada group.

It is also true that the best defence against a takeover is to act before the enemy strikes; in other words, take action which will deter a predator from making a move, such as selling off subsidiaries which do not fit the core of the business, or explaining the company's strategy to analysts in such a way that the share price rises to reflect an accurate, rather than an undervalued, view of its stock. Once a bid is made, it is hard to do this, because any disposals or other capital restructuring have to be approved by shareholders.

When it is clear that a takeover bid is likely to fail, those who have conducted the unsuccessful bid need to be on their guard. Almost certainly the predator will have built up a parcel of shares in the company, and will want to unload them at the highest price possible. That will not be possible if takeover fever has subsided, and the predator may be looking at a loss. In such a case it is normal to arrange a placement through brokers.

It has been known for an unsuccessful bidder to walk away from a failed acquisition with a large profit. Usually this requires barefaced cheek. This is what happened as a result of a visit on 20 November 1979 by the publisher Rupert Murdoch to his father's old office at the *Herald and Weekly Times (HWT)* newspaper group in Melbourne, Australia, where he cheerfully greeted Sir Keith Macpherson, the chairman and chief executive, with the glad tidings that his News Group was about to present the Stock Exchange with the terms of a A$126 million bid for just over half of the company. Since the offer valued *HWT*, the country's largest newspaper group, at A$100 million more than News Group, Macpherson suggested that the whole idea was ridiculous.

Perhaps it was; one newspaper later suggested it was like a snake trying to swallow a sheep, and similar metaphors were used five years later when the entrepreneur Robert Holmes à Court made an unsuccessful bid for Australia's largest company, BHP, an attempt that was described, colourfully, as 'trying to rape an elephant'. Murdoch, however, knew what he was up to. He wanted *HWT* desperately – ever since his father, whose genius had built up the paper, had died. But he suspected that he would not get it, even though News Group offered A$4 a share, a premium of A$1.26 on the market price.

His suspicions were correct. His bid caused panic at the head-quarters of another newspaper group 400 miles away in Sydney. John Fairfax Ltd, a conservative family concern, had a minority stake in *HWT*, and its newspapers were bitter rivals of Murdoch's. Apart from the extra power Murdoch would gain if he controlled *HWT*, he would become a partner of Fairfax in two other major enterprises, Australian Newsprint Mills, the country's only newsprint manu-facturer, and Australian Associated Press, the national news agency, both controlled jointly by Fairfax and *HWT*. Fairfax instructed its brokers to buy all the *HWT* shares it could muster to thwart Murdoch, and the price rose quickly to well above the A$4 that Murdoch had offered.

Within two days Fairfax had laid out over A$50 million and had acquired 15 per cent of *HWT*. The shares stood at A$5.52. Murdoch knew that he was beaten, but astutely spotted a lucrative way out. Instead of conceding defeat, he instructed his brokers, J. B. Were and Co., to continue buying shares but on a much more limited scale. At the same time he commissioned another broker, May and Mellor, to unload the 3,500,000 shares he had already purchased. The Fairfax people, convinced that Murdoch was still a buyer, snapped up the lot, paying top prices, only to face the humiliation of hearing that they had been outwitted and that Murdoch had quit, using one of his own newspapers to condemn the Fairfax 'rescue' of *HWT* as 'two incompetent managements throwing themselves into each other's arms at the expense of their shareholders'. Maybe, but the real point was that Fairfax was determined to stop Murdoch at any price, and paid dearly for it. When the shares settled back down at a lower price, Fairfax had lost over A$20 million, plus the interest on the A$50 million laid out to acquire the stock.

Several years later, Murdoch got his prize, as a result of some spectacular blunders by Warwick Fairfax, a junior member of the Fairfax family, whose dealings in the junk bond market lost him the empire his grandfather had built. The trick is that your opponent has to hate the idea of losing his beloved company so much that he will pay almost anything to keep it.

In most contested takeovers the issue of who wins is decided by institutional investors, as the major shareholders. In Britain they are not quite as fickle as in the United States, but increasingly the institutions are under pressure to perform.

Corporate raiders

Politicians and others who do not know how markets work often condemn speculators as parasites. The canny speculator can also put economic frailties to the test, as did George Soros when he figured correctly in the late summer of 1992, that the pound did not have the strength to be locked into Europe's exchange rate mechanism. Corporate raiders achieve the same impact with companies, especially when they spot that the break-up value of a company, the sum realised when all its assets are sold, may be considerably more than its market capitalisation, or share value.

Investors in the eighties and nineties made a lot of money following corporate raiders, and still do so today. One technique, popular at the time, was called appropriately 'Copycat'. It involved studying the moves of renowned old-style raiders like T. Boone Pickens, and emulating them. They were twenty-four hours behind, of course, but those who tracked the money masters in a bull market seldom fared badly. Those who wanted to limit risk used stock options. When this worked, they made big profits.

In the United States in which the leveraged takeover has been a favourite technique, a great deal of this activity was fuelled by borrowed money. A corporate raider would take a modest position in a large company, wait a short while, and then offer to buy the entire stock by making a takeover bid. Where would the corporate raider's small company raise these billions of dollars from, you may well ask. The answer: use the company's own money, through junk bonds.

Where there's junk there's money

The man in the street might suppose that those proposing to take over a company have the wherewithal to do so. After all, takeover merchants have always been painted as piranhas swallowing the small fry. This is not necessarily the case.

In the late 1980s, many takeovers were achieved with borrowed money, and in some instances this money was borrowed indirectly from the company that the predator was targeting.

Let me explain. Company X wishes to buy company Y, but has insufficient spare cash on its balance sheet to do so. Nor does it have enough security to offer its bankers, and it does not believe it can raise cash from its shareholders in a rights issue.

So instead it issues junk bonds, which are no different from any other interest-bearing security except that they carry a substantially higher than average interest rate. These bonds raise the capital required to finance a bid, and are normally secured against the shares of the company targeted. An investor buying junk bonds normally does so on the basis that his money is only committed if the takeover bid succeeds. If it is successful the corporate raider issuing the bond can afford to pay the higher interest rates because he will have the assets of the newly acquired company at his disposal. In other words, the strength of the victim company's balance sheet is its own downfall. If the corporate raider fails and is unable to get enough shares in the company in his sights, it is a fair bet they will have risen in the market, and he will have made a sizeable capital gain.

The use of junk bonds was championed most heavily in the 1980s by the Wall Street broking firm Drexel Burnham Lambert, where its greatest advocate was Michael Milken. By 1985 $27 billion worth of junk bonds had been issued, most of them through Drexels. In 1970 there had been only $7 billion worth of high-yield bonds outstanding, and most of that was for quality offerings. By 1989, at the peak of the junk bond craze, $201 billion of junk had been unloaded.

Many people imagine that the holders of junk were avaricious investors, dissatisfied with the more prosaic returns available on ordinary investments. They were not. At the beginning of 1989, 30 per cent of junk bonds outstanding in the United States were held by insurance companies, 30 per cent by mutual funds, and 15 per cent by pension funds. Many of them lost their money as the companies in which the junk was secured turned down. Drexels went bankrupt, and Michael Milken went to gaol. Junk bonds went out of fashion.

Poison pills

There are other forces at work in the leveraged takeover game which have caused grave disquiet, particularly for those who subscribe to the old-fashioned view that since a public company is owned by its shareholders it is reasonable to assume that their interests take precedence. The truth, of course, is a little different, as one of Britain's most fêted entrepreneurs was to find out in 1985.

In its heyday, more than half of Hanson Trust's income came from businesses in the United States. In August 1985, Lord (James) Hanson identified a major American company as a suitable case for takeover. The SCM Corporation was a solid if dreary conglomerate which manufactured outmoded typewriters, processed food, pigments and an assortment of other products. On 21 August,

Hanson Trust offered $60 in cash for each share in SCM Corporation, valuing the company at $755 million, well below its market capitalisation. Robert Morton, an analyst, told me at the time that this was 'in the mould of Hanson acquisitions: SCM is exactly the kind of company he goes for, a company which has already undergone a great deal of rationalisation and sorting out, which perhaps has not been fully realised by the shareholders'.

The SCM management was horrified. Here was a lord from England buying their company at rock-bottom value. From all the precedents, it was clear that, before they knew where they were, they would be looking for new jobs. Fortunately for them, the board saw matters the same way, rejected the Hanson bid, and refused even to talk to Hanson's US chief Sir Gordon White, despite several invitations to do so. It hastily called in its financial advisers, Goldman Sachs.

However, it was not Goldman Sachs that came to the rescue of SCM's beleaguered management, but Wall Street's largest broking house, the financial conglomerate Merrill Lynch. Merrill Lynch's capital markets division, headed by a young go-getter, Ken Miller, was hungry for new business, and skilful in organising what have become known as leveraged management buyouts. Within a few days, Miller and his team had come up with a means whereby, at the stroke of a pen, Hanson could be thwarted, the SCM management could save their jobs, and Merrill Lynch would receive a large fee.

On 30 August, only nine days after Hanson's bid, a new company was announced – legally a partnership between the SCM Corporation's management and Merrill Lynch, but funded by the Prudential Assurance Company of America. It offered $70 a share – $10 more than Hanson – for 85 per cent of the SCM shares, and promised to buy the rest out of SCM profits at some future date through the issue of junk bonds which, it was hoped, would also trade at about $70. A confidential Merrill Lynch paper described the deal as representing 'one of the most asset-rich leveraged buyout opportunities we have ever encountered'. For Miller, much was at stake: if he pulled off the deal it would be the first time that a leveraged management buyout had been successful against a tender offer for cash.

The wily Merrill Lynch team hoped that Hanson would withdraw, leaving them with the business, but they took steps to make sure they would still make money if he did not. A clause was written into the contract with SCM providing for a $9 million fee should the bid be topped leading to the termination of the arrangement. This was to be in addition to the basic fee of £1.5 million for fixing the deal in the first place.

Hanson had no intention of giving up. On 3 September, Hanson Trust increased its offer to $72 a share. Unlike the first offer, which valued SCM at a bargain-basement price, this was a much more attractive offer for shareholders. It was also all in cash. Accepting the offer would not involve the risk posed by the Merrill deal which, from the shareholders' point of view, meant waiting around for junk bonds and future profits which might never come.

It looked as if Hanson had won. But having made sure their $9 million fee was in escrow, Merrill's Miller and his team then came up with a much more ruthless way of frustrating the English lord's ambitions. They would strip out of SCM Corporation its two most potentially profitable businesses, in the belief that the Englishman would either lose interest or be left with a crippled company.

This tactic has become known as the use of the 'poisoned pill', although a more appropriate metaphor might be that of a scorched earth policy. In this instance, the SCM management and Merrill Lynch increased their leveraged buyout offer to $74 a share, but subjected it to a new condition: if Hanson or another party got more than a third of SCM shares, Merrill would have the right to purchase the two most thriving parts of the SCM Corporation – the pigments and processed food businesses – at knockdown prices. These businesses, described as the 'crown jewels', would then be run by the same SCM management. What was left in SCM would be hardly worth having. Merrill Lynch also took a retention fee of $6 million, investment banking fees of $8 million, and dealer-manager fees of $2.75 million, in addition, of course, to the $10.5 million already paid.

The next morning Hanson Trust withdrew its $72-a-share offer, and spent $200 million buying SCM shares on the New York market; within a few hours it had acquired 25 per cent of the company. But on 16 September Merrill Lynch acted again. With the Manufacturers Hanover Bank working as agent, it put the shares of the crown jewel subsidiaries in escrow, and apparently beyond Hanson's reach. At this point the lawyers took over, with the action moving to the New York District Court in Lower Manhattan. In the end Hanson Trust lost the case, but the verdict was reversed in the subsequent appeal. The English lord had won, but only after gritty determination.

Discussion in the United States since has ranged over whether the law courts are really the place to decide such matters, as well as whether the frenzy of takeover activity should be allowed to waste scarce investment capital, to inhibit innovation, and to force managers to sacrifice long-term goals for the good of the quarterly balance sheet. And should management be able to conspire with its preferred bidder to frustrate a better offer for shareholders? Some of these issues will be discussed later, in Chapter 16. Kathryn Rudie Harrigan, Professor of Strategic Management at the Columbia University Business School, talked to me about the increasingly common tendency for stock market takeovers to be decided in courts of law: 'It is just one more in a string of devices that managers and their investments bankers have come up with to avoid being taken over when they do not want to be.'

Is this new trend likely to be damaging to shareholders? Professor Harrigan thinks perhaps not, in that values are often forced up by what is essentially a game: 'It is a game, and it is a game that is played with great ritual, and is being played in many, many companies these days. It is often cheaper to acquire something than it is to build it from the ground up.' But she does believe that business will suffer in the end:

> I think it is damaging to the long-term health of the business, because when you are so busy satisfying these short-term requests of the financial community, who are looking for instant gratification from their investment, you often cripple the long-term ability of the company to be able to reposition itself to remain competitive in a changing environment.

Professor Harrigan also believes that the concepts of poison pills and crown jewels could be exported to Britain:

> The two capital markets are becoming very similar in the way that people operate within them, and the kinds of expectations they have of the companies whose equities they hold. And more and more of the equities are held by institutional investors, who have this kind of short-term expectation, and they want to see this quick pay-off on their investment. I think the kind of behaviour we see here, with these leveraged buyouts, will undoubtedly be appearing also in your stock markets.

As we move further into the twenty-first century, it seems inevitable that there will be many more multi-billion-dollar takeovers. The activity of the year 2000, when the value of mergers and acquisitions worldwide was a record $3.5 trillion, up from $3.3 trillion in 1999, was subsequently dampened down by the recession.[5] But after the shock waves that followed the destruction of the World Trade Center in New York on 11 September 2001, it seems inevitable that there will be consolidation in the world airline industry, while some global rationalisation of the financial services industry seems long overdue. But when stock market prices are volatile, there is a disincentive to merge, because most deals are done involving shares rather than cash. Time Warner shareholders found this out to their cost; the AOL shares they accepted in payment for their company slumped in value within minutes of Wall Street digesting the news.

Breaking Up is Hard to Do

Company divorces or break-ups, more politely referred to as 'de-mergers' have, of late been as fashionable as takeovers. In the seventies, conglomerates were all the rage, large corporations stringing together a variety of businesses in totally unconnected industries. A good example of a modern conglomerate that still exists and thrives is General Electric, one of the United States' top five corporations, which until recently was headed by the legendary manager Jack Welch. Inside GE are corporations involved in electrical products like lighting, aircraft engines, corporate leasing, insurance, television and Hollywood studios. There is no logical link, but Welch's mantra was that GE should be either number one or number two in any business it was in, or not be in it at all. Where businesses did not make it, he looked for buyers.

In Britain, Pearson was once a conglomerate with properties as varied as Royal Doulton China, the *Financial Times*, Longman, Penguin, Tussaud's waxworks, Chessington Zoo, Lazards investment bank, some Texas oil exploration companies, and the French Latour winery. Under the leadership of Marjorie Scardino, most of these businesses have been sold off, leaving Pearson as a more focused publisher, with particular strength in education following the acquisition of Simon and Schuster, the American market leader.

Very often, de-mergers are organised so as to restore focus to a company so that it can concentrate on what it believes it does best. In other cases they can become a useful way of raising money from a

---

[5] Thomson Financial Services.

particularly successful and perhaps undervalued subsidiary. News Corporation did this with British Sky Broadcasting, which it still controls but which is separately quoted on the London Stock Exchange. ICI did the same with its pharmaceuticals division, de-merging it to form Astra Zeneca.

De-merging normally helps shareholder understanding since financial analysts are able to get a much better sense of performance when numbers are not buried within a group's profit-and-loss statement, or an integrated balance sheet.

LIVERPOOL JOHN MOORES UNIVERSITY
LEARNING SERVICES

12   Selling the Family Silver

It's like selling the family silver.
> Former British Prime Minister Harold Macmillan,
> speaking in the House of Lords

I am not able to say myself whether it will be worth all the labour involved in privatisation. I do not know. I think we shall find out only a lot later on.
> Sir Denis Rooke, former chairman of British Gas

Get it out . . . get it sold.
> Kenneth Baker, one-time chairman of the Conservative Party

Privat: Middle English proverb from Latin, privatus, not belonging to the State, not in public life, deprived of office, from the past participle of private, to deprive, release.
> *American Heritage Dictionary*

Twelve Russians waited patiently in line for what, for them, was the sale of the century. This was not the type of queue so familiar in the 1960s and 1970s for bread, meat or items of everyday clothing. The Muscovites had come to buy shares in one of the country's best-loved concerns – the BBC, or Bolshevik Biscuit Corporation, which, in earlier times, had held 12 per cent of the Soviet market for cookies.

Each of them clutched a voucher worth 10,000 roubles, issued by the Russian Government and entitling the holder to exchange it for shares of equivalent value in any enterprise offered for sale by the Ministry for Privatisation. Advising the ministry were dark-suited experts from two Western financial institutions, Credit Suisse First Boston, and the European Bank for Reconstruction and Development. As they advanced to bid for their shares, the shabbily dressed men and women paid scant attention to the documentation set out on the tables before them. But their questions showed their relish for their proposed investment, as they asked: 'What will the return on capital be?', 'What are your profits?', 'What are your marketing plans?'

That day in 1996 was the first time in Russian history that ordinary men and women had been able to bid for shares. Though the sale was not reported on television news bulletins in Europe or America, history was being made. Three years earlier, confounding Lenin's predictions, communism as practised by the Soviet Union and its Warsaw Pact allies had collapsed, leaving an economic shambles as serious as that faced in Germany at the end of the Second World War. New, democratically elected leaders sought to rekindle their economies by resorting to privatisation: putting the ownership of enterprises into the hands of individuals and private institutions rather than under the control of the state. Unfortunately, most individuals cashed in their vouchers, and it was not long before many of the significant enterprises in Russia were back in the hands of their former bosses, who used their not inconsiderable savings to buy control. Thus party hacks became oligarchs, conveniently shedding their Communist Party sympathies as they joined the world of capitalism.

Even so, privatisation has come a long way since it was pioneered in Britain by Margaret Thatcher's Conservative government on the idea of the management guru Peter Drucker – it is now a philosophy which has swept the world. One by one, governments have been divesting themselves of great state-owned corporations. Britain led the way in ridding the taxpayer of the burden – and the public servant of the responsibility – of huge utility businesses like power and gas supply, telecommunications and airlines. Now privatisation has reached Africa, Asia and Latin America.

Alas, in Britain a brilliant idea has been poorly executed, with the result that very few members of the public have ended up with more than a handful of shares. Instead of encouraging saving, privatisation bred stagging – making a capital gain by selling equity at a profit immediately upon acquisition. The issues were priced too cheaply, and the City made huge profits, leaving many ordinary families with the feeling that share-trading was not for them. Yet privatisation has not been without its achievements. Many of the private companies are much more efficient than they were as state corporations. There is no longer a dismal wait for a telephone to be installed, or for the electricity man to read your meter. More to the point, instead of costing the government and the taxpayer money in subsidies, the majority of privatised companies make healthy profits, and pay tax on them. Privatised companies account now for more than 20 per cent of the FTSE index and their tax bill is almost exactly equivalent to the amount they were consuming in subsidies.[1] In Australia, Britain, France, Germany, Italy, Japan, Singapore, Portugal and Spain, the top companies are all newly privatised.[2]

Despite disappointments, it is unlikely that the burst of interest in share ownership, particularly among the working classes, would have come about if the British Telecom float had not taken place, with its hype, touring road shows, television campaign and gimmicks like bonus shares and vouchers to help pay the phone bills.

Even more hype went into the sale in December 1986 of over four billion shares in British Gas, with the introduction to the nation's television screens nightly of an ubiquitous but enigmatic character called Sid. Clever if unsubtle advertisements by the Young and Rubicam agency urged viewers to 'tell Sid' about the opportunities for the public to buy shares in British Gas. One even had a pigeon fancier releasing his bird and saying, 'There y'are, my darlin', just go and tell Sid.' Right to the end of the campaign, Sid was never to be spotted; in the very last advertisement, a near-demented potential shareholder was seen climbing a mountain peak and peering through the mist crying 'Sid!' at a shape that turned out to be nothing more than a startled sheep.

The British public accepted the offer gratefully – and why not? As with British Telecom, the Government had priced British Gas attractively and with a forthcoming election in mind – those who sold quickly were rewarded with a capital gain in excess of 20 per cent, and those who held the stock could look forward to cheaper fuel bills with the prospect of gas vouchers in addition to normal dividends. For every hundred shares bought, investors received a voucher worth £10 payable over a two-year period.

Once British Gas was safely out of the way, the Government set about another major sale, that of British Airways. This was followed by British Steel, the nation's electricity industry, the water authorities, and the railway network. *The Economist* saw it as 'the largest transfer of property since the dissolution of the monasteries'. Most of those who invested in privatisation stocks have found it a good investment, though almost everyone would have done better had they sold their shares at the peak of the bull market in 1999.

Those who bought into the original BT privatisation would have

---

[1] *Privatisation International*, December 1998.
[2] William Megginson (Professor and Rainbolt Chair in Finance, University of Oklahoma), *The Impact of Privatization on Capital Market Development and Individual Share Ownership*.

made a big profit on the 130 pence launch price had they sold before the end of the nineties bull market, realising 750 pence a share, equivalent to a return of almost 30 per cent a year, more than six times the savings rate of a building society. But those who kept their shares, probably because they were in a tax-efficient vehicle like a PEP, would have seen them fall to below the 400 pence mark. This illustrates the need to try and sell out at the top of the market.

Some privatisation shares have been poor performers. British Steel was one of the worst. Floating at 125 pence in 1988, they fell to 40 pence by 2001, so investors would have lost two thirds of their money. The only bonus was a 35 pence special bonus in 1999 when the company merged with Hoogovens to become Corus, its present name. Railtrack has been another sorry story. With its reputation in tatters after major rail crashes on main lines into London, the Blair government rightly allowed it to drift into receivership.

By contrast, BP shareholders have seen a huge rise as Sir John Browne's skilful management transformed it into a world-class company, acquiring Amoco, Arco, and Burmah Castrol on the way. Table 12.1 shows the performance of privatisation stocks.

Table 12.1 How Privatisation Stocks have Performed

Name	Date	Price	Price Oct 2000	Price Feb 2002	% change
BT	1984	130	727	240	185
British Gas	1986	135	173	286	212
BAA	1987	122	582	619	532
British Airways	1987	125	292	194	155
Powergen	1991	175	500	763	436
Railtrack	1996	380	1098	0	–380
Scottish Power	1991	240	536	431	180

Privatisation Methods

At this point it is worth stepping back a little to review in more detail how privatisations have been carried out. In theory, businesses that belong to the state belong to the people. Prime Minister Tony Blair, for instance, constantly refers to 'our National Health Service'. Many of the businesses that have recently been privatised were once before in private ownership, and then bought for our benefit through compulsory purchase, better known as nationalisation. The railway companies, Britain's post-war steel-makers, and several motor manufacturers such as Austin, Morris and Rover were all bought for our benefit by left-of-centre politicians who used our taxes and borrowed funds to expropriate them from their owners. In the former Soviet Union and in Eastern Europe the state simply declared private profit illegal, and stole all businesses from their traditional owners. The politicians then ran these concerns as if they belonged not to the people, but to them. Most nationalised industries in Britain ran at a loss, so the taxpayer was called upon to make up the shortfall.

With the arrival of Thatcherism, the politicians decided to hand back to us businesses the people were supposed to own, but instead of giving them back, they made us pay for them. This meant spending tens of millions of pounds in fees to intermediaries in the City of London, which helped them through a sticky patch which cost the rest of us dear. When we had spent our savings to buy these businesses back from ourselves, the Government decided to give some of us some of the money back through tax cuts, so that we would re-elect them.

Share issue privatisations

Share issue privatisations have been the most common method of privatising state-owned corporations. They have much in common with an initial public offering (IPO), discussed in Chapter 11, in that a detailed prospectus has to be drawn up, and approved, with all the same legal and disclosure requirements. They differ in that many share issue privatisations have been of very large businesses, such as BP Amoco, now one of the world's top three corporations, and a range of telecoms companies, including BT, Nippon Telecom and Telegraph, Deutsche Telekom, France Télécom, Telefonica and Telstra. As with large IPOs, shares are issued using a mixture of placement and offerings. Usually a significant proportion of a privatisation is offered to the public, with some shares reserved for employees. The remainder is placed with institutions. These institutions – or sometimes other institutions – also underwrite the privatisation; in other words, agree to buy the shares from the government selling the enterprise if there is not sufficient public interest. In practice, very few underwiters in privatisations have been called into action, as the majority of privatisations have been oversubscribed. Where this has happened, there have been two outcomes: allotments have been cut back, with the number of shares available to the public being rationed; or shares pre-allocated to institutions have been clawed back to increase the allocation to the public.

There are many reasons why the public may oversubscribe to a particular privatisation, but two predominate. The first is that although promoting the issue through advertising and other forms of publicity is normally banned, most privatisations have been accompanied by expensively funded advertising campaigns about the enterprise itself. In Britain, for example, the privatisation of British Airways coincided with hugely extravagant television and press advertisements promoting the self-styled 'world's favourite airline'. The same happened with gas, water, electricity and telecoms. None of the advertisements broke the law because they did not urge the public to buy the shares, but the City promoters have learnt the art of extracting maximum promotional value while staying within the strict legal limits. With such hype associated with the big-ticket privatisations, it is not surprising there was such great public interest.

Secondly, the price set for the great privatisations was always low enough to appear to be a bargain. Governments wanted privatisations to be a success, providing the public with a feel-good factor. The rapid rises in prices that followed most privatisations provided proof that many government businesses were sold too cheap.

Other forms of privatisation

Although share issues have been the most common form of privatisation in Britain, many other techniques have been used. Too numerous to mention here, they were outlined in my book *Selling the Family Silver*.[3] Two of them, however, stand out – selling the enterprise in whole or in part to an existing corporation; and issuing vouchers.

Selling off bits of nationalised industries has been and will always be a matter of controversy. Nowhere has this been more evident than in the privatisation of the railways in Britain. The privatisation of British Rail, arguably the least successful of all of British privatisations, is a story in itself which could fill twice the number of pages in this book. Much of the controversy that still surrounds this unhappy event is over the decision to split British Rail into an infrastructure company, Railtrack, and operators, train companies like Virgin Rail and Great Western. But even before this, bits of

[3] Colin Chapman, *Selling the Family Silver: has privatisation worked?* (Random Century, 1990).

British Rail were being sold off. Some down-at-heel British Rail hotels were handed over to major hotel operators for very low sums, and are now being valued by their new owners at thirty to fifty times what they cost. The old British Rail headquarters at Marylebone is now the prestigious Landmark Hotel. Similarly Sealink, the cross-Channel ferry operations of British Rail, was sold to rival P&O, and today, even after the introduction of the Channel Tunnel, is valued at more than five times what it cost. The debate continues as to whether these assets were sold too cheap, or whether they are now worth much more because they are better run.

The voucher system was common in countries where the populace was thought not to have either the money or the interest in buying privatisation shares, but was entitled to benefit. There have been many variants on the Russian scheme described earlier in this chapter. Suffice it to say that most voucher holders appear to have cashed in their shares, so that the equity designed for the public ended up with large investors. Essentially, though, this has also been the outcome of share issue schemes.

Even so, the fact that there are many more shareholders in the world today undoubtedly owes much to privatisation. Many of the largest privatisations, such as those in telecoms, created millions of new shareholders, particularly in European countries where share ownership was low. Tabel 12.2 shows some of the largest privatisations. France Télécom created nearly four million new shareholders, and 3.4 million took up shares in Crédit Lyonnais. Deutsche Telekom drew in three million to share ownership. Eight years on, many of these sold out, but millions remain.

Table 12.2

Company	Country	Market Value $mm
BP Amoco	Britain	173,870
NT and T	Japan	156,770
Deutsche Telekom	Germany	115,023
British Telecom	Britain	107,142
NTT DoCoMo	Japan	106,140
France Télécom	France	79,925
Telecom Italia	Italy	55,446
Telstra	Australia	63,890
Telfonica	Spain	51,150

Source: William L. Megginson, Professor and Rainbolt Chair in Finance, University of Oklahoma

Privatisation: Privileges for the Workers

Few employees have fared so well as those working for privatised concerns in Britain, for in almost all cases they were offered privileged treatment on both price and allocations.

Let us look at just one example: the employees of Northumbrian Water, the most oversubscribed of the ten new water companies. Those who did not live in Northumbria were restricted to just 100 shares each, and even the customers were allocated only 200: hardly worth the bother, and almost a waste of time. Those who worked for the company, however, had every reason to smile, for they were entitled to apply for and receive up to 5,000 shares. Workers at the other water companies received the same preferential treatment.

The Northumbrian shares were priced at 240 pence, payable in instalments, but water employees were able to invest at a 10 per cent discount. When trading started on the share markets, the opening price showed a premium of 60 pence a share. A worker taking his full allocation would have shown a paper profit of about 84 pence per share.

The water workers – along with other employees of privatised concerns – have also enjoyed other special privileges denied to others, the most significant of which is exemption from the punitive taxation imposed on their counterparts who work for other companies seeking extra capital through rights issues. Although companies offering rights issues normally allocate employees' shares through the distribution of the so-called pink forms signifying a priority offer, those workers who take advantage of this have to pay tax as PAYE on the premium to the issue price when the share starts trading, as if it was income. Indeed, so unfair is this rule that most employees end up having this tax deducted from their wages before they are able to dispose of the shares. The workers of privatised companies face no such intolerable burden.

The 90,000 workers of British Gas were also given generous treatment, which cost the taxpayer a total of £54 million. Each employee was awarded £70 worth of shares, plus a further £2 worth for each year of service. Those able to invest their own money were given two free shares for each one bought, up to a limit of £300 worth of free shares. Those inclined to dig deeper into their savings could buy up to £2,000 worth at a 10 per cent discount. Pensioners were also each given about £75 worth of free shares. This was in sharp contrast to the parsimony of British Telecom, whose employee shareholders missed out.

In all the major privatisations so far, the majority of employees have taken up their entitlements, though many later sold or reduced their holdings. Foolishly perhaps, most employees sold their holdings on the market, rather than to work colleagues or trade unions, for had they adopted this latter course they could have wielded more influence in their companies. To some extent this happened in the case of British Airways, where 5,000 employees gave their union a proxy vote over their shares.

Sale by Mutual Consent

Just when the flow of British privatisation bargains had dried up another trend emerged. It was called – in another massacre of the English language by public servants – demutualisation. For years the building societies – among Britain's most established institutions – had competed with each other in a mad scramble for a prime space in the high streets. They had been operating, literally, for the mutual benefit of their members.

Building societies were created to enable people to buy houses. At its simplest, the concept of the building society movement was that some members lent their savings to the societies at one rate of interest, while others borrowed money at a higher rate to purchase their homes. The money accumulated because of the difference between the two rates, both of which moved up and down more or less in line with market forces, went to pay for expenses, or to boost reserves. While the societies noisily defended the level of management costs and the need to establish visibility in the high street through branch networks, many felt there were inefficiencies in the system. (Actually, the relative efficiency of many building societies pointed out the inefficiencies of the high street trading banks.)

This principle of mutuality also extended to a large number of life assurance companies. Their difference between income and expenditure also went towards building up lavish reserves, generous staff benefits for employees, especially senior management, and bonuses for policy holders possessing with-profits endowment policies. Quite often building societies worked alongside the assurance mutuals, encouraging individuals to purchase homes on an interest-only basis with the capital repaid on the maturity of the endowment policy.

This inefficient form of home purchase was for many years encouraged by the Government, which made both the interest charges and endowment assurance premiums tax-deductible, thus conferring a substantial benefit to the higher-paid at the expense of those who could not afford to buy property.

As successive governments stripped away most of these tax benefits, both building societies and life assurance mutuals found they had to compete in the real world, and many of them did so very well. The Conservatives also introduced legislation to encourage competition in the financial sector, and many organisations from both groups felt they would be unable to hold their own against public liability companies.

Many, but not all, also felt they would be best able to compete by being on level terms, and becoming fully listed public liability companies with the ability to raise funds on the stock market. One of these came from the East Anglian city of Norwich, where not only is it the biggest source of employment but in 1995 surprised the local community by offering a job to every school leaver in the county of Norfolk with A levels.

For all its humble origins, the Norwich Union, at the time of its flotation, was a global business with branches worldwide. Its approach to demutualisation was especially bold, because not only did it offer its members, those holding with-profits policies, a free windfall of shares worth between £800 and £4,000, depending on the size of policy, but it also raised about £1.8 billion of new money with an additional offer to policy holders. By the time it had joined the Stock Exchange and its shares were trading on 16 June 1997, it was one of Britain's top fifty companies, worth around £5.5 billion. By 2000 it had been merged with two other companies, Commercial Union and General Accident, to form Britain's largest insurance group, CGNU.

13   Market Movers and Mavens

Within seconds of a takeover bid being announced, a company's profits tumbling, a central bank lowering or raising interest rates or the share price of a company moving up or down on any of the world's major markets, investors everywhere in the wired-up world will hear of it. Financial news travels faster than anything else.

Usually the professional investors hear first, and pay for the privilege. They also have the benefit of the instant interpretation of a highly specialised team of analysts and chartists. Until recently the ordinary investor was far behind the professional in the information chain, but the arrival of the world wide web on the Internet has made things less disadvantageous for the private investor. Government regulators have also contributed, although the objective of levelling the playing field is still far from being achieved.

In Chapter 3, I discussed at length how shares are valued, and now it is time to look at the forces that change these values. It will quickly become apparent that there is no one group of movers and shakers, as the conspiracy theorists of the anti-capitalist movement would have you believe. Share movements are not dictated by a secret cabal of business leaders meeting on an American or European country estate guarded by hitmen and Rottweilers. Nor do exclusive summits such as the annual meeting of the World Economic Forum in Davos dictate the shape and flow of the markets in the days or weeks that follow their annual 'talkfest' in the Swiss Alps. I participated in nine out of ten of the most recent summits, and while these are valuable networking events that make it possible to exchange views and predictions with hundreds of influential decision-makers, there is little or no evidence that they are the instigators of successful collusion and market manipulation. Markets are moved by a variety of factors.

No one predicted that global financial insanity would prevail in 1998 and 1999 in the valuations of some Internet stocks. (They should not be described as technology stocks, because there is little that is technological about them.) Equally, only a few predicted that the Internet bubble would burst as swiftly as it did. The Asian meltdown that followed the collapse of the Thai baht in 1997 was not foreseen by the Central Intelligence Agency, the International Monetary Fund or the World Economic Forum, despite the very substantial knowledge of these organisations and their staff or members.

Investor sentiment, the most powerful force in price movements, often reflects inexplicable shifts in the public mood. The bear market that coincided with the arrival of President George W. Bush in the White House in January 2001 was fuelled by a quite sudden decision by Americans to stop buying things, particularly computers and other consumer electronics products. This was not because Americans earned less, because they didn't, and they also had Bush's promise ringing in their ears of more money in their pockets through tax cuts. Even when Bush swiftly delivered on his promise and pushed through the tax cuts, Americans failed to rattle the tills on Main Street, and proved just as recalcitrant when the Federal Reserve reduced interest rates not once but several times. Investors talked of recession, and sold stocks. The falling stock market created its own clouds of gloom, and the economy slowed further.

Governments, Central Banks and Politicians

Across the world, this group has probably the greatest single influence on markets, but we need to be careful and distinguish between what governments do and what politicians say. It is a sad commentary on modern politics that all too often words are not matched by action. Before the euro was launched as a common currency for some member nations of the European Union, many of Europe's political leaders prophesied that it would become a strong currency, even rivalling the dollar. Those investors, particularly Americans and Britons, who bought shares or funds in Europe upon the creation of 'Euroland' (the countries in the European Union which have agreed to operate a common currency) quickly found that any gains they made in share values were more than wiped out by the declining value of the euro. Most finance ministers are sensible enough never to comment publicly on currency rates; those who do usually get it wrong. Beware of political leaders predicting the rise or fall of a currency, because the opposite will usually happen. Reuters, the news agency, now always inserts 'says' or 'predicts' in any report of this kind – 'Blair says', 'Schroder predicts', for example – so as to distance itself from the claim.

However, government actions are another story. Markets are moved by publication of a raft of government statistics, and by changes in interest rates. Changes in interest rates have the most impact. Governments in the United States, Britain and Euroland leave the setting of interest rates to their central banks – in other words, the Federal Reserve Board, the Bank of England, and the European Central Bank respectively. The rise or fall of interest rates is the key instrument of monetary policy, and these three central banks are independent, and quite capable of making decisions which can be and often are against the political inclinations of ministers. Tightening monetary policy by raising interest rates and therefore discouraging borrowing and spending and encouraging saving is a key weapon against inflation, but often results in job losses. When an economy is in recession, lowering interest rates, as did Alan Greenspan, chairman of the Federal Reserve, in 2000 and 2001, is supposed to stimulate spending and fuel economic activity.

Thus a drop of half of 1 per cent in basic rates, the yardstick by which all other rates are set, is usually seen as a stimulus for equities, while rising interest rates damage share markets. When the return on bonds, a more risk-averse investment, rises to a level that wipes out the average equity premium, the higher return one gets for greater risk, investors move out of equities into bonds until the position stabilises.

In Britain, decisions on interest rates are taken by the Monetary Policy Committee, a group of economists and other experts chaired by the Governor of the Bank of England, which usually meets over two days each month. After the meeting the Governor announces the decision – no change or a rise or fall – and often holds a news conference. The minutes of the meeting, summarising discussions and shedding more light on decisions, are published at a later date.

Next in line of importance is the annual Budget, produced by the Chancellor of the Exchequer and delivered to Members of Parliament in the House of Commons in March. This is where changes in taxation are announced, as well as a progress report given on the nation's economy. The Budget is a peculiar ritual in Britain. It is preceded by weeks in which the Chancellor and his senior officials in the Treasury are in purdah – their description, not mine – and consider a variety of pleas from pressure groups such as the Confederation of British Industry, the Institute of Directors, and the Trades Union Congress. It is rather like a shaikh's majlis, with the supplicants noisily proclaiming their needs and the Treasury mandarins nodding sagely and keeping quiet. The period of purdah begins early in the New Year at a large country house, and continues through long and sometimes argumentative evenings at the Treasury's mausoleum in Whitehall. By the time the Chancellor has packed his secrets into a faded red dispatch case and carried them into the Commons, the financial community is in a state of high expectation, fuelled by Budget leaks and media comment. By tradition the Chancellor sips at a glass of whisky as his message unfolds. Every piece of news is flashed on to television screens, and the market reacts.

There are other British Government decisions that move markets, but nothing with the impact of interest rate or budgetary changes. However, foreign government or quasi-official events also have an impact. The two most watched by traders are the decisions of the Federal Reserve Board on American interest rates, where any change impacts global markets, and the deliberations of the European Central Bank, which governs interest rates in Euroland.

The Analysts and the Ratings Agencies

Once upon a time the analyst was the office introvert, who spent his day hidden from view in a corner behind a pile of dusty papers, fretting over obscure charts while his broking colleagues got on with the business of trading shares. Now, though sometimes held in low esteem by a few of the more self opinionated members of the trading desks, analysts are high profile.

They have their strongest impact with their estimates of companies' performances, and buy or sell recommendations on individual shares. Major companies report their results to the London Stock Exchange and other exchanges on a quarterly basis, and others half-yearly. These events are eagerly anticipated, and when results are published, usually in the early morning before trading starts, they nearly always lead to share movements, unless they are, to quote a much-used phrase, 'in line with analysts' expectations'.

The rules provide that companies publish their results through the main exchange on which they are listed before discussing them with anyone. What that usually means is that within seconds of publication, a company's chairman, chief executive or finance director – and often all three – will be hosting a breakfast for analysts who follow the company. Sometimes specialist company reporters from the broadsheet newspapers will also be invited, although more often this group have their own less detailed question-and-answer session, which usually concludes with one-to-one interviews between the chairman and business television channels. The comments to analysts and the media will also impact on the markets because almost certainly the company executive will be asked for a forward-looking statement.

After the meetings the analysts will head back to their offices to brief their colleagues on the trading desks, although if what they have heard excites them they will use their mobile phones. They will then enunciate their opinions to the outside world, through media interviews, newsletters and the Internet.

In between results announcements, companies sometimes issue statements about their outlook, with the most important of these being profit warnings. A profit warning will always depress a company's shares, and may well impact on an entire sector.

Analysts usually work in sectors, such as telecommunications, media, oil and gas, or banks, in which case their focus is usually limited to a handful of major companies, and their work highly specialist. These men and women tend to be as knowledgeable about a company as those in the company itself, and they are usually highly respected.

According to a recent survey their average age is thirty-three, and a typical member of the fraternity will have spent six and a quarter years in the business, and three and a half years with his or her firm.[1] Fundamental research and field trips take up to two thirds of their time – and they spend a surprising amount of time on marketing activities, frequently talking to the media. This partly explains why analysts, especially those who appear often on radio and television, are not universally admired, particularly by the chairmen of the companies upon whose operations they comment.

Some companies also run away-days or weekend trips with analysts and selected financial journalists. Carlo de Benedetti, when chairman of Olivetti, favoured Florence, where the men and women from broking houses across Europe could sample fine art, good food and Tuscan wine. British Airways sometimes flies opinion-makers in the City to a variety of exotic overseas locations in the old but not mistaken belief that the further away from home, the closer the mind

---

[1] Ranking of UK Investment Analysts, Extel, 1999.

might be concentrated on the subject in hand. Many German companies favour a day in Rhineland vineries followed by a stiff morning of financial presentations at head office. Golf days for susceptible business editors are popular in Britain, while I have also heard of weekends spent 'curling' in the Scottish Highlands.

As and when they complete their detailed studies of the companies they watch, analysts will issue recommendations. These will not just be 'buy' or 'sell', but will include other terms such as 'strong buy' and 'hold'. These recommendations will be widely reported, and will inevitably lead to price shifts.

Securities analysts have now formed an industry in their own right, and have their own professional body. It is a highly competitive business, and one in which the rewards can be considerable. There are even annual contests for best analysts and broking firms, sector by sector. The best-known survey, the annual Extel Ranking of UK Investment Analysts, run by Thomson Financial was started in 1973 by Continental Illinois, and is based on a detailed questionnaire sent to investment managers of the major institutions. Only four out of ten bother to reply in detail, but this still makes almost a hundred, with over £600 billion of funds in their care, and the survey is self-perpetuating, as the winners can count on many a new job offer and a stream of telephone calls from journalists, merchant bankers, accountants and others anxious to tap their expertise.

A similar analysts' Oscar awards takes place in New York, under the aegis of *Institutional Investor* magazine. Across the Atlantic it seems much more of a one-horse race. Merrill Lynch, the world's largest broking firm once nicknamed 'the thundering herd', has won the award for each of the past three years, and for sixteen of the twenty-six years the contest has been going. The US survey is the result of 1,500 interviews with professional investors.

More detached from the markets are the credit rating agencies, of which Moody's, and Standard and Poor's are the best known. They grade a company's financial health by a star system. Triple A is at the top, triple C is risky. Both these agencies also rate country's debts – or the chances of creditors being repaid. Their approach is somewhat different from that of the mainstream stock market analyst, whose objective is usually to make a value judgement on a company's future prospects and profits. The ratings agencies are more concerned with the strength of a company's balance sheet, the level of its debt, particularly the ratio of debt to assets, and its ability to meet its liabilities to bond holders and others who have lent it money.

Nevertheless, ratings agency reports are an invaluable guide for the equities investor too.

The Chartists

Unlike the 'health warning' section of financial services advertisements, chartists believe that past performance really is a guide to the future of share price movements, and go out of their way to prove that this is the case. Chartism goes in and out of fashion, and some of the best chartists – or technical analysts, as they are sometimes called – command respect and a large audience whenever they make a presentation.

The chartist is particularly interested in market peaks and troughs, and believes that these high and low points can be predicted with a reasonable degree of certainty. Expressions like 'points of resistance' are important. Just as it is possible to foresee that house prices cannot rise beyond a certain point (because the ratio of borrowing to average income becomes too high) or that prices can fall no further (because demand will rise from those on lower earnings), so stock market chartists are convinced that it is possible to assess a share's intrinsic value.

By carefully plotting price movements over a period of time – an easy process with high-speed personal computers – a chartist can spot a trend, and recommend a time to buy or sell. That is the theory; in fact, chartism is fallible. The chartists failed to predict the great stock market crash of 1987, but then so did most other so-called experts.

Those who wish to learn more about the charms of chartism would do well to go to their nearest business bookshop and browse through some of the many titles available. An easier option might be to use the *Financial Times* to plot the performance of the main indices, and to look at shares that, year after year, appear to better it. If you have a PC, there are some interesting and inexpensive computer programs that enable you to do this.

The Gurus

More colourful than chartists are those rich individuals who have made fortunes out of the markets – George Soros, Peter Lynch, Warren Buffett, Ron Brierley, to name but a few. They have an impact in several ways. First, anything they say is likely to move markets, and not one of them could be called shy. Secondly, their actions are watched closely by other investors, and mimicked. Thirdly, many investors try and build a portfolio that tracks that of the gurus, in the hope that they too can become super-rich.

Warren Buffett, affectionately known as the Oracle of Omaha, is America's leading investment authority. From a small and unpretentious office in Omaha, Nebraska, he has bought and sold shares to achieve a personal wealth of over $10 billion. Buffett, self-effacing and gracious, runs his investments through his company, Berkshire Hathaway. His 'buy and hold' investment strategy is, according to his friend Peter Lynch, built round 'determining the intrinsic value of a business and paying a fair or bargain price: he doesn't care what the general stock market has done recently or will do in the future'.[2]

How can the average investor employ Warren Buffett's methods? According to Lynch, Buffett 'never invests in businesses he cannot understand or are outside his "circle of competence".' Says Lynch:

> All investors can, over time, obtain and intensify their 'circle of competence' in an industry where they are professionally involved or in some sector of business they enjoy researching. One does not have to be correct very many times in a lifetime as Warren states that twelve investment decisions in his 40-year career have made all the difference.[3]

Buffett went out of fashion temporarily when he decided not to invest in the new economy and dotcoms. Some commentators wrote him off as out of touch, the once great investor who did not 'get' the new economy. Buffett refused to accept the trendies' new metrics, epitomised by the use of acronyms like EBITDA, earnings before interest, tax, depreciation and amortisation. Such measurements were used to grossly inflate the share price of Vodafone, the British-based mobile phone company, which in 2000 soared on an EBITDA of £7.04 billion. The reality – its profit and loss – was a loss of £8.09 million. When reality set in, Vodafone's price collapsed. Buffett asked scornfully: 'Who do those who use EBITDA think pays for the capital expenditure that generates depreciation – the tooth fairy?' As Internet stocks crashed, Buffett had the last laugh. In his 2001 annual

---

[2] Robert G. Hagstrom, Jnr, *The Warren Buffett Way*, John Wiley and Sons, 1995.
[3] Ibid., Introduction by Peter Lynch.

letter to shareholders, he commented wryly that he had 'embraced the 21st century by entering such cutting edge industries as brick, carpet, insulation and paint. Try to control your excitement!'[4]

For many years Henry Kaufmann was one of the most influential voices in Wall Street. Armed with a doctorate in banking and finance, Kaufmann helped build up the research department of Salomon Brothers, the largest investment bank in America in the latter part of the last century. In the seventies and eighties his predictions on interest rates, inflation and other economic indicators were hugely prescient and widely followed. Paul Volcker, one of the more renowned chairmen of the Federal Reserve Board, praises Kaufmann for his 'depth of thinking'. An extract from Kaufmann's autobiography illustrates this quality:

> Financial markets are in many ways a microcosm of the people and societies they serve. Though measured in sterile figures, they embody and reflect much of the drama of the human condition: from the quest for comfort, security and wealth to the impulses to take risk and ensure the future and to compete and cooperate. The extremes of market movement reflect the extremes of human nature and human emotion: from optimism and elation to pessimism and despair. In the financial markets, as in life, rationality prevails most of the time.[5]

Investor Relations Managers

Companies themselves like to publish more information then ever before about their operations, and the rise of the specialist broking press has been such that the financial directors of large companies, and their public relations men, often spend more time wooing brokers' analysts than talking to financial journalists. Many companies employ an investor relations manager, whose job it is to keep both institutional investors and analysts informed of the more favourable aspects of the company. They now have their own body, the Investor Relations Society. Many of its members have lavish expense accounts, and jet in and out of two or more European capitals a day, expending great energy and charm on their subjects. Things can, however, go wrong. I remember the investor relations

---

[4] Berkshire Hathaway annual report, 2001.
[5] Henry Kaufmann, *On Money and Markets. A Wall Street Memoir*, McGraw Hill, 2000.

executive at Olivetti wringing his hands at an unfavourable broker's circular on his company written by a very presentable woman analyst, and crooning down the phone: 'How can you do this kind of thing to me?'

In recent years, increasing attention has been paid by the major European companies to soliciting investment in the United States, and those who have neglected this aspect of financial public relations have done so at their cost.

An example is provided by ICI, which maintains a full-time investor relations executive in New York to keep analysts at both institutions and broking firms up to date with the company's financial affairs. Some of the information is printed material, but another aspect of the job is to organise an annual road show to five American cities. There are also quarterly meetings allowing all major US analysts to meet the company's finance director and other top members of staff, and visits are arranged for those who wish to tour ICI's operations in Britain.

In recent years, the demands on company investor relations staff have grown considerably as institutions and analysts have sought greater insights and direct access to company managements, especially the finance director and the chief executive. The London Stock Exchange believes that these two executives should now expect to spend two months a year on investor relations, this time including telephone and face-to-face briefings with analysts, meetings and lunches with institutions and press contacts, post-results road shows, set pieces such as annual meetings, and hosting company visits by analysts and investors.

> Any company which does not provide it [access to senior management] will inevitably be seen as unresponsive and secretive, and will see its share rating suffer in the long-term. In essence the institutions usually own the business, and expect the management to reflect this by being available to report to them . . . as a company becomes more international, involving road-shows across Europe and even the United States, the appetite for European stocks is growing rapidly. The finance director will also get constant calls from a range of brokers, asking him or her to come and meet their institutional clients and those visiting from overseas. Unfortunately it is very hard to turn any of these down – the problem being that you have a business to run at the same time.[6]

---

[6] *A Practical Guide to Investor Relations*, London Stock Exchange. April 2000.

Investor relations is particularly crucial for smaller quoted companies. Why does it matter? 'The answer is simple,' says the LSE guide. 'There are 1,500 other smaller stocks out there all battling for attention. Compound that globally and there's enormous choice. You have simply got to get seen.'

Most companies use financial public relations firms and their corporate brokers to help them, but these people's services do not come cheap, with £200 an hour being a usual charge. Many financial public relations professionals are former financial journalists, and therefore can talk the language of both the finance director and the analyst. They also tend to be skilful at discussing the state of their clients' businesses without upsetting the regulators.

Two areas of investor relations call for considerable skill – correcting wrong price forecasts published by analysts, and handling company visits. The first needs a great deal of subtlety, because in advance of a company's results the person handling investor relations cannot give detailed figures for fear of breaching the FSA rules. He can break these rules even by a too precise correction. If things go bad and the company publishes a profit warning, there is a danger the stock price will collapse. If he talks up the stock, he will be in trouble also.

Visits by institutions are even more difficult, because if their representatives do not like what they find, they will sell your shares. There is nothing personal in this; the institution is under pressure to perform within quite short time periods and will be vigilant for any sign of weakness. So visits to a factory cannot just be left to an amiable plant manager buying a steak and kidney pudding for his guests at a local pub. Preparation by the company's finance director – and his presence at the visit – is a prerequisite, and it does not look good if the man from head office demonstrates that he has not been to the factory, and is not known by the local staff. The finance director will also have to do some homework into the institution. What does their portfolio consist of? Why did they buy into our company? Do they have cash to invest further? Is there a new fund manager, and if so where did he come from?

Investor relations people spend a large part of their time courting analysts. It has become customary for companies, particularly large companies, to make life as comfortable as possible for analysts, transporting them *en bloc* or individually to expensive country hotels, where it is possible for them to socialise with directors and senior management as well as to talk shop. A thorough briefing of analysts immediately after a company's results are published can be crucial in getting a good press, for increasingly newspapers are dependent on the views of analysts for comment. Expectations can be lowered if profits are going to be bad, and vice versa.

Financial public relations companies like to think that they are a cut above their counterparts in the West End who deal with products and services, and they probably are. Their senior people certainly exude more style, and maintain larger expense accounts. Their role is also much more important. There are legal obligations on companies who make financial changes to inform the press, and someone has to ensure that announcements are hand-delivered or sent electronically round the City at the right time, usually before market trading starts or in the late afternoon. There can be no question of sending out details of an acquisition, or a rights issue, on an embargoed basis.

But City PR advisers are no mere messenger boys. In many cases they are the eyes and ears of a company chairman, and occasionally his voice. Some company chairmen are gregarious and well-connected individuals, able both to project a positive image and to be sensitive to public opinion. The majority are not. A good PR person will be able to keep the chairman and directors informed of shareholders' opinion, what the newspapers are saying and, increasingly important, an assessment of political, Whitehall and Brussels opinion. If needed, he will be able to lobby politicians on the company's behalf. In major takeover activity, or in rights issues, the public relations man will also become a valuable aide to merchant bankers and stockbrokers.

Brokers' Circulars

These days almost all the share broking houses run their own publishing operations, providing material in print as well as on the web, though Internet users will, of course, be able to read it first. Still, brokers pride themselves on being able to get their publication out fast. On Budget day, for instance, some broking firms, as well as a few firms of accountants, will have their analysis of the Chancellor's measures in the hands of important clients long before the newspapers arrive.

Brokers' publications fall into two categories. There are regular weeklies or monthlies which contain a detailed review of the major

economies and their financial markets, and offer a number of recommendations. Their forecasts have a high reputation for accuracy,
usually better than the Treasury's. Amongst the regulars are Morgan
Stanley's and Merrill Lynch's monthly outlooks, which are always
good reading. There are regular specialist publications also, such as
Salomon Brothers' *Financial Futures*, and *Options Analysis*. Then
there are sector or subject reports, which look at either a company or
an industry in great detail, and come up with recommendations.

Financial Advisers

With such a wealth of information available, to whom do today's
investors turn for knowledge, and from whom can they obtain the
most reliable advice? It is an obvious question, and it is perhaps
the one that is most frequently asked by those with more than a
few pounds to invest. It is also one of the hardest questions to
answer.

One quite correct answer is no one. In the end the investor,
whether the chief investment manager of a large insurance company
or a widow in Worthing, has to make the decision as to which is the
best vehicle for improving the value of their savings. It is possible,
even for those who do not consider themselves financially literate,
to have cheap access to a great deal of information, and even that
is sometimes of less use than a hunch or an everyday observation.
For instance, anyone who has watched the development of Britain's
high streets over the past ten years will have noted the rise of Tesco.
You may not make a quick profit on Tesco shares, but they will
grow.

But this is to avoid the real question. To whom can one turn? A
bank manager, stockbroker, accountant, building society manager,
perhaps. All have their place and purpose, but none of them is
necessarily a good investment adviser. Today's bank managers prefer
to lend money than to give investment advice, steering customers in
the direction of in-house unit trusts, which have not been the best
performers. Accountants are useful tax advisers, and usually save you
the cost of their fee, but when one seeks investment advice from
them, they can start talking about complicated accountant-run
pension schemes for the self-employed, and property trusts. Building
society managers live or die by the balances on deposit in their
branches, so it is not easy to accept their views as impartial. This

leaves stockbrokers, who can be either good or bad advisers, but mostly are a mixture of both.

Regrettably, very few large stockbrokers seem to want to service individual investors, and an increasing number of firms will not deal with them at all, unless the clients are very rich. This short-sighted approach is in contrast to the interest shown in small investors in the US, where share shops are common. But it is typical of the patronising attitude of many in the City towards the average member of the British public.

It may well be that Britain will follow the example of the United States. There, sharebrokers take their business to the public, and in almost every prosperous suburb there will be one or more open-plan broking offices, laid out rather like a large travel or estate agent, where members of the public may call, enjoy a cup of coffee, and discuss their investments with a consultant. There is plenty of literature available, including both brochures and financial magazines; Wall Street prices run continuously on television monitors, and there is a friendly and unpressurised atmosphere.

It is a pity that one of the few equivalent places in Britain's high streets appears to be the betting shop. The emergence of independent financial advisers should have led to the development of money shops, but not very many exist. For the most part the advisers stick to insurance broking, leaving share dealing to the banks and big securities houses.

14 Getting Too Much: the Information Overload

It is not long since private investors rightly complained that they were starved of adequate and timely information. Even with a subscription to the *Financial Times* or other periodicals they simply could not get enough of it. They were at a substantial disadvantage to professional and institutional investors with information at their fingertips. These days an average investor on a limited budget can access the same information as that available to the professionals. The problem is there is so much of it that it is easy to become overwhelmed and confused by information overload.

There is only one way to cope with too much information, and that is to be selective, searching for quality and taking the time to assimilate only media content that adds value to the investor's decision making process. In my view that means looking for analysis and comment that has an intelligent perspective, a good example being the daily Lex column of the *Financial Times*, or the acid comments by Neil Collins, the City Editor of the *Daily Telegraph*. There are other worthwhile columns in the press, but there is a lot of chaff, even in the *FT*, that has little import for investors.

A primary requirement is fast and easy access to prices, preferably in real time. These need to be set in a historical perspective. Good charts are important, as is perceptive analysis by a credible observer. Achieving this means accessing all forms of media.

Everybody has a personal preference. When I am in Britain during the working day I prefer to have Bloomberg Television quietly in the background, supplemented by ready online Internet access to web sites like ftmarketwatch.com and advfn.com. I read the *Financial Times* and one of the other broadsheets. At weekends I like *The Economist*, *Sunday Business* and *Shares* magazine. I do not bother much with mainstream television's news, believing its coverage of business to be flimsy and superficial, despite recent expansion in this sector. This is a personal preference. Each investor should experiment to find the media that suits his or her portfolio.

Television

Most people in Britain, including those at the top of the pile, use television as their primary source of news. But there are only two channels that provide active and full-time coverage of business and finance, Bloomberg Television, and CNBC, an acronym which stands for Consumer News and Business Channel. Both are American-owned. Bloomberg's founder and owner is an extraordinary entrepreneur, Michael Bloomberg, whose main business is the Bloomberg terminal for professionals. CNBC, part of the American network NBC, is owned by General Electric. Both have substantial operations in Britain, and can be seen on cable or satellite for a basic subscription of about £10 per month. CNBC is perhaps slicker and more telegenic than Bloomberg, but has much more American content than its rival. After the European lunch hour it switches its attention to Wall Street. Since the Dow Jones Company, publishers of the *Wall Street Journal*, are shareholders in CNBC, it has the benefit of access to the *Journal*'s senior editorial staff, though it makes surprisingly little use of this substantial competitive advantage.

Bloomberg's London-based channel has a much stronger focus on the United Kingdom. While it will carry frequent live reports from the New York Stock Exchange and NASDAQ, it never forgets that its viewers are British investors. It has separate channels for France, Spain and Italy. The strong team of presenters impress with their knowledge of the markets, and handle breaking financial news with competence and flair. Bloomberg also has split screens, which is an advantage. Just under two thirds of the surface is dedicated to the actual television output, mostly live financial news and comment. To the right of the screen is a panel containing the time, and the actual state of three or four share market indices. This panel is rotated every five seconds and includes both the value and the percentage change for the FTSE 100, the FTSE 250, the All Share Index, the FT Futures, the techMark, the DAX from Germany, the CAC-40, the Dow Jones Industrial Average, the NASDAQ, NASDAQ Futures and a variety of currency cross rates.

Thus in a couple of minutes a viewer can get a complete global take on how things stand. Below this and across the screen is the first of two tickers, which contains a scrolling list of real-time share prices for the major markets mentioned earlier. Beneath is a second ticker line of less prominent indices. The final strip, across the foot, scrolls breaking financial, company and sporting news. Many television professionals do not like the display, and there are some who find it confusing. However, there is no other broadcaster as effective as Bloomberg in providing current and pertinent information.

Other cable and satellite broadcasters that cover business with a number of daily programmes include BBC World, BBC News 24, CNN, and Sky News, but their output will not satisfy those who want to be able to access information in real time whenever they want it. Terrestrial or mainstream broadcasters in Britain provide little of interest to investors. What business coverage they do provide is aimed at the general public. After all, that is their remit.

The Internet

The Internet has to be the best primary source of information for those who wish to follow the markets: in fact, for many it will suffice as the only source. The web has the advantage of being available twenty-four hours a day, seven days a week, and most of its content is free, though there are some sites that charge and are worth the subscription. The issue for investors is which sites to pick on grounds of reliability and objectivity.

Again, each and every user will develop a personal preference, and these preferences will depend on whether you are a day trader, frequent trader, occasional investor, or just an interested observer. There are several types of site to be considered:

- pure news providers
- those that contain market prices, breaking news and other hard information as well as providing access to a number of investment tools to help you manage a portfolio. These sometimes call themselves portals, implying that they provide a gateway to other relevant sites
- those that are built out from print publications, where much, if not all, of the content is culled from the newspaper or magazine
- those provided by companies, with a special section for their stockholders
- web sites of official or regulatory bodies such as the London Stock Exchange, the Financial Services Authority, and NASDAQ

Pure news providers

There are only a few of these, and they display an understandable reluctance to provide more than a small amount of their output free of charge to non-paying customers. The exceptions are AFX News and Bloomberg News, whose output is bought and recycled by many web portals, and whose web sites are an excellent source of breaking news, AFX is a wholly-owned subsidiary of the state-owned French news agency Agence France Presse, but is based in London. Its site, afxpress.com calls itself 'tomorrow's newspaper today', and conveniently groups stories in sectors to make access to specialist subjects easy. However, it does not have the analytical content of a newspaper, and is very much a basic service. Bloomberg.co.uk has greater depth, more analysis, access to share prices, delayed by fifteen minutes, and the opportunity to look at clips of interviews in video and audio. For those who prefer a more worldly view of global business and are happy to accept only limited coverage of companies and markets, then reuters.com is also worth a look.

Business portals

These will be the most useful web sites for investors and others interested in the stock markets. The dotcom boom and subsequent crash saw many new ventures started and quickly fold. One of the most high-profile was thestreet.co.uk, the British version of the American site of the same name. Though quite competent and useful, its backers, which included Rupert Murdoch's News Corporation, decided to pull the plug on it before it became established.

Three good sites which have survived, at least up to the time of writing, are advfn.com, stockhouse.co.uk and ftmarketwatch.com. ADVFN stands for Advanced Financial Network, and it provides a superb service, with real-time prices, detailed charting, a chronological record of company statements, and a bulletin board about each listed share. It also provides all the detailed fundamentals, such as earnings per share and net asset value per share. A recent development has been the introduction of 3D graphics so that instead of looking at a set of numbers, you can watch any change in market numbers impact other indicators. The chairman says:

> A good way of trying to describe it without showing it to someone is if you can imagine a flight simulator where you have got a mountain range and each mountain is a company and you completely find what the data is you are looking at there, so the height of the mountain could be the market cap of the company.

That could be connected say to a live share price, so the mountain will be going up and down as the share price goes up and down. You can trigger it off, so that it flashes red if there is any news that applies to that company or there is a lot of volume traded in that company at any one time. You can fly around this in 3D and fit thousands and thousands of companies on one screen and see instantly what is going on. Suddenly something flashes or pops up, what the hell's going on there. Click on that mountain or the company and up will come all the full fundamental information of that company and the historic price, share price and of course the live share price.[1]

ADVFN advertises itself as the first company to bring affordable professional-level data to the mass market, and it does just that, putting to shame many of the larger and longer-established financial information companies, most of which do not even offer real-time prices.

However, it does not provide any analysis or comment, and for that, ftmarketwatch.com is superb. For many years the *Financial Times* struggled with its own web site, spending millions of pounds on its development with little obvious improvement. Then the *FT*'s parent, Pearson, decided to import to Britain the concept of the American financial portal, cbsmarketwatch.com, owned by the CBS television network. It set up a joint venture with CBS and named it ftmarketwatch.com. The move was inspired, because not only did the new venture do well, but it also resulted in a radical shake-up and improvement in the *Financial Times*' own site, ft.com. The only problem is that the site is so popular that sometimes connectivity is difficult or even impossible.

Ftmarketwatch has its own journalists, and tends to look ahead rather than studying the past. It has news alerts, company reports and sector guides. It is available in English and German, and is unashamedly directed at the investor. Its structure is a masterpiece of Internet design: for example, you can read the news categorised as most recent, by sector, by mergers and acquisitions, and by other classification. Each news story contains the company's stock market code, so that investors can trade immediately without having to waste time looking it up. Another button, 'market pulse', takes you to exactly that – detailed reports on the state of the major stock markets. There is another section for official announcements made

---

[1] Michael Hodges, chairman of advfn.com plc.

by companies to the major stock exchanges. On ftmarketwatch you can build your own portfolio in a user-friendly way, and get its current value at any time. It is possible to subscribe to a number of additional services, including one which examines in detail all small companies listed in AIM.

Stockhouse.co.uk has been in business since the early days of the Internet, and also enjoys a strong following, having many of the qualities of both the previously mentioned sites. It too allows you to build and update your own portfolio, and you can receive news via e-mail with portfolio alerts. It has particularly good access to more than 600 media sources.

Another site worth a regular visit more for its commentaries than for facts and charting tools is that of The Motley Fool, an organisation that has strong anti-establishment credentials, and regularly expresses profound scepticism about the marketing antics of the big players (www.fool.co.uk). While not as thorough as its United States parent, it contains many common-sense comments, such as this example two weeks after the 11 September 2001 disaster, when the perceived wisdom was to slash the value of insurance shares:

> In the current market then, as you might expect, one of the hardest-hit sectors is insurance companies. Clearly with such a major disaster there will be some gigantic payouts to be made yet the effect of this is not shared out equally amongst the companies. But the knee-jerk reaction of the markets is to cream them all at first, creating potential opportunity. There may well be companies out there that have virtually no exposure at all, hit by indiscriminate dumping of anything smelling remotely of insurance. This is where deep crisis players must look. Similarly those that have some exposure may still be oversold.
>
> Insurers are an obvious hunting ground, but look at banks that have fallen. This makes no sense at all and is a good example of a potential crisis situation. Why would Lloyds as one example be a poorer-quality share the day after all this than before? I cannot see any reason. If anything, banks may profit from the presumably enormous rebuilding programme that will be commenced by the ever-resourceful Americans who, as I know them, will not permit this tragedy to alter their way of life.[2]

Acts of terrorism such as the attacks on the World Trade Center and the Pentagon depressed all shares, and those companies in crisis

---

[2] www.fool.co.uk, 22 September 2001.

before the event are likely to remain in crisis for some time. But good companies with solid businesses might be expected to benefit substantially in the medium term. The Motley Fool's logic made a refreshing contrast to some of the more apocalyptic comments to be found elsewhere.

Within these web sites and many others are bulletin boards where investors can participate by exchanging tips and opinions about the stock markets. These sites have a wide following, although any tip offered on a bulletin board needs to be treated with caution. Some tips are genuine; others are ill-concealed attempts to ramp the price of a share. There have been instances when one person has sent a bulletin board several thousand e-mails on the same stock within a year. A harder scam to detect is when someone tries to ramp a stock using multiple identities, either concurrently or in a planned sequence. Another more subtle scam is to respond to any negative remarks about a share you favour with an upbeat comment. Most bulletin boards have technology in place to try and identify those perpetrating scams. Sally Yates of Stockhouse claims scams are rare.[3] I am not so sure.

Bulletin boards are fun to use, especially when enough people take part to make a session a genuine exchange of views, as on the recent decline of British Telecom. But no one should expect comments on share values to be any more reliable than those of soccer supporters' clubs on their teams' prospects. Even so, research seems to indicate that bulletin boards have a big following.[4]

Company web sites

Don't look to a company site to give you news about that company first. All price-sensitive announcements have to be made available to the market before being published on the Internet. That said, many company web sites are rich in information about their businesses and products, and a great deal of research time can be saved by making use of them. Investors seem to agree, for almost a third say they use these sites to obtain company information.[5]

The best sites will always have the most recent annual report, company announcements and press notices, and speeches made by the chief executive, downloadable in pdf format. Pdf files can be

---

[3] *Investors Chronicle*, 30 March 2001.

[4] A. C. Nielsen, *Investors Chronicle*, 30 March 2001.

[5] Survey for the London Stock Exchange by MORI, July 2000.

opened by a piece of software called Acrobat, available free from the web site of its maker, Adobe, or for a few pounds from any computer store. The information can then be printed out.

Some sites have special sections for investors, and include news stories that have appeared in the financial press about the company. Event calendars are often published showing dates for interim and annual dividend announcements, industry conferences and trade shows. Others go even further by providing transcripts of briefings to analysts. Pearson has a particularly good web site for investors, and includes video and audio of long briefings for analysts given by its chief executive, Marjorie Scardino, and finance director, John Makinson.

Voted best web site for the private investor amongst FTSE 100 companies in 2000 was that of the control systems firm Invensys (invensys.com). It has a very detailed statistics system, and a timely interview with the chief executive, downloadable in both video and audio. What I liked about it was that it looked forward rather than back, for example with an interesting preview of a conference in London on Building for the Twenty-First Century. Shareholders could quickly see that computer systems such as those developed by Invensys have much to contribute to the construction industry, and might be expected to benefit from new schemes.

Other notable corporate sites are those of Barclays, BP-Amoco, British Airways, Logica, Sainsbury's, and Tesco. Most of these are third- or fourth-generation sites, rebuilt and redesigned after earlier efforts failed. Unfortunately, many companies have sites that are, by comparison, still primitive.

Many United States companies encourage questions from investors by e-mail, and hold timed briefings at which people may post their questions over the web and have them answered by a general forum. Further developments down the line are likely to be web-casting of annual and special company meetings, with proxy voting available on a corporate web site. This will create a much more level playing field for stock holders who may live far away from a company's home base. Also, information that might once have been restricted to investors in one country is now available to all.

The Financial Press

Newspapers and magazines are for perspective, comment and analysis rather than hard news, although if you are not interested in trading shares more frequently than once or twice a week, a selection of reading matter will provide much of what you need.

Amongst the dailies, the *Financial Times* is the newspaper the professionals read, and is the only one that provides a complete range of share prices, and detailed company news. It also has breadth in that it covers the major international companies as well as overseas economies and emerging markets. Alas, the *FT*, good as it is, is not without some weak points. Apart from the excellent Lex column, which has three or four short comments each morning, it is surprisingly thin on analysis, and does not have the kind of probing investigative commentaries one might expect from such a reputable publication. These essentials for investors can often be found in magazines like *Fortune*, and in some other international financial dailies, such as the *Wall Street Journal* in the United States and the *Australian Financial Review*. The *Wall Street Journal* has a European edition, *Wall Street Journal Europe*, but unfortunately it is a poor relation of its illustrious American parent.

Among the broadsheet dailies in Britain, *The Guardian*. *The Independent*, *The Times* and the *Daily Telegraph* all have solid business sections, although, as might be expected, their focus is mostly British. Under its present city editor, the *Daily Telegraph* has a biting and acerbic comment column, which is widely read. *The Times*, which once had a widely followed separate business section, now puts finance and business at the back of the main newspaper, behind the obituaries. It too has lively commentary, but seems to have cut back on interesting features, once the strength of the paper's business section. However, *The Times* is not afraid to introduce business into the main leader pages of the paper.

The broadsheet Sunday papers also have separate business and personal finance or money sections, but serious investors will want to buy the pink'un, *The Business*, which now has a separate *Sunday Investor* section. The other broadsheets are readable, but they lack the authority they once enjoyed when financial journalists like John Davis, Ivan Fallon, Robert Heller and Jeff Randall were regular contributors.

Magazines are a mixed bunch. A relatively new entrant, *Shares*, has the liveliest coverage, ahead of the racy headlines but staid though dependable reporting of the *Investors Chronicle*. *Shares* manages to be upbeat even when markets are depressed, constantly seeking out and recommending opportunities for its readers. The *Investors Chronicle* is thorough and not above controversy, particularly in its features. One I recall, headed 'Britain's Super Bosses', listed the merits of a group of men and woman who had, it claimed, 'turned round the fortunes of their flagging ships with spectacular results'. At least half of those mentioned had, in fact, done nothing of the kind, but then it is easy to be wise after the event. With any publication and its tips and advice, it is important for both the fledgling and the serious investor to do their own Internet research. A subscription to the *Investors Chronicle* or *Shares* can be useful, for it gives you the right to trawl the online archives of the print products, as indeed does *The Economist*.

15   Policing the Markets

*The financial planning industry is in many ways still in the days
of the Wild West. The marshal hasn't ridden into town, there's
mayhem in the streets, a lot of random shooting.*
  Scott Stapf, of the North American Securities Administrators'
Association

*Unless investigators can uncover a tape recording with
irrefutable evidence that Box told Cox to 'fill your boots', they
are banging their heads against a well-fortified wall of self-
interest which inevitably protects those who have made a
fortune by being ahead of the game.*
  Editorial in *The Business*

*As past and present cases show, consumers are often the first
victims of market failures or financial instability. We have only
to look at the fall-out from the bursting of last year's Internet
stocks bubble.*
  Howard Davies, chairman of the Financial Services Authority

At four o'clock in the morning of 23 October 1812, three men called
at the Popincourt Barracks in Paris with the devastating news that the
Emperor Napoleon had died beneath the walls of Moscow. It was a
plausible story – news from the campaign front took three weeks to
get back, and the French armies had just achieved a great victory at
the Battle of Borodino that had opened the gates to the Russian
capital. The men also said that the Senate had abolished the Empire
and appointed a provisional government, and was calling on the 10th
Cohort of the National Guard for support. Within hours, a huge
conspiracy against Napoleon was under way, and the Emperor's
leading supporters were thrown into prison.
  This story, described by Italian author Guido Artom, in his book
Napoleon is Dead in Russia, was the inspiration for one of Britain's
most notorious examples of share-market rigging. In the early
nineteenth century, only major news moved the fledgling stock

market, and it took headlines like 'Napoleon Set to Invade' or, better still, 'Napoleon Dead' to cause a shock.

Since, even in the days before the telegraph, old news was no news, stockbrokers often placed faithful retainers in the port of Dover to listen to the rumour mill, watch the sea, talk to fishermen and report back regularly. So when, on 21 February 1814, Colonel de Burgh, alias Charles Random de Bérenger, turned up in Dover in a red uniform, claiming to be aide-de-camp to General Lord Cathcart, and reporting the death of Napoleon and the fall of Paris, the news reached London at the speed of a pony and trap. Although foreign reporting was severely limited in those days, along with share ownership, there were those in London who had heard of the earlier, unsuccessful conspiracy against Napoleon, and the subsequent execution not only of the plotters, but also of the soldiers who unwittingly carried the message. They were therefore very much on their guard against such stories. But Colonel de Burgh had an elaborate cover story, a detailed account of how Napoleon had been butchered by the Cossacks. He had also made a point of going directly to the headquarters of the Port Admiral in Dover to apprise him of the facts. Surely, said brokers, it must be true.

Prices on the Stock Exchange shot up, as the wealthy clients of brokers received the news, apparently confirmed by handbills distributed in the streets of London. They were not to know that these had also been handed out by de Bérenger who had himself taken a coach to the capital to collect his gains, estimated at about £10,000. It was, of course, all pure fiction, but note that those who lost out had been contacted by brokers, who were themselves often privileged possessors of inside information.

Not much changed in the following 175 years. Until recently it was those 'in the know' who stood to make rich pickings from speculative trading on the Stock Exchange. Latter-day frauds on similar lines to that perpetrated by de Bérenger were common in the early 1970s, during the so-called Australian mining boom. Reports of a nickel strike by an obscure, barely known and usually recently listed mining company would reach Sydney as a result of a tip from Kalgoorlie, a remote dusty gold town in Western Australia. Confirmation was impossible, but the word flashed round, and the price of the stock shot up. I once worked on a magazine where the financial editor would return from lunch, very excited, and shout something like 'Bosom's Creek has struck nickel' before rushing to the phone to buy shares. Some brokers made a point of reserving shares for journalists, who could be counted upon to write favourably about a mining prospect which, more often than not, when the geologists' report arrived, turned out to be nothing more than a hole in the ground or a stick marking a spot in the desert. Fortunes were made and lost.

Much of the activity was 12,000 miles from the geologists' trowels. Each day, as soon as the London Stock Exchange opened there was feverish activity as investors sought to cash in. Many had their fingers badly burned, and the two-year 'boom' earned Australian brokers a bad reputation which took years to live down. As one merchant banker who frequently visits Sydney put it: 'The Aussies saw it as a way of getting their own back on the Poms.'

Ramping stocks was not confined to those on the fringe of share markets. Writing in the *Observer* on 5 September 1971, under the headline 'Digging up the Dirt', I reported how an Australian Senate Committee investigation into the series of mining collapses and false claims in that country had severely shaken investors' confidence.

One thoroughly dishonest practice disclosed to the Committee was the purchase of huge blocks of shares in early trading by certain brokers, using their house accounts. By lunchtime, word would be round the markets that a particular share was on the move, and the broking house would unload its newly acquired holding at a substantial profit. Those shares that remained unsold would be allocated to clients for whom the firm held discretionary accounts, at a substantially higher price than the firm had paid for them, thereby enabling it to make a profit at its clients' expense. To add insult to injury, the clients would be charged brokerage, but usually would be none the wiser, for they would see from the *Australian Financial Review* that they had apparently obtained the shares at the 'market price'.

The Committee's report makes interesting reading, even years after the inquiry. It scrutinised in detail the accounts of one stock-broking firm that had gone into liquidation, only to find that about 80 per cent of the firm's trading was on its own account, and that its income from commission amounted to only a minor proportion of turnover.

Another prominent Sydney stockbroker, who was also a director of two major mining companies, was exposed for trying to have one of the companies taken over by a joint venture operation, in which his stockbroking firm's affiliated investment house had a stake. Evidence to the Senate Committee revealed that the stockbroker had planned the takeover without informing the company chairman or his fellow directors, and that an associate company of his firm was to act as the underwriters.

Let us move back to London, and to Thursday 13 June 1985. It was a typical summer Thursday on the Stock Exchange. Trading was languid, as is so often the case at this time of the year. Then came a sudden burst of activity, much to the curiosity of a party from a Norfolk Women's Institute that was visiting the public gallery that day. Someone was buying large blocks of shares in Arthur Bell and Sons plc, and their price rose by 14 per cent.

The visitors had to wait until reading their Saturday edition of the *Eastern Daily Press* to find out why. Guinness plc had made a bid for Bell on Friday the 14th, and on the eve of that takeover offer, someone had got wind of what was going on, and had been buying Bell's shares furiously in the hope of a quick profit. Yet insider trading is strictly forbidden both by the law, which since 1980 has made it a criminal offence, and by the rules of the Stock Exchange. Despite that, as a practice, it is still widespread.

According to the magazine *Acquisitions Monthly*, the share prices of takeover targets rise on average between 20 and 30 per cent in the month before a bid. Over 90 per cent of prices move before a bid. One reason for this may well be that astute investors have spotted, from their own research, likely targets for takeover. Passing insider information is more likely.

To combat this, the Stock Exchange maintains a special squad of men and women at its Throgmorton Street offices to try to track down insider traders. This means questioning those suspected of using inside knowledge to make money, and putting the evidence before the Exchange's Disciplinary Committee.

New and powerful computers allow the squad to spot erratic price movements in London and on other major international markets, and they have the authority to question anyone who works for a member of the Stock Exchange, which, of course, includes a large number of international banks and other financial conglomerates. Their computers have instant access to all Stock Exchange transactions over the previous six months, and they may manipulate the database by asking over a hundred questions.

But just like detectives from the regular police forces, they rely more on hot tips from informants than on the craftsmanship of a Sherlock Holmes. The number of tips runs at about ten a week. Many of them come from market makers spotting something suspicious. Since market makers can lose thousands of pounds by incorrect pricing, they are very aware of phoney figures.

The Stock Exchange also has the backing of compliance officers employed in securities houses. These men and women make sure that both the Stock Exchange rules and their own house rules on share trading are strictly observed, and if they spot an irregularity in a transaction involving another firm, they usually report it to their opposite number.

Some companies are stricter than others in observing the code of conduct staff must obey when buying and selling stock on their own account. Chase Securities insists that all deals are placed through the company, and that compliance staff are notified. At most securities houses the phone transactions of all dealing staff are logged, so that investigators can, if they wish, find out who telephoned whom and when. Some firms have taken this a stage further and record the telephone calls of all staff.

A mixture of recorded conversations and the alertness of the London Stock Exchange's surveillance unit has already been responsible for trapping several insider traders. Just before the Mecca group bid for Pleasurama, the casinos and restaurant company, the members of the unit spotted that there had been an increasing amount of trading in Pleasurama. Their suspicions were further aroused when they received calls from market makers in some leading broking firms drawing their attention to the fact that something irregular must be going on. Compliance officers at several houses were phoned, and after a tape at Morgan Grenfell had been played, it was discovered that a tip had been passed on by a female member of Samuel Montagu's corporate finance team. This was the department involved in advising Mecca on its offer. The other banks then listened to their own tape recordings, and the woman plus two others who had used the information were unceremoniously sacked. The three had stood to make a useful sum of money from trading on inside information. That they were caught owes much to their own greed and the vigilance of the surveillance squad. If they had been more cautious and less avaricious, their dealings might well have passed unnoticed.

Even so, many insider traders escape detection. One particular problem is the use of nominee companies in offshore tax havens as the trading vehicle. The Stock Exchange team of former policemen, computer consultants, stockbrokers and accountants say they often follow good leads only to come up against obstacles when a block of shares is purchased by a nominee company. 'We can see no way at the moment of busting offshore companies without international cooperation,' I was told. 'All the old names are always there – the Cayman Islands and so on. But it is not only in the Caribbean or in Liberia that this problem exists – much closer to home, in the Channel Islands or the Isle of Man, we have just no hope of getting behind the nominee thing.'

At the time of writing, it is fifteen years since the notorious Guinness scandal, but insider trading is still rife and largely undetected, even in very major takeover bids involving corporations of the highest reputation. Ahead of an announcement in September 1999 by the NatWest banking group that it intended to bid for the Legal and General insurance group, the latter's price shot up by 10 per cent in value as 41 million shares changed hands in a single day. The Stock Exchange announced the inevitable inquiry, and there were rebukes to the adviser banks, Schroders and J.P. Morgan, but as *The Business* said, there did not 'seem a hope in hell of tracking down the culprits: by mid-afternoon on Thursday even the shoe-shine boy on Liverpool Street station knew that L and G was a takeover target'. The newspaper commented:

> That extraordinary affair, which resulted in jailings and a swath of new rules and regulations, was supposed to have marked a turning point in stock market ethics. But for all the huffing and puffing of high-minded governments and handsomely rewarded City regulators, the age-old practice of trading on 'well sourced' information is as prevalent today as it was in the go go 1980s.

The Securities and Exchange Commission

Policing the markets has traditionally been conducted in two ways: through self-regulation by quasi-official bodies set up by stock exchanges in consultation with governments, and by official agencies staffed by professionals. More recently the professionals have taken over as governments have concluded that regulatory systems need to be run by full-timers with no vested interest in any company within the securities industry.

The most feared and respected of these agencies – and the most important given the size of the American market – is the United States Securities and Exchange Commission (SEC), which protects the interests of America's estimated 50 million investors. Although its authority is technically limited to policing the securities industry in the United States, its tentacles are spread much wider, extending, for example, to the conduct of American investment institutions in their operations outside the country.

The SEC, with a staff of 1,800, was established in July 1935, some six years after the Wall Street Crash of 1929. A Congressional investigation found that there had been stock manipulation on a huge scale, blatant dishonesty, and insider trading, and the SEC was established with sweeping powers over the securities industry.

Now all corporations have to file quarterly financial returns, and much more detailed annual ones, with the SEC, as well as informing it promptly of any facts or important events which might affect the market for the company's stock. Federal laws require companies intending to raise money by selling their own securities to file with the Commission true facts about their operations. The Commission has power to prevent or punish fraud in the sale of securities, and is authorised to regulate stock exchanges. The law under which it operates lays down precise boundaries within which directors, officers and large shareholders may deal in the stock of their companies.

In its time, the SEC has notched up some notable successes in prosecuting corporate crime. In August 1968, it filed charges of securities fraud against fourteen Merrill Lynch officers and employees. In the end Merrill Lynch publicly consented to an SEC finding that it had used advance inside information from the Douglas Aircraft Company for the advantage of preferred institutional clients, defrauding the investing public of an estimated $4.5 million in the process – no mean sum at the time.

The Securities and Exchange Commission is a mecca for bright young lawyers who wish to make their name as determined investigators, and then, as often as not, get out into lucrative private practice with the SEC name on their credentials.

However, while the SEC has a reputation as a vigorous force, and has claimed many scalps, it is severely constrained in its activities by a shortage of funds. Although it collects fees from registered investment advisers, it has to hand over a large share of the proceeds to the United States Treasury. It has only about 300 enforcement officers to cover the whole of the United States, and the section which deals with the investment management and mutual funds industry has an inspectorate of only about 60 people.

Although this latter group undertakes about 1,500 spot checks each year on investment advisers, it is not surprising that many confidence tricksters escape unscathed. Officially there are about 17,000 registered investment advisers in the United States, so on average each gets a spot check once a decade, during which time many will have sold their businesses on. But these figures include only the registered advisers. The Consumer Federation of America (CFA) believes that there could be about half a million people acting as unofficial financial advisers, while even the Securities Administrators Association accepts that there are 250,000. Many of these not only claim to offer investment advice; some of them actually manage clients' money.

The SEC also depends greatly on a number of self-regulatory bodies to fulfil its task. For the most part stock exchanges police the activities of their members, and each has an investigations branch. The New York Stock Exchange, the American Stock Exchange and the National Association of Securities Dealers (NASDAQ) all work in close cooperation with the SEC.

The SEC has much wider powers than Britain's Department of Trade, and has much more inclination to utilise them. The DTI so far has been reluctant to utilise its power to force open bank accounts and to demand documents, though this may change. But the SEC may subpoena individuals and companies in the US, and demand sight of their bank accounts. Outside America it has agreements with the British, Japanese, Swiss, Cayman Islands and other governments to gather information, and it can also call for sanctions to be imposed on the US branches of uncooperative foreign banks. Not only may offenders be prosecuted, with penalties as high as three times the illicit profits, but the SEC will turn over all the evidence it has gained to civil litigants who have been disadvantaged as a result of someone's insider trading. As the *Financial Times* pointed out, the SEC's achievements highlighted 'the passivity of the DTI'.

Even these powers are inadequate when one considers the definition of the modus operandi of an insider trader provided by the *Financial Times*:

> The would-be insider trader gets a job with the corporate finance department of a merchant bank active in mergers and acquisitions. Always travelling via a third country, he visits two tax havens, Panama and Liechtenstein, which have resisted foreign pressure on their secrecy laws. In each country he sets up a trading company, and opens bank accounts in two or three

banks in their names. He only uses banks with no operations or assets in Britain or the United States. He never tells the banks his real name, but arranges for them to deal through a large London broking firm whenever they receive coded instructions over the telephone.

When he picks up inside information, he always trades alone using a call box. He never trades in large amounts, but may break up a transaction into a series of deals from different accounts. He avoids the mistake of trading just before a bid announcement – it makes the market makers vengeful.

Curiously, though, it was the SEC's biggest coup, catching Ivan Boesky, the self-styled 'king of the arbs', that provided the DTI with some of their best leads into City fraud this side of the Atlantic.

Arbs, or arbitrageurs, are people who buy stocks short-term when pricing is in transition, in the hope of making a great deal of money as they move up. They come to the fore in a takeover: after a bid has been made, arbs buy as many shares as possible in anticipation of a higher bid. When the higher bid comes, they sell. Arbs also work in between markets, for example when a company's stock is quoted on both the Australian and British exchanges. If the price moves up in Australia they buy the stock in London hoping the price will rise there also.

Boesky was brought to book after the Securities and Exchange Commission netted Dennis Levine, a senior executive of a famous Wall Street broking firm, Drexel Burnham Lambert, for insider trading. During an extensive investigation and interrogation of Levine, their quarry engaged in some judicious plea bargaining, providing a large amount of information to the regulators. The upshot was that Levine pleaded guilty, paid back $12.6 million in illegal profits, and implicated Boesky. Like Levine, Boesky also 'co-operated' with the prosecutors, but he was fined $100 million, barred for life from working on Wall Street, and ordered to dismantle his $2 billion firm.

Boesky was one of the biggest and best-known speculators in the feverish takeover business in America, using a phenomenal network of contacts to make huge profits through arbitraging. Like Levine, he also 'cooperated with the authorities', which is a euphemism for becoming a supergrass in order to keep out of jail.

The Financial Services Authority

For years, the game of cricket was played in England by amateurs, and control of the financial services industry was conducted in the same manner. There were a large number of self-regulatory organisations with strange acronyms and even more incomprehensible rulebooks. Essentially it amounted to the prefects controlling the boys with a somewhat light touch. However, as more and more scandals burst upon the City, and as it became clear that the old Stock Exchange motto of 'My Word is My Bond' was not a mantra that had a universal following, the politicians took over and passed laws to create a monolith, the Financial Services Authority (FSA). The FSA established itself comfortably in a podgy tower under the shadow of Canary Wharf well before most of its powers became operational, and it is becoming increasingly clear that rooting out scandals and slapping miscreants on the wrist is only a minor part of its operations. So wide has it spread its tentacles over the entire operations of the investment and personal finance industry, so all-embracing are its functions, that Britain, once the least regulated of the major world economies, has become about the most smothered.

The process that led to the final creation of the FSA was a classic one – first an official inquiry, then recommendations for the establishment of a variant of the American SEC, a rejection of this in favour of a highly complex voluntary system, followed by a more onerous regime than anyone originally thought necessary. Meanwhile the original concerns that consumers were being sold products and services either that they did not want or which were unsuited to their financial needs, and that City insiders were making unreasonable profits from their inside information – remain to this day. The story of the arrival of what some City professionals acidly refer to as the 'thought police' at Canary Wharf is worth telling briefly.

Earlier editions of this book gave a detailed account of the work of the official inquiry under Professor Jim Gower, which did an extremely thorough job. However, the Conservatives, led by Margaret Thatcher, while accepting that putting trust in a handshake was not enough to stop people being cheated, were ideologically opposed to the establishment of a new professional regulator.

Thatcher and her Chancellor, Nigel Lawson, a former financial journalist, wanted the City to police itself – and, in spite of Professor Gower's misgivings, believed it could. But Whitehall decided an umbrella organisation was needed to oversee this self-policing, so the Securities and Investment Board was created, staffed by professionals and headed by a former civil servant, Sir Kenneth Berrill. The SIB sat on top of a plethora of self-regulatory bodies – one of which was the Stock Exchange – and tried to make sure they drew up rulebooks and made their members stick to them.

The result was an amorphous set of overlapping bodies each with sets of regulations that were so complex that even the regulators were thoroughly confused. Many of the self-regulatory bodies had names based on hideous acronyms, such as LAUTRO (Life Assurance and Unit Trust Regulatory Organisation), IMRO (Investment Management Regulatory Organisation), and FIMBRA (Financial Intermediaries, Managers and Brokers Regulatory Association). The Securities Association was created to take over the regulatory role of the Stock Exchange.

The Securities and Investment Board and these other bodies had to follow a number of guidelines laid down by the Financial Services Act. For example, approved investment businesses had to be 'competent, financially sound and to offer best advice' after 'getting to know' the customer.

Berrill could have chosen to leave the definitions vague, and trust the self-regulatory bodies to interpret the law in a reasonable way. Instead, rather in the manner of an American contracts lawyer who anticipates that everything in a deal will go wrong, he drew up very detailed rules, so there could be no ambiguity about what was permissible.

The result was that practitioners faced some of the most extensive, expensive and taxing conditions imposed on any sector of industry. Whereas the American Declaration of Independence runs to only 1,337 words, and the ten commandments to a mere 333 words, the rulebooks of SIB and the self-regulatory organisations contained more than a million words.

It was not long before this panoply of regulation was severely tested, and found wanting, in what became known as the Barlow Clowes affair. In the summer of 1988, thousands of investors reading their daily newspapers were startled to discover that the money they had set aside for pensions or other long-term savings had vanished. Barlow Clowes, the company to which it had been entrusted, was being liquidated. This might, in the history of personal investment, be a familiar story, but what made matters worse was that most of the funds lost were commuted lump sums from life savings or redundancy payments. The majority of the investors were elderly.

What was also particularly interesting about this scandal was that it embroiled both financial advisers and the Government. It was not just a question of investors being cheated of their savings as a result of sharp practice by a fund management group. Many of the 11,000 who lost a major part of their life savings did so after being advised to invest in the Barlow Clowes fund by professional independent financial advisers who should have known better. Their defence was that Barlow Clowes had been licensed by the Department of Trade and Industry after suspicions had been raised about the firm's activities.

Barlow Clowes was built up as a low-cost management group. Its funds were not designed to attract the reckless, but the cautious investor seeking a better return than a deposit account in a bank or building society. The attraction was that expert managers would consolidate investors' cash into interest-bearing deposits, principally British gilt-edged securities. That indeed was the intention of the fund's chairman, Peter Clowes, but, alas, he succumbed to the temptation of using some of the cash along the way for sumptuous living, including yachts and fast cars. The sorry tale finally ended in the criminal courts. Peter Clowes spent a number of years in prison, and the regulators had learned the lesson that even the thickest of rulebooks does not prevent investors being fleeced.

Widespread concern about the complexity of the regulatory system led to Sir Kenneth Berrill being replaced by David Walker, a former executive of the Bank of England, who simplified structures and, while relaxing some aspects of regulation, toughened up others. Even so, there continued to be concern about the efficiency of self-regulation, and in 1996 and 1997 a series of pensions scandals came to light. These scandals were not examples of blatant fraud, like Barlow Clowes, but the product of uncaring and greedy salesmen from well-known life assurance companies. Incentivised by large commissions, these salesmen persuaded middle-aged people to relinquish their income-based pensions for money-value schemes, where the total worth varies according to the price of the securities that make up the portfolio. Many people were persuaded to make the change, with the result that most of them could expect a large downturn in their potential pension incomes. This led to a large number of the companies being fined, and forced to retrain their sales forces.

When Tony Blair's revitalised Labour Party was elected to government in 1997, one of its first acts was to announce the establishment of the Financial Services Authority, which Blair intended should become a 'world class regulator'. Headed by a former deputy-governor of the Bank, Howard Davies, the FSA took over banking regulation from the Bank, and integrated the work of the Securities and Investments Board and all its subsidiary self-regulatory organisations. When Davies met the former chairman of the American Federal Reserve Board, Paul Volker, the big American greeted him with a laugh and the comment: 'Big job, I just hope you can retain your sense of humour.' To his credit, Mr Davies does appear to have done exactly that, with a series of speeches that mix solid messages with wit.

The FSA is not a government department, nor is it publicly funded. Ingeniously, it is a private company whose income comes from levies on the businesses in the financial service industry, and from fines. Its aims are clear enough and defined by law:

- *Market confidence*: maintaining market confidence in the financial system
- *Public awareness*: promoting public understanding of the financial system
- *Consumer protection*: securing the appropriate degree of protection for consumers
- *Reduction of financial crime*: reducing the extent to which it is possible for a business carried on by a regulated person to be used for a purpose connected with financial crime

The FSA is politically accountable through the Treasury. The latter appoints the chairman and the board, which must have a majority of non-executive directors. The FSA has to provide Parliament with an annual report, and hold an annual public meeting. There is also a committee of non-executive board members with clearly defined responsibilities, including ensuring the economic and efficient use of the FSA's resources and setting the pay of executive board members.

The FSA chairman is convinced of the benefits of a single regulator.

> We believe this makes sense for us, given the growing integration of our financial markets and the growth of large cross-sectoral

conglomerate institutions, which comprise banks, insurance companies, securities firms and investment managers under the same corporate umbrella. The longer we have worked with this single model the more convinced we are that it makes sense.[1]

Compared with the shambles of the previous regime, there is a lot of common sense about the FSA. It cannot run amok, creating rules and regulations without regard to their practical impact on the various practitioners in the industry, and it has tried to create a regime that is cost-effective. It also appears to realise that there is no sense in having rules which cannot be enforced. As Davies says:

> Our legislation also imposes on us a particular model of consultation. If we wish to introduce a new regulation, or indeed change an existing provision, we must produce a careful cost-benefit analysis and consult both on that analysis and indeed on the justifications we seek for our proposals. Where the industry makes criticisms, we must respond to them formally, explaining why we do or do not accept their points.[2]

Another aspect of the FSA approach has been to adopt a risk-based strategy, identifying and assessing threats – for example, when it appears that a situation in a company or sector is likely to spiral out of control. But this approach did not enable it to identify a crisis at Equitable Life, until 2001 one of Britain's most prestigious life assurance companies, where mismanagement led it to close its doors to new business, cut bonuses, and impose higher exit penalties on those deciding to withdraw their money.

One of the most controversial aspects of the FSA's new powers is its role in informing and educating the public. There are those who feel this is not the job of a regulator. Others argue, and I share the view, that given the poor record of the stockbroking community and the City generally in this area, it is good that someone has been delegated the task formally. Even before the organisation was formally set up, the body established to foreshadow it had already done some valuable work in this area, consulting on and publishing a Consumer Education Strategy, which concentrated on education for financial literacy and the provision of consumer education and advice. It also set up a Consumer Education Forum to provide the FSA with

---

[1] Howard Davies, chairman of the FSA, in speech to Grimaldi Forum, Monte Carlo. July 2001.
[2] Ibid.

advice on its consumer education strategy and work programme; published a series of guides for consumers, for example on financial advice and pensions; and established a single point of enquiries for consumers, which deals with up to 2,000 telephone calls a week.

Though politically accountable, the FSA has been given a raft of powers. These include information-gathering powers, powers to require firms to make regular returns or notify particular events, powers to commission expert reports – for example from accountants – and arrangements for direct reporting to the regulator by a firm's auditor or actuary.

But the body says it will not be heavy-handed or bureaucratic, preferring to develop its risk-based approach to supervision. As part of this approach, it says it seeks to 'focus regulatory attention on those firms and activities likely to pose the greatest risk to consumers and markets'.

The FSA has two main investigation powers. The first allows it to conduct general investigation of the affairs of an authorised person and its group, where there is good reason for doing so. The second allows investigations into a wide range of matters where there is the suspicion that particular offences have been committed or provisions of the Financial Services Act breached. The FSA can also go to court for a warrant enabling the police to enter and search premises in support of these investigative powers.

As this edition went to press, the Financial Services Authority's powers were further enhanced by the British Government taking the decision to transfer to it the regulatory powers of the London Stock Exchange. The exchange officially lost its powers as a result of its decision to incorporate as a public company, but the move, announced by Gordon Brown, the Chancellor of the Exchequer, also followed several years of criticism.

One of these criticisms surrounded the failure of the exchange to create a suitable regulatory environment for the smaller companies, concentrating its firepower on the FTSE 100 companies that dominate the market. The example of the weakness of the Alternative Investment Market (AIM) compared with the proven success of the Neuer Markt in Germany is cited by critics. Others, though, fear that enlarging the FSA's role still further will lead to its expansion into a large bureaucracy.

Howard Davies is adamant that his organisation will not become a burdensome bureaucracy, and points to the decision to stop routine compliance visits to financial service companies, concentrating instead on areas that pose the greatest risk to investors. Davies has said that he will adopt a strategy that will:

> identify, prioritise and address risks to the FSA's four statutory objectives: to maintain market confidence, promote public understanding of the financial system, secure appropriate consumer protection and reduce financial crime. After identifying and classifying risks to objectives, the next task is to assess the likelihood and importance of a particular risk. This helps establish priorities when allocating resources.[3]

Compensation and the Ombudsman

A new compensation scheme provides compensation if an authorised firm is unable to meet its liabilities to investors, depositors or policy holders. The scheme is being operated by a company separate from the FSA, but accountable to it. The Authority says its aim is 'to provide a reasonable level of compensation to individual customers and small businesses that have suffered loss as a result of the collapse of a bank, building society, insurer or investment firm'. This is a good idea because it is simpler than the system it replaced, providing a single point of entry for consumers.

The same principal has been applied in setting up the Financial Services Ombudsman (FSO), which replaces eight separate ombudsman schemes. As with the compensation scheme, it is being run by a separate company which will be legally and operationally independent of the FSA but will be required to report annually to it on the discharge of its functions.

Other Watchdogs

Other watchdogs that have an impact on the markets are the Office of Fair Trading and the Competititions Commission. The latter will creak into action if the Government decides that a possible takeover may be against the public interest because it will substantially reduce competition in the marketplace. It will conduct an investigation and report back to the Department of Trade and Industry, which will then decide whether or not to allow the takeover or merger to go ahead.

---

[3] *Financial Times*, 13 July 2001.

The Office of Fair Trading, as its name implies, investigates alleged unfair trading practices.

There is also a plethora of regulators whose job it is to watch over privatised monopolies or near monopolies. They rejoice in a series of unattractive acronyms, such as OFWAT (water), OFGAS (oil and gas), and OFTEL (telecommunications). They have power to restrict price increases, and to generally poke their noses into the corporations they regulate. In doing so they often get up the noses of the bodies under their scrutiny, which lobby government with ever-increasing frequency but usually without effect.

A body called the Better Regulation Task Force believes that the regulatory touch on the former nationalised industries would be more effective if it were to be lighter. It says that the new corporations replacing the former public utilities provide better services, and only a few of a left-wing persuasion would dispute that, with the possible exception of the railways, which are bad now but were also bad before. But Lord Haskins, the task force's chairman, believes that the terms of reference of the regulators have become overloaded with additional burdens, and has described them as 'unworkable'.[4] He argues that the complexity of regulations make them 'confusing and easy to exploit', that they have not been conducive to encouraging badly needed new investment, and that regulatory bureaucracies have been created. 'The complexity,' he says, 'encourages game-playing and leaves consumers confused and suspicious.'[5]

---

[4] *Financial Times*, June 2001.
[5] Ibid.

16   Eyes on the Ball

*Am I sorry for the institutional investors? Not at all. The greed
and fashionable short-termism of the City was the underlying
cause of this catastrophe.*

William Rees-Mogg, The Times

*It remains widely acknowledged that concerns about the
management and strategy of major companies can persist
among analysts and fund managers for long periods of time
before action is taken.*

Report to the Treasury by Paul Myners, 2001

The stark headline on the main editorial page of *The Times* caught
my eye immediately. 'Marconi is the victim of greed and stupidity', it
read. The author, William Rees-Mogg, a former editor of *The Times*,
a member of numerous committees and a former deputy-chairman of
the BBC board of governors, was at his thundering best, going on to
describe how the management of Marconi, formerly known as GEC,
had destroyed shareholder value.

> The previous management, headed by the legendary Arnold
> Weinstock, had created a formidable range of good businesses in
> sectors from defence, through electrical engineering, to advanced
> electronics. GEC had a strong balance sheet, and a mountain of
> cash, and, in the last five years of Weinstock's leadership, its share
> price had doubled. Much of Weinstock's success was attributed
> to a textbook style of management, which could be best described
> as 'delegation with accountability'. He allowed his managers
> considerable freedom to run their businesses, but once a month
> called them to account if their numbers departed from budget. By
> this means of control he was also able to spot the danger signal
> fundamental to any business model: if the profits continue to rise
> when the flow of cash is falling away.[1]

When Weinstock retired, his successor, George Simpson, inherited

---

[1] *The Times*, 9 July 2001

a buoyant company. There was, however, a problem. According to Rees-Mogg: 'The City wanted more. The City wanted GEC to spend the cash and go for growth. The City wanted an excuse to make the shares a glamour stock. As a result, in the words of an insider: "George did not manage the company, he managed the share price."' The result was the collapse of Marconi's share price to little more than one eighth of its value a few months earlier. The chief executive, John Mayo, was ousted, and the man he had replaced, Lord Simpson, reinstated, only to find himself sacked two months later. The Financial Services Authority launched an investigation into Marconi's decision to fail to notify a £220 million quarterly loss for two months, while the press combed the wreckage of the company for detailed evidence of how a highly paid management could perform so badly.

Rees-Mogg's conclusion was that:

> I feel sorry for the employees, whose jobs have been lost by incompetence at the top, and sorry for the private shareholders. I also feel sorry for the pensioners and others whose funds have been invested for them in Marconi shares. Am I sorry for the institutional managers? Not at all. The greed and fashionable short-termism of the City was the underlying cause of this catastrophe.

This is spot-on, and opens up a new issue which has only gained prominence in the last decade. What can be done to protect large numbers of small shareholders when the losses they suffer are not the result of fraud, dishonesty or cheating by company directors or management, but are well beyond the normal boundaries that could be expected from the mantra of 'risk and reward'?

Let me illustrate this by asking you to test two suppositions. It is reasonable to assume that by buying a share in a company you may lose money: you may buy at the wrong time when shares are at a peak, the company may make mistakes (as when Marks and Spencer misjudged the market), the unexpected could happen (as when a series of fatal rail crashes ruined the reputation of the rail industry in Britain). The stock markets are often casualties when there are international crises, and investors switch from securities to cash or gold.

Managers are also human and fallible. If they take no risks, they are unlikely to succeed, unless they are running a firm of undertakers. The job of management is to run the company entrusted to them as efficiently and profitably as they can, for the benefit of the shareholders. They are, after all, accountable to the shareholders. Or are they?

This leads to the second supposition. The shareholders own the company, right? They call the shots, appoint the board of directors, monitor the management, call managers to account for failures, and make sure they are paid what they are worth, enough to provide a powerful incentive to perform well, but not so much as either to overburden the company with an excessive salaries bill or to create envy and discontent among the rest of the staff. Here we have a problem, because small shareholders own such a tiny proportion of a company's stock that they really have no voice. However, the big investment institutions have plenty of clout, keep their eye on the ball, and make changes where needed. Or do they?

As you will have guessed, it is in the second supposition that the deepest problem lies. As Lord Rees-Mogg indicated in his prescient article, the institutions are simply not doing their job. Worse than that, they have failed miserably. Julian Franks, Professor of Management at the London Business School, told a seminar that 'Corporate governance in Britain is awful. The changes that have been made in recent years are marginal.'[2]

Corporate governance is the somewhat ugly term given to making sure a company's management keeps its eye on the ball. In recent years thousands of words of corporate-speak have been devoted to it, to little avail. The Institute of Directors has put it at the heart of its activities, trying to encourage companies to appoint better-qualified non-executive directors. It has established a new qualification, obtainable only after examination, of 'chartered director', in the belief that if boards include outsiders with a strong focus, managements who stray or perform badly will be called to account.

There has also been a drive to induce institutions to involve themselves more in how companies are run, although as William Rees-Mogg has remarked, all too often they do too little too late. There have been numerous committees of inquiry looking into corporate governance – the most prominent being Cadbury, Greenbury and Hampel – culminating in the publication of a code in June 1998.[3]

[2] Seminar at the London Business School, June 2001.
[3] Combined Code of the Committee on Corporate Governance, 1998.

As a result of this, there have been interventions – as in the Marconi case and when major companies like British Airways and British Telecom have run off the rails. However, most institutional investor action, which is normally taken discreetly behind the scenes, has only occurred too late. In BT's case, inducing the chairman, Ian Vallence, to step down was too late to prevent hundreds of thousands of investors losing a large proportion of their savings.

It is doubtful whether institutional investors or the fund managers employed by them are qualified to run companies, any more than other professionals such as barristers or architects are. They are certainly in no position to second-guess full-time corporate management. However, they do spend a lot of time lunching with these self-same managers, and visiting their companies, usually not at their own expense. They also examine strategy, and test management assumptions. Too often, when they identify potential problems, they remain silent. It is not much for the rest of us to expect that when they spot trouble they should take action, rather than sitting on their hands. The Myners Report came to the same conclusion: 'Intervention requires persistence and a thick skin, perhaps raising issues repeatedly over a period of time with firmness until concerns are addressed. Merely meeting senior management and expressing polite reservations about strategy is not sufficient, if it is not effective.'[4]

Some institutional investors believe it is their business not to get involved in top level management, but to vote with their feet; in other words, simply to sell the shares of companies they think are badly run. They agree with the celebrated American investor Warren Buffett that when they see 'gin rummy managerial behaviour' they should dump stocks.[5] The trouble is that this may be difficult if they hold a share as part of a tracker fund. Another widely held fear is that if investors become too involved in the machinations of a company – and then decide to buy or sell its stock – they could be branded as insider traders, liable to prosecution. This issue alone has become a major subject for discussion – at what point does contact inside a company put an investor in a privileged position?

---

[4] Report to the Treasury by Paul Myners, 2001.
[5] Berkshire Hathaway annual report, 1983.

Executive Pay

Another very big issue for the stock markets is the conduct of senior executives, particularly those on very high earnings. Chief executives are often referred to in the tabloid press as 'fat cats', and rightly so. In recent years, while average earnings in Britain have been rising by between 3 and 4 per cent a year, slightly ahead of inflation, the pay of chief executives in large and medium-sized corporations has been going up by 16 per cent annually. In a few cases the bosses have justified pay rises four times that of their workers on the grounds that a large slice of the increase has come from predetermined bonuses or share options. Unfortunately, all too often the higher pay has not been earned, and there have been many instances where chiefs have been paid more for achieving less.

In the year 2000, directors' salaries rose by an average 8 per cent during a period when the FTSE 100 index fell by 10 per cent, and there is some evidence that as share prices continued to fall through 2001, senior executives' pay went on rising.[6] There are many examples, some of them grotesque, of boardroom salaries rising as companies fell from grace.

Bonuses and Options

Not long ago it was unfashionable to give employees, even executives, shares in the company, and bonus scheme were preferred. There was an obvious reason for this: bonuses could be capped. A typical scheme would offer a 10 per cent of salary bonus for reaching budget, a further 10 per cent for going 10 per cent better than budget, and a maximum 30 per cent for achieving 25 per cent more than budget. Some bonus schemes, which worked on a return on capital deployed basis, were sensible and rewarding, but too many were flawed. A senior manager could, for example, have achieved budgeted sales targets while allowing the cost of achieving these sales to overrun greatly. Another could have cut costs to achieve budget, throttling growth prospects in the process. So more recently it has been fashionable to give executives – and sometimes whole staffs – share options. The job of the remuneration committee would be

---

[6] Executive Remuneration Review, May 2001.

twofold – to set a strike price, the amount at which the option could be exercised, and a strike date.

How it works

In 2000 Clive's company gave him 5,000 share options at a strike price of £5 per share, exercisable in 2005. The present price is £7.50. So he has already made a notional gain of 50 per cent. Were he able to buy the shares he would outlay £25,000 but be able to sell them for £37,500. The company does well, and in early 2001 the shares stand at £15. It is too early for him to exercise his option; had he been able to do so he would have made a profit of £50,000, or 300 per cent on his outlay. But then the market falls, and the shares are quoted at £4.90, at which point his option is worthless, unless they move above the £5 mark again.

There are many parallel situations to this, particularly in the TMT – telecoms, media and technology – sectors. Potential fortunes have been lost, perhaps temporarily, perhaps forever.

What some crafty executives did in early 2001 as markets fell was to persuade boards to 'redraw the lines'; in other words, to reduce the strike prices for existing options, so that they could still hope to make a profit in the future. Wouldn't it be great if ordinary shareholders could do that; in effect saying 'We overpaid for those shares and would like to be able to do the deal again at a lower price.' It's akin to saying 'We overpaid for that BMW, now let us have it for 20 per cent less!' Needless to say, those who are trying to uphold proper corporate governance were not amused.

In good times, when shares seem always to be going up, the issue of executive pay is often sidelined. But when economies are slowing, when job losses mount, and when public opinion becomes restless, then the money flowing into the bank accounts of the fat cats will dominate discussion on corporate governance.

17   Greed and Fear

The final step towards understanding how the stock markets work is to grasp that in the end the two prime motivators are greed and fear. Greed drives us to grab more if we think the price is cheap. Fear makes us risk-averse in case we lose everything we have.

In turn these senses of greed and fear feed off news and information that might affect our share or bond holdings in any given company or country. The greatest fear of all is war, except perhaps for those manufacturing arms, who stand to gain from increased sales. But war destroys assets, both human and physical, and neither can quickly or cheaply be replaced. Bankruptcy also terrifies shareholders, because normally they lose their entire investment. That 'safest' of investments, Railtrack, turned out to be one of Britain's greatest losers. After bankruptcy come strikes, floods, management incompetence, competition from new or cheaper products, changes in consumer habits, and even changes of public mood. News of developments in any of these areas is likely to increase fears that what seemed to be a sound investment last year or last week may now no longer be the case.

Similarly, there are developments that impact on greed. Sharply rising house prices motivate people to jump on to the property bandwagon for fear that they will miss out on a capital gain. The dotcom hype of the turn of the century led tens of thousands of people to pay high prices for shares in companies that not only had never turned a profit but also never looked as if they could. Martha Lane Fox managed to persuade City of London accountants who should have known better that the assets of lastminute.com were worth tens of millions of pounds, with the result that thousands of investors overpaid for shares that were worth very little.

These days, the value of our shares is governed not just by what goes on within a company or inside national boundaries. Disconnected events on the other side of the world can affect our savings for good or ill. Nothing we own – whether it be shares, property or gold – is immune from the upshot of developments elsewhere. Such is the impact of globalisation.

Globalisation has become a hot political topic, and fuel for a motley group of anarchists, Marxists, environmentalists and other protestors who have a grudge against the present state we live in. But globalisation is not the product of transnational corporations or secret cabals of the supposed masters of the universe. It is the inevitable outcome of technological change. Because technological change is spread unevenly across the planet, it is unavoidable that its benefits are not universally felt. Hence the digital divide that the United Nations and many caring people lament.

The most significant technological change has been in the speed of communications. Data, including information, now moves via satellite from one part of the planet to another in microseconds. The announcement of an exploratory oil drilling in Borneo or the collapse of an insurance company in Melbourne will be known in London or New York immediately.

Similarly very large sums of money can be transferred from one country to another in seconds. This has made it possible for those with funds invested in another country to withdraw them immediately. This could be on a whim, although it is more likely to be because of bad news, or a falling currency. Sudden outflows tend to destabilise the country or company from which they are withdrawn.

Fixed investments in service industries such as call centres, cannot be set up or shut down at a moment's notice, but they are fairly mobile, and many of them have been moved from expensive locations like London or Frankfurt to other cities where labour is plentiful and cheaper. Norwich, Newcastle and Edinburgh are all areas which have seen employment in call centres grow. More recently these services have moved beyond national borders. When you make a reservation on British Airways your call could be answered in one of a number of countries, depending on the time of day or night and the volume of calls. If you order a Dell computer from an advertisement in an English magazine, the 0800 number will route you to Ireland. One of Britain's largest insurance groups runs its claims operation from a suburb of Mumbai, India. The cost of switching calls down a leased line to India is much less than employing clerks in Southend-on-Sea. And if labour costs rise sharply in Mumbai, the activity can always be switched in a few months to somewhere cheaper where communications are good, possibly Bangladesh or South Africa.

Manufacturing companies are not so mobile. Once millions of pounds has been invested in new plant, machinery, and skilled labour

– often supported by substantial tax incentives from governments – it takes a major board decision to write it off by closing or moving the business. But it happens. Two German automotive giants, Daimler Chrysler and BMW, have moved capacity away from Europe to South Africa. If you buy a Mercedes-Benz C-series in Britain, it will have come not from Stuttgart but from East London in South Africa. The two largest American manufacturers, General Motors and Ford, have both ended passenger car production in Luton and Dagenham respectively. Over the next decade it is likely there will be more moves of this kind, but they will not happen quickly.

Even less mobile are people. In the eighteenth century, large numbers of Europeans crossed the Atlantic to create and build what is now the United States. After World War II many British families migrated to Australia and were provided with transportation for £10. Large numbers of Africans, Asians and West Indians came to Britain. These days migration is tightly controlled. In a perfect economic world, people would move from countries where there is little or no work to those where jobs are plentiful. As it is, only millionaires and those with skills in demand – such as doctors, nurses, computer programmers and systems analysts – can easily switch countries.

This partly explains why globalisation is less than perfect. The other reason is that economic forces are not benign, and can damage a country as effectively as a hurricane can wreck an unprepared community. It is important to understand this, because it helps to explain how those who work in a copper mine in Zambia – or have shares in the company that owns it – can be badly hurt by a seemingly unconnected event in South East Asia. That same event may decimate profits at British and American banks, and cause millions of pensioners to see their savings plunge.

Far-fetched? Let me provide you with a real example. The key date in this case is 8 December 1997. On that morning the people of Thailand woke up to find that their currency had fallen by 40 per cent. Their government had closed all but two of their fifty-eight large finance houses, sparing them the indignity of going bankrupt. Panic set in as many Thais realised they would be losing their life savings. The panic spread throughout the Asian region as share prices plunged in a slide that became known as the Asian meltdown, the most serious crash for ten years.

How this all happened is a salutary lesson in how globalisation works. It should also reinforce in investors the age-old advice never to believe a politician's promise or the mouth-watering hype that regularly comes from the marketing departments of the financial services industry.

The Thai government had made a solemn pledge ten years earlier that the country's currency, the baht, would remain fixed to the dollar at the rate of 25 baht to one dollar. They did this for sound reasons: the dollar is by far the world's most significant currency, and by aligning their currency to it they would attract investors, who would be reassured that whatever happened, they could exchange their money back to the American greenback at the same rate they had moved it in. The Thai government promised to use whatever measures were needed to keep the dollar exchange rate at 25 bahts.

So what happened? In the early years things went well. Foreign investors and lenders were only too willing to move money to Thailand because returns were higher than in the main dollar market, the United States. And Thai banks and businesses were happy to pay slightly more to borrow dollars because it enabled them to finance expansion, particularly in property such as shopping centres, housing developments and tourist resorts. Everyone gained, especially as exports were strong through the high shipments of electronic products and earnings from package holidays.

The feel-good factor spread through the country as more jobs were created and the people had more money to spend. The new affluence led to a spending and borrowing spree. People took on new mortgages, using the money that their banks had borrowed in dollars. There was an increase in sales of prestige cars and other luxury goods, most of them imported from Europe or Japan. Gradually the country's healthy balance of payments surplus went into deficit. The central bank, however, was able to handle this by encouraging more international borrowings, and the continued flow of money into the country was sufficient to maintain the current account (the country's balance sheet) in surplus.

This did not last for long, because the products of many other countries in the region in competition with Thailand became cheaper. The currencies of Japan, Malaysia, Singapore and Taiwan were not pegged to the dollar, and as they floated downwards, goods from these countries fell in price in international markets. Gradually Thailand's exports slowed, whereas had the baht also been a floating currency, they would have stayed competitive.

By the mid 1990s, Thailand's current account deficit – a figure reached by subtracting export earnings from import costs and adding interest payments on international loans – was at a record 8 per cent of gross national product, one of the highest anywhere in the world. A current account deficit must be funded by an equally large flow of funds from overseas. The government was advised to devalue the baht to maintain equilibrium, but instead it repeated its pledge to keep the rate. Interest rates rose to encourage more foreign capital, but this served only to make borrowing more expensive and thus slow down the economy as business leaders put off spending decisions.

By now the international ratings agencies, Moody's, and Standard and Poor's, which operate a kind of weather forecast on the financial health of countries and companies, were becoming more negative about Thailand. A triple A rating means rock solid and risk-free; a triple C is very worrisome. Anything below that is a basket case. International financial institutions and wealthy investors watch these ratings on a daily basis, and when Moody's downrated Thailand, many of them decided it was time to pull their money out, and return it to the safe haven of the United States.

These sudden outflows forced the government in Bangkok to crack, and they abandoned the fixed exchange rate, allowing the baht to float down to its real value in the global marketplace. Within two hours it had lost 40 per cent of its value. This meant that the property developers and others who had borrowed in dollars found not only that their interest bill was rising but that, expressed in baht, the amount they owed had soared beyond their worst nightmares. A debt of 2.5 million baht ($US100,000) had become $4.6 million. For most borrowers, the debts were now greater than the value of the developments for which they had taken out the 'cheap' loans. There was only one course to take: declare bankruptcy and default on the loans.

There is an old adage which says that if you owe a bank a thousand pounds you are in trouble; but if you owe them a million they are in trouble. And so it proved. The banks became insolvent, and most were shut down.

In their concrete and glass fortresses in London and Wall Street, those controlling the billions of dollars entrusted to them by investors, savers, and pension funds quickly became very nervous. If Thailand, one of Asia's brightest 'tiger' economies, could collapse, could there be others?

South Korea operated a floating rather than a fixed exchange rate, and had a strong current account surplus. But some of its investment banks had borrowed large sums of short-term money overseas and reinvested it in Korea. These short-term borrowings far exceeded the government's foreign currency reserves. The outlook for South Korea's currency, the won, looked bleak, so international investors played safe and dumped their investments.

The Seoul stock market plunged, and soon Asian contagion had brought big falls to Taiwan, Singapore, Malaysia, Hong Kong, and an already weakened Japan. Money withdrawn moved into the safety of United States Treasury bonds, with the huge repatriation into the dollar pushing its value upwards. Because many essential commodities, like petroleum, are sold in dollars, this increased prices for the hapless Asian tigers, so dependent on oil for their energy.

Unnerved by events in Asia, fund managers examined their portfolios in every other emerging market for signs of weakness. South Africa and Russia came under particularly sharp scrutiny. In South Africa the currency, the rand, was weak, crime was rampant, and Thabo Mbeke, about to take over as president from the legendary Nelson Mandela, was an unknown quantity. Sell, said those looking for safety.

The position in Russia was much worse. Many international investors had poured money into Russian bonds or lent money to Russian companies on the basis of business plans of dubious value. Some of these plans had been drawn up by international management consultants seemingly more intent on a quick fee income than long-term growth. Strong sales forecasts were not met as Russian manufacturers realised that demand for shoddy products once dumped on central European countries through Comecon, the Soviet sponsors of the Common Market between European members of the Warsaw Pact, simply did not exist.

There was a bigger problem. Much of the money lent to Russian entrepreneurs vanished as it was converted back to hard currencies and found its way into Swiss bank accounts. Money laundering became a highly profitable industry: even official money channelled through the International Monetary Fund 'disappeared'.

It became increasingly clear that Russians might never be able to pay back many of the loans so rashly entered into by global banks, but there was reasonable confidence that the then president, Boris Yeltsin, would honour his administration's pledges. It was not to be. In August, the Kremlin announced that the Russian Federation had no choice but to default on its debt. The rouble crashed, and world stock markets plunged.

If savers and investors become ultra-cautious, risk capital ends up in short supply, and new developments suffer. People's buying habits also change. They are less inclined to splash out on new cars, new homes and new gadgets. Manufacturers, seeing demand falling, lay off workers, and this in turn sets off another vicious circle of excess caution. From these actions bear markets are born.

18   Conclusion

Most of the Earth's assets – and to some extent property beyond our planet – are owned not by rich individuals, but by us, as shareholders. We may not know it because these assets, which could be land and buildings, aircraft and ships, corporations and supermarkets, may be largely in the hands of the big institutions. However, most of these institutions are reinvesting our savings, contributed through pension schemes, unit trusts, trades union dues and other forms of collective investment. So if ownership of companies is widely spread, who actually really controls them? Who, to borrow a Wall Street phrase, are the masters of the universe? The question is not an easy one, and the debate over management and control will become one of the enduring issues of the twenty-first century.

Let us first look at this issue by way of the interesting example of British Airways. The airline was once owned by the state; in other words, the people of Britain. The Government sold it through privatisation, and it ended up belonging to thousands of private shareholders, the airline's staff, and institutional investors, British and foreign. Some of the money raised was return to the public, through tax cuts, but most of it went into the Treasury's coffers. At the time there seemed to be absolutely no doubt as to who pulled the strings at BA. Management was firmly in the grip of the chairman, Lord King, and his chief executive, Colin Marshall.

For a while BA was the world's most profitable airline, making serious money. The Government not only saved the heavy subsidies it had previously spent to prop the airline up, but also gained from tax paid, giving it a double payback. But a few years ago, after the chief executive, by then ennobled as Lord Marshall, had succeeded King as chairman, BA's fortunes flagged and its share price fell sharply.

The big investment institutions that formed the largest group of shareholders in BA became restless, but their ire was directed less against Marshall, who had maintained strong connections in the City through many interlocking directorships, than against the man who had replaced him as chief executive, Robert Ayling. Under pressure from these institutions, Ayling was forced to resign, even though

Marshall and the board endorsed his policies. He was replaced by an Australian, Rod Eddington, who reinforced Ayling's policies of concentrating on business traffic at the expense of economy passengers. BA's share price fell further, to half the level it had been under Ayling, but to date there have been no calls from the institutions for a change in policy, or Eddington's head.

Consider another point. British Airways, under its articles of association, published when it was privatised, must be under British control, and a majority of its shareholders must be citizens of the European Union. This is so that it can remain a British carrier, and be subject to air agreements made between Britain and the United States and other countries. At the last count, 43 per cent of its shareholders were not British, and three quarters of the foreigners were Americans. Amongst the institutional shareholders, Americans were hugely prominent. One of the three institutions listed as holding more than 3 per cent of BA shares is Franklin Templeton, a United States mutual fund managing over £150 billion for nine million Americans.

This is not an attempt to paint a picture of huge American influence over British Airways or any other company, for good or ill. It simply serves to point out that when managers of large companies look over their shoulders at those who exercise control over them, these forces may be far from their own back yard. The representatives of these institutional investors will probably know very little about the airline business, or any other business. Almost certainly they will never have run a company, or sat on an executive board. But they will be numerate, understand balance sheets and profit-and-loss accounts, and will often have an eye to short-term gains rather than long-term advantage, a perception that may be totally opposite to that of management and employees.

Nor can institutions be relied upon to be consistent in their approach. Inconsistency is rife, as we saw in the example of British Airways. They waver. They are fickle. They are subject to mood swings, and are often unduly influenced by personal relationships and contacts. If they were simply hard-headed number crunchers, then managements would know where they stand. When the personable and hard-driving Marjorie Scardino took over at Pearson, she was flavour of the year amongst City institutions, long before her reputation had been earned. At the height of her achievements, and after restructuring Pearson in the manner that everyone had said was necessary, she went out of fashion. By the time this edition is printed, one hopes she may be in favour again.

The same inconsistency can be seen in institutions' approach to whole sectors. The titanic institutions of Wall Street and London were the ones that pushed their funds and their clients into dotcoms and telecoms companies that became grossly overvalued. The small investor was carried along in the stream, fed by media hype flowing from the word processors of unquestioning financial journalists, themselves fed by analysts working for institutions seeking to make a placement or initial public offering. Having made their killing, these same institutions were in the vanguard of those dumping stock and pouring scorn daily on new media and technology companies, including those that were soundly based.

Institutional investors are big beasts in a jungle, and there is no point in pretending otherwise. Many of them are not even very good investors, for as has been repeatedly pointed out, most of them underperform the stock market index in the countries in which they operate.

That is bad enough, but whether they are the right people to push the managers about is highly debatable, especially as they are also very inconsistent about it. Many large institutions are benign, preferring not to get involved, arguing that their best bet, if they are unhappy with a company's performance, is to sell their share-holdings. Others move with hesitation, often stepping in too late. There is the salutary tale of Marconi, told in Chapter 16. The problems at British Telecom were there for everyone to see months, even years, before the institutions reluctantly acted to persuade Sir Ian Vallance to take an overdue retirement. Confirmation of the slowness of institutional investors to act when companies are performing badly comes from a recent academic study. In what is claimed to be the first comparative evaluation of the role of share-holders, bidders in takeovers, and executive directors in disciplining managements of poorly performing companies, it found that 'in the UK most parties, including holders of substantial share blocks, exert little discipline, and that some actually impede it'.[1]

There are other groups who watch over managements with a varying degree of interest and effectiveness, and these are what have now come to be called stakeholders. They include employees, who

---

[1] Julian Franks (Corporation of London Professor of Finance, London Business School), Peter Moores (Professor of Management Studies, Said Business School, Oxford), and Luc Renneboog (Assistant Professor of Finance, Tilburg University, the Netherlands), *Who Disciplines Management in Poorly Performing Companies?*, London Business School, 2001.

provide the human resources and whose future is linked to the success of the company; rightly, they expect to be kept informed about its prospects. Gone are the days when ambitious trades union leaders used to talk about 'co-determination', whereby a company would be run by a committee drawn from a board of shareholder representatives and one selected by employees. Even so, the European Union is still actively promoting the concept of employee participation, and sensible managements will not only promote share ownership among employees but also provide workers with detailed financial information on a regular basis, as well as consulting them about major changes.

Another important stakeholder group is the customers. Customers expect their support of companies to be reciprocated, and managers who ignore the wishes of their patrons do so at their peril, as dozens of companies have found to their cost, the most prominent in recent years being perhaps Marks and Spencer. Customer power is a growing force. Shell, Wal-Mart, the French perfume and liquor industry, Marks and Spencer, and Nike are among those who have fallen victims to substantial consumer boycotts.

The debate will continue for many years over the rightful role of each of these stakeholders. There is clearly a power struggle for control. It is not the kind of struggle we saw in the immediate post-World War II years, when Labour sought to take over the 'commanding heights of the economy', although that kind of psychology is much in evidence in the present British Government's desire to keep control of the National Health Service. The arguments are more subtle, and the lawyers are joining the party. As this book went to press, Unilever, one of the world's largest consumer companies, was well into a lawsuit against Merrill Lynch, the world's largest investment house, alleging that it had mismanaged its pension fund. If fund managers can be held legally accountable for poor investment decisions, they will be forced to become more interventionist in companies in which they have substantial holdings. And if that happens, life in the boardrooms and on the stock markets will be changed for ever.

Glossary of Terms

ADRs American Depository Receipt; see depository receipts.

AER Annual Equivalent Rate. Usually specifies the interest paid from current, deposit, or savings accounts. This new term replaces CAR (Compound Annual Rate), which denoted much the same thing.

AGM Annual General Meeting. The meeting of shareholders held each year to approve the accounts and to reappoint directors and auditors. Normally held twenty-one days after publication of the annual report. It must be held within eighteen months of the previous AGM. AGMs are often attended by private investors as an opportunity to question directors on a company's performance, prospects, and results.

AIM Alternative Investment Market. The London Stock Exchange's market for smaller, younger, and growing companies.

AITC Association of Investment Trust Companies. This is the industry body for the investment trust sector, and will provide investors with a great deal of useful information.

analyst Someone who studies particular stock markets or industry sectors, and makes buy or sell recommendations regarding the shares of specific companies within them. Such recommendations are arrived at through a combination of research, economic statistics, and visits to the companies themselves. See also **fund manager**.

Annual Report & Accounts The directors' report to shareholders, which sets out the details of the company's performance during the past year. Normally split into two halves, the important part is the back half, which contains the accounts. Once you have mastered how to read a balance sheet, you will find accounts a mine of information. Full details of directors' pay are included, along with much other financial information. The front half normally includes reports from the company's chairman and chief executives, but many of these are written by the corporate relations people and tend to be gratuitous publicity rather than useful information.

annual volatility Volatility is one measure used to assess the risk of a portfolio as it helps to describe the likely range of returns achieved by the fund. In statistical terms it is the standard deviation of the return distribution. Greater volatility of monthly fund returns means that there is a wider range of likely returns in the future, or greater uncertainty regarding the fund return. Most investors would equate this greater uncertainty with greater risk.

APCSIM Association of Private Client Stockbrokers and Investment Managers. This is the official body of stockbrokers and fund managers who specialise in providing investment services for private clients.

APR Annual Percentage Rate. The compounded rate used to give a standard comparison of the amount of interest you are likely to pay on loans, mortgages or outstanding credit card balances. This is a key figure, and should always be the one used to compare costs or returns on interest-bearing securities.

arbitrage The act of profiting from the difference in price when the same security, currency, or commodity is traded on two or more markets at different prices.

assets Another word for real possessions. Net assets are the difference between what you own and what you owe. Sometimes investments held in a portfolio are referred to as assets. Assets are also items a company owns, such as land, machinery, stocks, cash, and investments.

associated companies When one company has an interest in another company that represents more than 20 per cent but less than a majority of the voting rights in that company's share capital, then this is deemed an investment in an 'associated' company. The profits of the associated company are consolidated into the results of the company holding the investment. If the holding company has less than a 20 per cent interest, then only dividends received will appear in its accounts. If the holding company has over a 50 per cent interest, then the investment is deemed to be a subsidiary company, and its results and net assets will be fully consolidated in the holding company accounts.

at best order An instruction to a stockbroker by a client to buy or sell shares for the best price available.

audit A professional, independent examination of the accounts of a company. Accounts of all registered companies, whether listed or not, must be audited.

AUTIF The Association of Unit Trusts and Investment Funds, the industry trade body for unit trust and investment trust management companies.

balance sheet The statement featured in the Annual Report & Accounts that indicates the value of the company's assets and liabilities as of the end of its financial period. The balance sheet also provides details of the company's methods of financing.

base rate The core interest rate determined by the Bank of England in Britain, by the European Central Bank for those European countries in the European Monetary System, and by the Federal Reserve in the United States. Most other savings and borrowing rates are derived from base rate.

basket A contract or other derivative for the purchase or sale of shares, which comprise a pre-defined group of equities. It could be all equities in the FTSE 100, for example. You can also have a basket of currencies – for example the pound, euro and yen aggregated against the US dollar.

basket case Slang for a country that has debts exceeding its reserves, and is in need of international support. Sometimes used to refer to a company or companies in trouble.

bear An investor who sells a security in the hope of buying it back at a lower price. A bear market is a falling market in which bears would prosper.

bid-offer spread The difference between the price at which an investor buys unit trusts or shares and the price at which he sells them. The buying or offer price is usually higher than the selling price, and the difference between them may vary within the limits of a formula laid down by the Financial Services Act 1986.

bid price The buying price for securities in the market.

Big Bang 27 October 1986, the date when the rules of the London Stock Exchange were changed to allow corporate ownership and to abolish the role of jobbers as market makers on the floor of the Throgmorton Street building.

blue chip A popular term used to define a company regarded as being a sound and safe investment. The adjectives you normally associate with such a company are large, solid, well established, reputable and, perhaps, boring.

bonds Interest-bearing securities that entitle the holder to interest during their life, and repayment of the loan at maturity. In Britain, but only in Britain, government bonds are called gilts, short for gilt-edged securities. American government bonds are known as Treasuries. The issuer promises to pay bond holders a fixed rate of interest for a fixed number of years. Those bonds with a life of five years or less are known as 'shorts', while those with ten years or more are called 'longs'. Bonds are traded on all stock markets, and move up or down in line with interest rates.

broker A member of a stock exchange which provides dealing services with or without advice to the public, and which can also buy and sell shares on its own account.

bull The opposite of a bear. Bulls buy shares in the expectation of being able to sell them at a higher price. A bull market is a rising market. One of the longest bull markets in history came to an end in the year 2000.

call option The right, but not the obligation, to buy stock or shares at an agreed price up to a predetermined date in the future. One of the basic units of the futures markets.

capital An investor's savings and wealth or a company's share capital and reserves. Also sometimes used to describe a lump sum of money that is available for immediate use.

capital employed The funds employed by the company in its activities. On the balance sheet, the company's share capital, reserves, and debt represent capital employed.

capital gains tax A tax on the increase in value of assets sold in a particular year. Operates as a handicap to personal investors as it inhibits them from selling shares when circumstances dictate that they should.

capitalisation issue An issue in which funds from a company's reserves are converted into shares that are issued free of charge to the company's shareholders.

cash The value of all liquid assets employed in a business, either as ready cash or invested in short-term securities that can be quickly sold and turned into cash.

cash-flow statement The statement in the Annual Report & Accounts that indicates the sources of all cash, from both operations and external means of finance, for the financial period. The cash-flow statement indicates how cash has been used for trading, capital preservation, investment, and taxation purposes.

charts Graphs of share and market (index) performance used to determine relative trends and to identify likely future moves. Charts are key instruments in technical analysis. See also **technical analysis**.

City This term describes the London financial markets in the same way as Wall Street defines the New York financial centre. It used to mean the square mile within the operational control of the Corporation of London, but the term is now more generic to describe all of London's financial operations, including those in Docklands. It is similar in concept to the term 'Fleet Street', which means the national newspaper industry, though not one newspaper remains there.

commission The charge made by stockbrokers to individual investors for carrying out their buy or sell instructions. The charge may be either a percentage of the value involved or, for small deals below a stated and agreed value, a fixed amount.

contract note The paperwork investors receive from their stockbrokers confirming the terms of the deal that has been undertaken on their behalf.

convertible loan stocks Securities that pay fixed interest, but that can be converted into shares at a given price and at set times.

corporate governance The term used to describe the policies and procedures that a company's directors are expected to use in conducting the company's affairs and its relationships with shareholders. The directors are responsible as managers of the shareholders' interests in the company.

covered warrant A security issued by a party other than the issuer of the underlying asset, giving the holder the right to acquire a share or bond at a specific price and date.

creative accounting The term used to indicate accounting and financial reporting practices which, whilst not illegal, are intended to convey a circumstance or position that is either misleading or illusory, thus creating a perception of profitability or soundness that may not be wholly valid.

creditors, long All liabilities payable more than one year after the balance sheet date. This includes provisions, deferred taxation, loans, and debt (including convertible debt) repayable more than one year after the balance sheet date.

creditors, short All current liabilities payable on demand or within one year of the balance sheet date.

CREST The British electronic share settlement system that was introduced on the London Stock Exchange in July 1996.

current assets The value of the assets held at the balance sheet date that are represented by cash, or could be converted into cash within the next twelve months.

current liabilities The value of those liabilities at the balance sheet date that the company is obliged to settle within twelve months.

Debt Management Office (DMO) The part of the British Treasury that has responsibility for issuing gilts to fund the Government's borrowing requirement.

depository receipts Negotiable certificates that give evidence of ownership of a company's shares. Used to trade British and other non-American shares on the New York Stock Exchange, where they are known as ADRs.

depreciation The financial equivalent of wear and tear. Companies are allowed to deduct a certain amount from profits to allow for the decline in value of plant and equipment. Items like vehicles can be depreciated by 25 per cent of their value each year.

deregulation Removing or reducing restrictions in the hope that it will make a market more efficient.

discretionary account Account which allows a designated stock-broker or investment company to make investment decisions and buy or sell shares without consulting the account holder.

distribution The payments of any investment income generated by a fund. These payments may be made quarterly, half-yearly, or annually. Investors can usually choose to have the distribution paid to them or reinvested in the fund.

dividend The sum paid by the company to its shareholders as their financial reward for investing in the company. Dividends are usually paid half-yearly as 'interim' and then 'final' dividends.

dividend cover The amount of money a company has available from its profits to cover the cost of its dividends.

dividend per share The income a shareholder receives on each share owned in a company.

earnings per share An important and widely used indicator of the return on equity investment. Mathematically, EPS is calculated by dividing the total amount of a company's net profits by the number of ordinary shares issued.

equity The part of a company's share capital represented by ordinary, or voting, shares. Equities is a term often used for stocks and shares.

eurobond An interest-bearing security issued across national borders, usually in a currency other than that of the issuer's home country, most commonly dollars.

ex-dividend When appended to the share price as xd, it means that investors who buy the shares will not receive the already declared dividend. Conversely investors will receive the dividend when they sell them xd, even though they no longer hold the shares at the actual time of payment.

execution only Execution-only orders are fulfilled by stockbrokers who offer low commission rates but no advice.

Fed Common name for the United States Federal Reserve Board, America's central bank.

fiscal policy The use of taxation measures to influence a company.

flotation The occasion on which a company's shares are offered on the market for the first time.

Footsie The popular name for the FTSE 100 Share Index, the British stock market's main benchmark index, which measures the daily share price performance of Britain's top hundred public listed companies.

FSA Financial Services Authority, the agency appointed by the Government under the Financial Services Act to oversee the regulation of the financial services industry.

FTSE Index Three indices comprise the FTSE All Share index: the FTSE 100, FTSE 250, and the FTSE Small Caps.

fund General term for any investment vehicle which pools together the money of many small individual investors and invests it according to a defined set of investment aims and objectives. These include such investments as unit trusts, investment trusts, and pension plans.

fundamental analysis A method of researching the investment potential of a company.

fundamentals Usually refers to the underlying economic factors affecting a particular market, country or sector, and includes such aspects as industrial output, wages and raw materials costs, currency strengths or weaknesses, and trade balance.

fund manager A professional manager of investments in a pension fund, insurance company, or unit trust, or other individual fund. He or she makes the day-to-day decisions on what investments to buy or sell on behalf of the fund's investors.

futures A futures contract enables an investor to buy or sell securities or other goods at a future date at a predetermined price. The price is established between buyer and seller on the floor of an exchange, such as the London International Financial Futures Exchange (LIFFE), using an 'open outcry' system. The contracts themselves may be traded with third parties.

gearing Company borrowing as a proportion of funds. A highly geared company is usually seen as a riskier investment.

gilt-edged securities See **bonds**.

goodwill Intangible assets such as reputation or brand names.

growth companies Those companies that are expected to have continual growth, year on year, in their earnings per share.

hedging A strategy used to offset investment risk. Usually makes use of futures or options.

index-linked Indicates that an investment is tied to the rate of price inflation.

inflation The amount in percentage terms by which prices rise or fall year on year. In Britain the primary measure of inflation is the Retail Price Index (RPI).

initial public offering (IPO) The offering of shares in the equity of a company to the public for the first time.

insider dealing The purchase or sale of shares by someone who possesses inside information on a company's performance that has not yet been made available to the market, and which might affect the share price. In Britain, as in most western countries, such deals are a criminal offence.

intangible assets The company assets that are usually non-monetary in nature and without physical form, but which represent an expected future benefit. Examples of intangible assets include brands, patents, intellectual property, and goodwill on acquisition (the value placed on the acquired company's reputation and market presence).

interims The company's results for the first six months of its reporting period, which is usually its financial year.

investment club A group of like-minded individuals, friends, or colleagues who gather together for the purpose of investing in the stock market.

investment trust A closed-end investment fund that is a company listed on the Stock Exchange, and the purpose of which is to invest in other shares. Investment trusts often specialise in specific types of companies, in a geographic area, or in a single industrial sector.

ISA Individual Savings Accounts. The Government introduced ISAs in April 1999. ISAs are tax-efficient vehicles. There is no tax on dividends held within them, and capital gains taxes are not levied if the ISA remains in place for five years or more.

issue price Price at which shares are first offered to investors when a company floats on the stock market.

LIFFE London International Financial Futures and Options Exchange.

limit order An order submitted to an electronic order book with a specified size and price. The order is either held on the order book, or executed, either in part or in full, against any eligible order, with any remaining unexecuted portion being added to the order book.

liquidity The portion of an investment portfolio that is not fully invested, but is represented by cash holdings. Also, the level of continual buy-and-sell activity making up the market demand for shares and indicating the ease with which securities can be traded on the market.

listed company A company whose securities have been admitted to the London Stock Exchange and which has had to comply with the Exchange's listing regulations.

market capitalisation The value of a company as measured by the total stock market price of its issued and outstanding shares. In other words, the number of shares in issue multiplied by the current share price. Market capitalisation is widely used as a definition of company size and value.

market maker A Stock Exchange member firm that is obliged to make a continuous two-way price in the shares it follows. It is also used to describe a broker's employee who sets a price at which he is prepared to buy or sell shares on behalf of his firm.

merger The agreed integration of two companies, usually in the same industry, to create a new, combined entity with control still reflected in the ownership shares of the original companies

mid price The median (mid point) of the buying and selling spread quoted by the market makers. The price shown in the share price pages and market reports within the financial media, but not the price at which investors could necessarily expect to conclude a deal to buy or sell.

minority interest That part of a subsidiary company that the investing company does not itself hold or control. For instance, if a company has an interest in 87 per cent of the share capital of another company, then that other company is a subsidiary, and 87 per cent of its profits and assets will be featured in the consolidated accounts of the share-owning company. The 13 per cent not directly owned will be featured in the consolidated accounts as a minority interest.

monetary policy Influencing the direction of an economy through control of the money supply, usually by changing interest rates.

net asset value The net assets of a company divided by the number of shares it has issued.

net income Net income is pretax profits less taxation and other special charges. This is the amount that can be reinvested in the company or paid out in dividends or, usually, both. Those liable to lower rate or basic rate income tax will have no further liability to tax. Higher rate taxpayers will have to pay more when their tax return is due.

nominee A person or company holding securities on behalf of others. Those who use online or telephone brokerages almost always hold their shares through nominee accounts.

OFEX Off exchange. An unregulated alternative to the official stock market organised by J.P. Jenkins Ltd and targeted at smaller companies that have a potentially higher risk and thus prospects of higher rewards.

offer for sale A method of bringing a company to the market.

option You pay a published amount to have the option to buy or sell at a specific date in the future. Call options give their holder the right to buy a nominated number of shares at a specified price before a specified date. Put options allow the holder to do the opposite: sell at a set price before the nominated date. However, most people trade their options before they expire.

P and L Profit-and-loss account. The statement that details income, costs, profits and losses of a company.

par value The face, or nominal, value attributed to each of a company's shares, which form part of the security's title. Par value has no relationship whatever to either the value of the company at any given time, or the quoted price of its shares.

PE Price/earnings ratio. This is another important bellwether, calculated by dividing the market price of a company's ordinary shares by its earnings per share figure. This number, published for each share in the prices section of the *Financial Times*, provides a good insight into the market's expectations for the company's profits. It is used also to assess a company's performance against that of its peers. For example, in the food retail sector you will find major supermarkets have PEs that are different. If Tesco is on a lower PE than Sainsbury's, and you believe will outperform it, then you may conclude that Tesco's share price is too low, or Sainsbury's too high.

penny share A term applied to companies whose shares have a very low price, usually less than 50 pence a share. Many investors find penny shares attractive. A few pence gained can mean a good profit, but this argument applies conversely also.

PEP Personal Equity Plan. Introduced in 1987, PEPs are tax-efficient personal investment vehicles, which carry no income tax or capital gains tax on their investment returns. They were abolished and replaced by ISAs in 1999, but existing PEPs can continue, with profits reinvested on a tax-efficient basis. PEPs are slightly handicapped by high management charges.

plc Public limited company.

preference shares Shares in a company that usually pay a fixed rate of dividend. Though not as secure as bonds, they rank ahead of ordinary shares and are a way of creating unsecured debt. Generally frowned upon by stock exchanges, which prefer all shares to be equal.

preliminary statement An announcement made by a company prior to the publication of its annual results.

premium The potential profit on a share from its issue price; hence the expression 'trading at a premium'.

pre-tax profit The key figure reported by a company at half-year or year-end; the best measure of performance.

price-sensitive information Information that may impact on a company's share price and must be reported to a stock exchange.

private company A company that cannot offer its shares to the general public and is not listed on a stock exchange. Some companies that have once been public companies de-list, for various reasons, a recent example being the Virgin Group.

privatisation Conversion of a state-owned operation or enterprise into a publicly listed company, usually, but not always, as a result of the sale of its shares to the public.

Proshare An independent, not-for-profit organisation set up to encourage and support individual investment in the stock market by private individuals. It is committed to the provision of education in personal financial management and strongly supports investment clubs.

prospectus A formal document issued by a company when it first seeks entry to the Stock Exchange. The prospectus describes the company's business plan, financial background and details achievements and objectives. It also often includes an official forecast of future performance.

registrar An organisation contracted to maintain a company's share register.

rights issue This takes place when a company asks its shareholders for more money by offering them additional shares at a substantially discounted price. The money may be needed for expansion, or to reduce debt, as in BT's 2001 rights issue. Rights issues usually lead to a fall in share prices. For example, a two for five rights issue at 145 pence would allow existing shareholders to get two shares for every five they own at that price. Investment bankers normally underwrite rights issues, meaning that they take on the obligation of buying any newly issued shares not taken up by existing shareholders.

ROCE Return on capital employed. This is a key statistic often used in determining bonuses. It is the rate of return achieved by a company on the assets deployed in the business.

scrip issue Also known as a bonus issue, this occurs when a company issues additional shares to existing shareholders at no cost to them. Scrip issues usually result in a fall in price to reflect the additional number of shares in the market, but they can sometimes be effective in attracting additional shareholders, who buy in on the lower price.

SEAQ The London Stock Exchange's automated quotation system.

SEATS Plus This combines trading on the basis of orders (see **SETS**) and market making. It is used on the Alternative Investment Market, and on the main market where there are fewer than two market makers making a market in a given share.

securities Another name for shares and bonds, and other instruments with a money value.

SETS Stock Exchange Electronic Trading Service. Since October 1997, FTSE 100 shares have been traded through an electronic order book, rather than by market makers quoting bid and offer prices.

settlement Once shares have been traded, settlement is the process that transfers cash from buyer to seller, and share certificates (or electronic registration) from seller to buyer.

shareholders' funds The total of shareholders' capital invested in a company. Mathematically it is the sum of the original issued capital plus reserves created since incorporation.

small caps Another name for smaller companies, as measured by their market capitalisation.

spread The difference between the buying (offer) and selling (bid) price.

stag A person who buys new issues or privatisation offers in the expectation of selling them quickly for a good profit.

stamp duty A polite description of a government tax on share purchases. It is not applied to sales, though capital gains taxes apply where there is a profit.

stockbroker A person or company that buys and sells securities on behalf of clients; see also **broker**.

suspension A halt in trading ordered by a stock exchange either at a company's request or of its own volition. Trading may be suspended, for example, when a company is announcing very bad news, or a takeover announcement is imminent.

switching Moving an investment from one fund to another.

technical analysis A way of studying the investment potential of a company using mathematics. Share price and underlying financials are examined and compared rather than looking at news and other developments.

tender Tender offers are used when securities are auctioned to the highest bidder. As with property auctions, a guide price is announced, and then bidders offer their best price. Sometimes this is through an open option, more often through sealed bids.

tracker fund A professionally managed investment fund that uses a variety of techniques to emulate the investment performance of a specific stock market index.

turnover The volume of business, usually sales, of a company before cost deductions.

underwriter Not to be confused with an insurance underwriter, who assesses and takes on risk, an underwriter in the financial markets agrees to buy securities that are left unsold after a new issue, a rights issue, or a privatisation. Underwriters get a fee for taking on this obligation.

unit trust A collective investment or fund which, unlike an investment trust, is not quoted on the Stock Exchange, but which invests in securities. Units can be redeemed on a daily basis at the price quoted by the fund manager, and the money withdrawn reduces the amount of money available to the fund manager.

USM Unlisted Securities Market. The predecessor of AIM, it closed in 1996.

warrant A security which can be traded on stock markets and which entitles the holder to buy specific shares at a set price at a future date.

working capital Cash and other liquid assets needed to finance the everyday running of a company.

yield Another important measurement tool, which reflects the annual income as a percentage of current market capitalisation. If share prices fall, reducing the value of a company, yields move up.

Index

LIVERPOOL JOHN MOORES UNIVERSITY
Aldham Robarts L.R.C.
TEL. 051 231 3701/3634